DIABETIC AIR FRYER COOKBOOK

For Beginners

**2000 Days of Quick, Healthy Recipes
for Type 1 & 2 Diabetes,
Fits Prediabetic & Newly Diagnosed**

**Low-Carb, Low-Sugar Diet
with a 30-Day Meal Plan**

Deb Corbin

This book is for educational and informational purposes only and should not be construed as medical advice. The author has tried to provide accurate and reliable information; however, it is not a substitute for professional medical consultation. Always consult a healthcare provider before starting any new diet or health program, especially if you have a medical condition such as diabetes.

The recipes in this book are designed to be low-carb and low-sugar to support a healthy lifestyle for individuals with Type 1 and Type 2 diabetes and those following prediabetes or other health-related diets. Individual results may vary, and the nutritional content of each recipe should be tailored to meet your specific health needs. The author and publisher assume no responsibility for any adverse reactions, effects, or consequences resulting from using or misusing the information, products, or procedures presented in this book.

This book does not aim to detect, treat, cure, or prevent any disease. Readers should use the recipes and advice at risk and consult qualified health professionals.

CONTENTS

INTRODUCTION

Welcome to *Diabetic Air Fryer Cookbook for Beginners: 2000 Days of Quick, Healthy Recipes for Type 1 & 2 Diabetes*, your ultimate guide to enjoying delicious, diabetes-friendly meals while keeping your health in check. This book is designed specifically for those living with Type 1 and Type 2 diabetes, the newly diagnosed, or those managing prediabetes. You can nourish your body, manage your blood sugar, and enjoy your favorite flavors with the proper knowledge and tools. The journey to healthy eating doesn't have to be complicated. This book explores the advantages of using an air fryer. This fantastic appliance lets you cook with much less oil while achieving crispy and flavorful results. From breakfasts that jumpstart your day to savory dinners and guilt-free desserts, this cookbook offers 2000 days of balanced, low-carb, and low-sugar recipes that are easy to prepare and ideal for anyone looking to make healthier choices.

Managing diabetes can often feel overwhelming, especially when you're first diagnosed or adjusting to a new lifestyle. But it doesn't have to be. Having the proper tools, knowledge, and meal plan can still lead to delicious and satisfying meals that support your health. Whether you have Type 1, Type 2, or prediabetes, understanding how food affects your blood sugar is essential for effectively managing your condition. In this book, you'll find a collection of low-carb, low-sugar recipes designed to fit within a balanced diet to help keep your blood glucose levels in check. More importantly, you'll be introduced to a modern, convenient cooking tool—the air fryer—that makes preparing these meals easier, faster, and healthier than ever before.

Together, we will embark on a journey to reclaim your kitchen with the air fryer, creating diabetes-friendly meals that are quick to prepare and flavorful.

What You'll Find in This Cookbook

Simple & Accessible Ingredients: All recipes use easy-to-find, affordable ingredients stapled in most kitchens.

Diabetes-Friendly Recipes: Every meal is crafted with diabetes management in mind, focusing on low-glycemic ingredients, fiber-rich vegetables, and healthy fats.

A 30-Day Meal Plan: This step-by-step guide simplifies your transition into healthier eating and makes meal planning stress-free.

Nutrition Insights: All recipes are provided with comprehensive nutritional information for each recipe to track your intake of calories, carbs, protein, and more.

Diverse Flavors for Every Meal: From comforting breakfasts to savory snacks and indulgent desserts, our recipes offer a variety to excite your taste buds.

Recipes Crafted for Two Servings

Each recipe in this cookbook is designed for two servings, providing an ideal balance of convenience and portion control. This method makes meal planning more accessible, particularly for individuals managing diabetes or those who maintain a healthy and balanced diet. There are many reasons why this approach is beneficial, especially for those who want to keep a balanced, diabetes-friendly diet.

Convenient Portion Control: Managing portion sizes is crucial for anyone with diabetes, as consuming the right amount of food can help stabilize blood sugar levels and manage weight. This cookbook offers recipes designed for two servings, simplifying meal preparation without the need to measure and divide ingredients. You will know precisely how much to cook, making achieving your dietary goals easier and avoiding overindulging.

Ideal for Couples, Singles, or Meal Preppers: Whether cooking for yourself or sharing a meal with a partner or loved one, having recipes yielding two servings is practical and convenient. If you're cooking solo, you can enjoy one serving immediately and save the other for lunch or dinner the next day. If you're cooking for two, it's the perfect amount to satisfy both appetites without leaving behind leftovers to tempt you. Additionally, these recipes are great for meal prepping, allowing you to plan and reduce the time spent in the kitchen during busy weeks.

Minimizing Food Waste: Minimizing food waste is more important than ever. Preparing just two servings means you're less likely to have unused ingredients or leftovers that spoil in the fridge. This focus on efficiency is beneficial when working with fresh produce and perishable items. You'll use just what you need, keeping your grocery costs down and your meals fresh and vibrant.

Flexibility and Adaptability: Each recipe serves two, but measurements can be adjusted for larger groups. This flexibility ensures you can scale the recipes up or down depending on your needs without compromising flavor or quality. The recipes are simple, with easy-to-follow instructions that adapt a breeze.

WHAT IS DIABETES

Type 1 and Type 2 Diabetes

When discussing diabetes, it is essential to recognize the two primary types: Type 1 and Type 2. Although they share some commonalities, including how they affect blood sugar regulation, they are distinct regarding causes, management, and how they manifest in the body. Let's look at each type to understand how they differ and what managing your diet and lifestyle means, mainly using an air fryer for healthier cooking.

Type 1 Diabetes: An Autoimmune Condition

Type 1 diabetes is an autoimmune disease in which the immune system attacks the pancreas's beta cells, which produce insulin. Insulin is a hormone that allows glucose (sugar) from the bloodstream to enter cells and give them energy. Without insulin, blood sugar levels remain high, leading to potentially life-threatening complications.

Who It Affects: Type 1 diabetes can develop at any age but is commonly diagnosed in children and young adults. It accounts for approximately 5-10% of all diabetes cases.

Causes: The exact cause of Type 1 diabetes remains unclear, but it is believed to result from a combination of genetic and environmental factors, which may include exposure to certain viruses.

Management: Individuals with Type 1 diabetes need to administer insulin daily, either through injections or an insulin pump, to regulate their blood sugar levels. It is crucial to keep a close eye on carbohydrates and blood sugar levels.

Diet and Lifestyle Considerations: Type 1 diabetes patients constantly face difficulty managing their blood sugar. While an air fryer cannot eliminate the need for insulin, it can help to prepare healthier meals with less added fats and refined sugars. Using an air fryer to prepare balanced, low-carb meals can more effectively manage post-meal blood sugar spikes.

Type 2 Diabetes: A Metabolic Disorder

Type 2 diabetes is the more common form, accounting for about 90-95% of all diabetes cases. In this type, the body either becomes resistant to the effects of insulin or the pancreas fails to produce sufficient insulin to regulate blood glucose levels.

Who It Affects: Type 2 diabetes is more common in adults, but it's increasingly being diagnosed in children and adolescents due to rising obesity rates and sedentary lifestyles.

Causes: A combination of genetic predisposition and lifestyle factors, such as being overweight, poor diet, and lack of physical activity, contribute to the development of Type 2 diabetes.

Management: Unlike Type 1 diabetes, some people with Type 2 diabetes can manage their condition with lifestyle changes alone, such as diet and exercise. However, others may need oral medications or insulin injections.

Diet and Lifestyle Considerations: Managing Type 2 diabetes often involves losing weight, adopting a balanced diet, and staying active. An air fryer can be a game-changer: it prepares delicious, crispy foods with significantly less oil, reducing overall calorie and fat intake. By air-frying vegetables, lean proteins, and even diabetic-friendly snacks, people with Type 2 diabetes can better control their weight and improve their metabolic health.

Why Understanding the Difference Matters: Understanding the difference between Type 1 and Type 2 diabetes is essential for effective management. Individuals with Type 1 diabetes need insulin therapy to survive, whereas those with Type 2 diabetes may be able to control their blood sugar levels through diet, exercise, and medication.

A healthy, balanced diet is vital for both types. The recipes in this cookbook are designed to be diabetes-friendly, focusing on low-carb, low-sugar, and nutrient-rich ingredients that support stable blood sugar levels. The air fryer plays a crucial role by allowing you to prepare flavorful, healthy meals without the excess fat and calories often associated with traditional frying methods.

Whether you have Type 1 or Type 2 diabetes, the goal remains the same: to keep blood sugar levels in a healthy range and reduce the risk of complications. Using the air fryer and following the recipes in this book, you'll take a proactive step towards better health and enjoy delicious and diabetes-friendly meals.

Prediabetes

Prediabetes is a serious health condition in which blood sugar levels are higher than usual but not high enough to be diagnosed as Type 2 diabetes. It is a warning sign that diabetes could develop if no lifestyle changes are made, but the good news is that it is a stage where intervention can have a significant impact. By understanding prediabetes, you can take proactive steps to prevent or delay the onset of Type 2 diabetes and improve your overall health.

What Is Prediabetes? Prediabetes occurs when your body starts to struggle with processing glucose properly. In a healthy body, the pancreas releases insulin to help cells absorb and use glucose for energy. When you have prediabetes, your body either doesn't produce enough insulin or becomes resistant to the effects of insulin, causing glucose to build up in the bloodstream.

Blood Sugar Levels:

> **Normal:** Fasting blood sugar below 100 mg/dL (5.6 mmol/L)
>
> **Prediabetes:** Fasting blood sugar between 100–125 mg/dL (5.6–6.9 mmol/L)
>
> **Diabetes:** Fasting blood sugar 126 mg/dL (7.0 mmol/L) or higher

A diagnosis of prediabetes is a critical opportunity to make lifestyle adjustments and lower your risk of developing Type 2 diabetes and other complications, such as heart disease.

Risk Factors for Prediabetes:

Several factors can increase the risk of developing prediabetes, including:

Overweight or Obesity: Excess weight, especially around the abdomen, can make your body more insulin-resistant.

Sedentary Lifestyle: Physical inactivity contributes to weight gain and insulin resistance.

Family History: A parent or sibling with Type 2 diabetes increases your risk.

Age: The risk of prediabetes increases after the age of 45.

High Blood Pressure: Elevated blood pressure is often associated with insulin resistance.

Unhealthy Diet: Diets high in processed foods, refined sugars, and unhealthy fats can increase the likelihood of prediabetes.

Gestational Diabetes: Women who had diabetes during pregnancy have a higher risk of developing prediabetes.

Understanding these risk factors can empower you to make healthier choices and lower your risk of progression to Type 2 diabetes.

Signs and Symptoms of Prediabetes:

Prediabetes often has no apparent symptoms, making it difficult to detect without blood testing. However, some people may experience:

- **Darkened Skin Patches:** Areas of darkened skin, typically in the neck, armpits, or groin, known as acanthosis nigricans, may be a sign of insulin resistance.

- **Increased Thirst or Hunger**

- **Fatigue**

- **Frequent Urination**

Contact your healthcare provider for screening if you suspect you might be at risk.

Prevention and Lifestyle Changes

The great thing about prediabetes is that it's not a permanent condition. By making fundamental lifestyle changes, many people can prevent or delay the development of Type 2 diabetes. Here are some practical ways to take control:

Healthy Eating: Focus on a balanced, low-carb, low-sugar diet emphasizing whole foods, lean proteins, vegetables, and healthy fats. The recipes in this book are designed with these principles in mind, making it easier to prepare diabetes-friendly meals using an air fryer.

Weight Loss: Losing even a small percentage of body weight can significantly affect your blood sugar levels. Aim for gradual, sustainable weight loss through healthy eating and exercise.

Regular Exercise: At least 150 minutes of moderate exercise per week can improve insulin sensitivity and help manage blood sugar levels. Activities such as walking, cycling, and strength training are excellent options.

Stress Management: Chronic stress negatively impacts blood sugar levels. Consider practicing relaxation techniques like yoga, meditation, or deep breathing exercises.

Adequate Sleep: Poor or insufficient sleep is linked to insulin resistance. Aim for 7-8 hours of good-quality sleep each night.

How the Air Fryer Can Help Manage Prediabetes:

One of the biggest challenges for people with prediabetes is modifying their diet in a way that is both enjoyable and sustainable. That's where the air fryer comes in. It allows you to prepare delicious, crispy foods with minimal oil, making it an ideal tool for creating healthier versions of your favorite meals.

Benefits of Using an Air Fryer for Prediabetes Management:

Lower Calorie Intake: By reducing the amount of oil used in cooking, you can lower your overall calorie consumption, aiding in weight loss.

Healthier Fats: An air fryer makes cooking easy with healthier oils like olive or avocado oil, which can improve heart health.

Balanced Meals: The air fryer is perfect for preparing various dishes, from roasted vegetables to lean proteins, helping you maintain a well-rounded diet.

Quick and Convenient: The speed and ease of using an air fryer make it more likely that you'll stick to your healthy eating plan.

Final Thoughts: Prediabetes is a wake-up call and an opportunity to make meaningful changes. By understanding your risk factors and implementing healthier habits, you can take control of your health and significantly reduce your chances of developing Type 2 diabetes. This cookbook provides a variety of delicious, low-carb, and low-sugar recipes that use the air fryer to help you on your journey. From breakfast to dinner, snacks, and desserts, these recipes will support your goals and show you that eating well doesn't have to be sacrificed.

Newly Diagnosed Diabetic

You were receiving a diagnosis of diabetes, whether Type 1 or Type 2, can feel overwhelming. It's a moment that often comes with a flood of emotions, from confusion and fear to frustration and uncertainty. But remember, you are not alone, and being diagnosed is the first step towards taking control of your health. With the right mindset, education, and support, you can lead an entire and active life while effectively managing diabetes. This chapter will guide you through understanding your diagnosis, embracing healthy habits, and using practical tools like this cookbook to support your journey.

Understanding Your Diagnosis: The first step after a diabetes diagnosis is understanding what it means for your body. Diabetes is a chronic condition that affects how your body turns food into energy. Typically, the pancreas produces insulin, a hormone that helps sugar (glucose) enter your cells for energy use. However, in diabetes, this process is impaired.

Emotional Impact of a Diabetes Diagnosis: It's important to acknowledge that being diagnosed with diabetes is not just a physical challenge but also an emotional one.

If you're struggling emotionally, reach out to friends, family, or mental health professionals. Diabetes is a lifelong condition, but with the proper support and strategies, you can thrive.

Steps to Take After Your Diagnosis Here's what you can do right away to start managing your diabetes effectively:

Educate Yourself: Knowledge is power. Learn as much as you can about diabetes, how it affects your body, and what you can do to manage it. Speak to your healthcare provider, take diabetes education classes, or join support groups to gain insights.

Meet with a Diabetes Care Team: Your team may include an endocrinologist, a diabetes educator, a dietitian, and a mental health professional. They can provide you with a comprehensive care plan tailored to your needs.

Track Your Blood Sugar Levels: Monitoring your blood sugar is crucial for understanding how different foods, activities, and stressors affect your glucose levels. Your doctor will advise you on how often to check your blood sugar and what target ranges to aim for.

Create a Meal Plan: Food is a significant part of blood sugar management. Working with a registered dietitian can help you understand which foods to eat, how much, and when. The recipes in this cookbook are designed to be low in carbohydrates and sugars, making it easier to keep your blood sugar in check.

Incorporate Physical Activity: Exercise is a powerful tool in managing diabetes. It helps lower blood sugar levels and improves insulin sensitivity. Find activities you enjoy, whether walking, swimming, yoga, or strength training and aim for at least 150 minutes of moderate exercise each week.

Learn about Medications and Insulin: Depending on your type of diabetes, you may need medication or insulin to help manage your blood sugar. Your healthcare provider will explain how and when to take these and what to do in case of side effects.

Prepare for Emergencies: Learn how to recognize the signs of high and low blood sugar and have a plan for what to do in each situation. Keep emergency supplies on hand, such as glucose tablets for hypoglycemia and a medical ID bracelet indicating your diabetes status.

Why Diet Is Crucial in Diabetes Management

Diet is one of the most significant factors affecting blood sugar levels. As someone newly diagnosed, understanding how to make healthy food choices is essential. Carbohydrates, proteins, and fats all play different roles in blood sugar management:

Carbohydrates: The primary macronutrient that affects blood sugar. Focus on consuming complex carbs like whole grains, legumes, and non-starchy vegetables, and avoid simple sugars.

Proteins have minimal impact on blood sugar and help keep you feeling full. Incorporate lean proteins such as chicken, turkey, tofu, and fish into your diet.

Fats: Healthy fats from sources like avocados, olive oil, and nuts can support heart health, which is crucial since people with diabetes are at a higher risk of heart disease.

This cookbook provides a variety of diabetes-friendly recipes that cater to your new dietary needs. Using an air fryer, you can prepare meals that are lower in fat and calories while still being delicious and satisfying.

How the Air Fryer Fits Into Your Diabetes Management: One of the most valuable tools you can use as someone newly diagnosed with diabetes is an air fryer. This kitchen appliance can revolutionize cooking by providing healthier versions of traditionally fried or high-fat foods. Here's why it's beneficial:

Reduced Oil Use: The air fryer uses hot air circulation to cook food, which means you need only a fraction of the oil typically used in frying. This leads to lower calorie and fat intake.

Quick and Convenient: Managing diabetes can be time-consuming, especially when meal planning and preparation are involved. The air fryer cooks food faster than traditional methods, making it easier to whip up healthy meals in no time.

Crispy and Flavorful Meals: One of the most complex parts of a new diabetes-friendly diet is feeling like you're missing out on your favorite foods. The air fryer delivers crispy, flavorful results without excess oil, so you can still enjoy delicious meals without sacrificing health.

Moving Forward with Confidence: Being newly diagnosed with diabetes is undoubtedly a life-changing experience, but it's also a chance to prioritize your health and make meaningful changes. You can live a vibrant and healthy life by embracing a balanced diet, regular exercise, and proactive health management. The recipes in this cookbook are crafted to make meal preparation simple, enjoyable, and nourishing so you can take control of your diabetes one meal at a time.

Remember, you have the power to manage your diabetes and live life to the fullest. This cookbook and the strategies you learn will be essential for your journey to better health. Take it one day at a time, and know that small, consistent changes can lead to a significant impact. You've got this!

Managing diabetes doesn't mean giving up on your favorite dishes; it means finding ways to make them work for your health. With this cookbook, you'll discover how to create meals that taste amazing and support your overall well-being. Whether you're a busy professional, a parent looking to prepare healthy meals for your family, or someone new to cooking, these recipes are designed to be quick, flavorful, and enjoyable.

Let's embark on this delicious and healthy journey together. With your air fryer and this cookbook as your guide, you'll learn how to create meals that bring joy and health to your table. Here's to cooking savvy, eating well, and living vibrantly!

THE POWER OF THE AIR FRYER

Living with diabetes requires careful attention to diet and lifestyle choices, and making changes in the kitchen can significantly impact your overall well-being. The air fryer is one of the most transformative tools to add to your healthy cooking routine. It's a versatile, convenient, and health-promoting appliance that can simplify meal preparation while supporting diabetes management goals. This chapter explores why the air fryer is a fantastic choice for people with diabetes and how it can help you prepare delicious, satisfying meals without compromising your health.

Less Oil, Lower Calories: One of the most significant advantages of using an air fryer is that it requires significantly less oil than traditional frying methods. While deep-frying can turn otherwise healthy foods into calorie-laden meals, the air fryer uses rapid air circulation to create a crispy, golden exterior with just a fraction of the oil. For people with diabetes, consuming fewer unhealthy fats and calories is crucial for maintaining a healthy weight and controlling blood sugar levels. By reducing the amount of oil used, you can still enjoy crispy, flavorful foods like

French fries, chicken wings, and roasted vegetables without guilt.

Better Blood Sugar Control: High-fat, high-calorie foods can lead to insulin resistance and weight gain, making it harder to manage blood sugar levels. Air frying provides a healthier alternative, enabling you to create meals that are lower in fat and more diabetes-friendly. The air fryer is also excellent for preparing nutrient-dense, fiber-rich vegetables essential for stabilizing blood sugar. Foods cooked in an air fryer retain more nutrients than traditional frying methods, ensuring you get the most out of your healthy ingredients.

Easy Preparation of Low-Glycemic Foods: When living with diabetes, focusing on low-glycemic index (GI) foods is essential to prevent spikes in blood sugar. The air fryer is perfect for cooking these types of foods efficiently. Vegetables like Brussels sprouts, cauliflower, and sweet potatoes, which have a moderate to low glycemic index, can be roasted to perfection in the air fryer, bringing out their natural sweetness and flavors without adding unnecessary sugars or unhealthy fats.

Portion Control and Meal Prep: The air fryer makes cooking meals in controlled portions easier, helping you stick to a balanced diet. It's perfect for quick, single-serve meals or small batches, making it ideal for people who want to manage their food intake. Plus, meal prepping with an air fryer is a breeze. You can prepare various healthy snacks and meals for the week in no time, making it less likely that you'll reach for processed or high-sugar convenience foods.

Promotes a Balanced Diet: An air fryer allows you to cook various dishes, from lean proteins to fiber-rich vegetables and healthy snacks. This versatility encourages a well-rounded diet, which is crucial for managing diabetes. For example, the air fryer can prepare crispy kale chips, roasted chickpeas, or low-carb zucchini fries for snacks and make perfectly cooked salmon or chicken breasts for dinner. By incorporating diverse nutritious ingredients, you can keep your meals exciting and enjoyable while staying committed to your health goals.

Quick and Convenient: Managing diabetes often means planning meals carefully and following a regular eating schedule. The air fryer speeds up the cooking process, making it easier to prepare healthy meals without spending hours in the kitchen. This convenience benefits those with busy lifestyles who need quick, nutritious options that don't require much cleanup. The air fryer's efficiency allows you to whip up delicious meals in minutes, helping you stay on track with your dietary needs.

Reduced Formation of Harmful Compounds: When fried at high temperatures, foods can produce harmful compounds like acrylamide, which is linked to various health concerns. The air fryer minimizes the risk of forming these compounds compared to traditional frying, making it a safer option for preparing crispy foods. Reducing harmful substances is beneficial for people with diabetes, as it helps support overall health and reduces the risk of complications associated with the disease.

Delicious and Satisfying Meals: One of the challenges of following a diabetes-friendly diet is finding healthy and satisfying meals. The air fryer creates deliciously crispy textures and enhances the natural flavors of your ingredients, making your meals more enjoyable. From crunchy vegetable sides to juicy, seasoned proteins, the air fryer delivers satisfying results that can make sticking to a healthy eating plan much more appealing.

The air fryer is a game-changer for anyone looking to improve their diet, but it's particularly beneficial for people managing diabetes. This kitchen appliance is a powerful tool in your diabetes management toolkit, allowing you to prepare low-oil, nutrient-rich meals that taste incredible. It promotes healthier eating habits, simplifies meal preparation, and provides a way to enjoy your favorite foods without compromising your health.

As you explore the recipes in this cookbook, you'll see how easy and rewarding it is to use the air fryer to create diabetes-friendly meals. From crispy snacks to hearty dinners, the air fryer will become your go-to for quick, delicious, and health-conscious cooking. Let's begin this journey to better health—one air-fried meal at a time!

PRINCIPLES AND TIPS FOR DIABETES-FRIENDLY EATING

Managing diabetes starts with understanding how food impacts your body and making choices that stabilize your blood sugar levels. In this chapter, we'll cover the basics of diabetes-friendly eating, focusing on the role of macronutrients, the importance of a low-carb, low-sugar diet, and mindful eating strategies. You'll also find tips for stocking your kitchen with ingredients and substitutions that fit your new lifestyle.

Macronutrients Explained: Balancing Carbohydrates, Proteins, and Fats for Blood Sugar Control

The three main macronutrients—carbohydrates, proteins, and fats—play distinct roles in your body, and balancing them is critical to controlling blood sugar levels.

Carbohydrates are the most essential macronutrient to monitor when managing diabetes because they immediately affect blood sugar. Foods high in carbohydrates include bread, pasta, rice, and starchy vegetables like potatoes. While you don't need to eliminate carbs, choosing complex carbs like whole grains, legumes, and non-starchy vegetables can help you avoid blood sugar spikes.

Proteins help repair tissues and keep you feeling full longer, which can aid in weight management—a crucial aspect for Type 2 diabetics. Lean protein sources such as chicken, fish, tofu, eggs, and legumes are *best*. *Protein* also minimizes blood sugar, making it a vital part of a balanced diet.

Fats provide energy and help your body absorb essential vitamins. However, not all fats are created equal. Saturated and trans fats can raise cholesterol levels and increase the risk of heart disease, which people with diabetes are already more prone to. Instead, focus on healthy fats like olive oil, avocados, nuts, and seeds. These fats can help keep your heart

healthy and stabilize blood sugar levels when consumed in moderation.

Balancing these macronutrients in each meal ensures your body receives the nutrients it needs while maintaining blood sugar control.

Low-Carb, Low-Sugar Diet: Tips on Lowering Sugar Intake and Focusing on Low-Glycemic Foods

A low-carb, low-sugar diet is essential for keeping blood sugar levels stable. Reducing sugar and simple carbohydrates can help prevent the dramatic spikes and drops in glucose that are challenging for people with diabetes. Here are some tips to help lower your sugar intake:

Choose Low-Glycemic Foods: Foods with a low glycemic index (GI) release sugar more slowly into the bloodstream, helping to prevent sudden spikes. Examples include non-starchy vegetables, whole grains like quinoa and barley, legumes, and fruits like berries and apples.

Cut Back on Sugary Drinks: Beverages like soda, fruit juices, and even some flavored waters can be loaded with sugar. Opt for water, herbal teas, or unsweetened drinks instead.

Use Natural Sweeteners: To satisfy a sweet tooth, consider natural, low-carb alternatives like stevia, monk fruit, or erythritol. These sugar substitutes have minimal impact on blood glucose levels.

Read Labels: Hidden sugars are everywhere, even in foods you might not expect, like sauces, salad dressings, and processed snacks. Be diligent about reading labels and choosing products with no added sugar.

Focusing on whole, minimally processed foods and limiting your intake of sugary products will help you maintain stable blood sugar levels and improve overall health.

Portion Control and Mindful Eating

You are managing Portions and Recognizing Hunger Cues. Even when eating healthy foods, portion control is critical for managing blood sugar and weight. Recognizing your hunger and fullness cues and practicing mindful eating can help prevent overeating, which can cause post-meal blood sugar spikes.

Understand Serving Sizes: A portion is not necessarily the same as a serving. For example, while you may be served a large plate of pasta at a restaurant, the serving size is just 1/2 cup. Please pay attention to serving sizes and stick to them as closely as possible.

Use Smaller Plates: One simple trick is to use smaller plates and bowls, making your portion sizes look more satisfying without overeating.

Eat Slowly: It takes about 20 minutes for your brain to register you're full. Eating slowly helps you avoid overeating and gives your body time to recognize when it's had enough.

Check Your Hunger: Before reaching for food, ask yourself whether you're starving or eating out of habit, boredom, or stress. Recognizing true hunger versus emotional hunger can help you make better choices.

By practicing portion control and eating with intention, you can prevent blood sugar spikes and keep your eating habits in check.

Common Ingredients and Substitutions

You are stocking Your Pantry with Diabetic-Friendly Options. Having the right ingredients makes it much easier to prepare diabetes-friendly meals. Here's a guide to some everyday ingredients and the healthier substitutions you can use in your recipes:

Flours: Instead of all-purpose flour, opt for almond flour, coconut flour, or whole grain flours like spelt. These lower-carb options can help manage blood sugar levels.

Sweeteners: Replace sugar with natural, low-glycemic sweeteners such as stevia, monk fruit, or erythritol. Avoid artificial sweeteners like aspartame or saccharin, as they can have adverse health effects.

Grains: Instead of white rice or pasta, choose whole grains like quinoa, brown rice, or farro. For an even lower-carb option, use cauliflower rice or zucchini noodles.

Dairy: Full-fat dairy products like cream and cheese can be enjoyed in moderation, but if you want to reduce fat, opt for Greek yogurt or plant-based alternatives like almond or coconut milk.

Oils: Choose heart-healthy fats like olive oil, avocado oil, or coconut oil instead of butter or margarine, which can contain unhealthy trans fats.

Simple substitutions like these make it easier to prepare meals that support your health while satisfying your taste buds.

Understanding the Glycemic Index: A Key Tool for Diabetics

Understanding foods' glycemic index (GI) can be a game-changer in managing diabetes. The GI ranks foods based on how quickly they raise blood sugar levels after consumption. Foods are categorized as low, medium, or high GI, allowing diabetics and those managing prediabetes to choose foods that support steady blood sugar levels.

The glycemic index (GI) measures how carbohydrates in different foods affect blood glucose levels. The scale ranges from 0 to 100, with higher numbers indicating foods that raise blood sugar levels more quickly.

Low GI (55 or less): Foods that cause a gradual rise in blood sugar. These include most vegetables, whole grains, beans, legumes, nuts, and fruits like apples, berries, and cherries.

Medium GI (56–69): Foods that cause a moderate rise in blood sugar. Foods like bananas, oats, sweet potatoes, and brown rice fall in this category.

High GI (70 or above): Foods that cause a rapid spike in blood sugar. Foods like white bread, instant rice, and sugary snacks cause quicker glucose spikes.

By choosing more low-GI foods, people with diabetes can enjoy more stable energy levels and better blood glucose control.

Understanding and using the glycemic index in food choices is particularly beneficial for those with diabetes, as it allows for:

Steady Blood Sugar Levels: Low-GI foods help to maintain stable glucose levels, minimizing blood sugar spikes.

Improved Energy: Low-GI foods gradually release glucose, providing sustained energy rather than quick spikes and drops.

Making the Glycemic Index Work for You: Tips and Recommendations

It's helpful to consider several factors that can influence the GI of foods to use the glycemic index best. Here are some recommendations for interpreting GI and incorporating low-GI foods into your diet.

Weight Control: Low-GI foods are often more filling and nutrient-dense, which can help with weight management, a key component of diabetes control.

Pair High-GI Foods with Low-GI Foods: Mixing high-GI food with low-GI food can help moderate the impact on blood sugar. For example, pair white rice (high GI) with a protein source like chicken breast (low GI) and add vegetables (low GI) to balance the meal.

Fiber Slows Down Digestion: Foods high in fiber, such as whole grains, vegetables, and legumes, generally have a lower GI. Fiber slows down the digestion of carbohydrates, leading to a slower release of glucose. Adding fiber-rich foods to meals helps lower the glycemic load of a meal.

Healthy Fats and Protein Moderate Blood Sugar Response: Fats and proteins have little to no impact on the glycemic index. Including healthy fats (like olive oil, avocado, or nuts) and proteins (such as fish, lean meats, or legumes) with each meal can help reduce blood sugar spikes.

Choose Whole, Unprocessed Foods: The more processed a food is, the higher its GI. For example, instant oatmeal has a higher GI than steel-cut oats because it has been processed to cook quickly, which increases its effect on blood sugar.

Be Aware of Ripeness in Fruits: Fruits' GI can change as they ripen. For instance, a green banana has a lower GI than a ripe banana. Choosing fruits that are not overly ripe can help manage blood sugar levels better.

GLYCEMIC INDEX

Low Glycemic Index (GI ≤ 55)

These foods cause a gradual rise in blood sugar levels, making them ideal for sustained energy and stable blood sugar.

Chickpeas – GI 10	**Cherries** – GI 20	**Tomatoes** – GI 15	**Greek yogurt (unsweetened)** – GI 12
Lentils – GI 29	**Apples** – GI 36	**Peanuts** – GI 14	**Sweet potatoes** – GI 54
Milk – GI 31	**Oranges** – GI 43	**Steel-cut oats** – GI 55	**Leafy greens (spinach, kale)** – GI 15
Barley – GI 28	**Pears** – GI 38	**Carrots** – GI 39	**Whole-grain pasta** – GI 42
Quinoa – GI 53	**Grapefruit** – GI 25	**Green peas** – GI 39	**Berries (strawberries, blueberries)** – GI 25

Medium Glycemic Index (GI 56-69)

These foods cause a moderate rise in blood sugar and are best eaten in smaller quantities or balanced with low-GI foods.

Bulgur – GI 55	**Kiwi** – GI 58	**Oatmeal (quick-cooking)** – GI 66	**Potatoes (boiled)** – GI 56
Pineapple – GI 66	**Beets** – GI 64	**Basmati rice** – GI 58	**Sweet corn (boiled)** – GI 60
Raisins – GI 64	**Papaya** – GI 60	**Butternut squash** – GI 51	**Honey** – GI 58
Corn – GI 60	**Grapes** – GI 59	**Bananas (ripe)** – GI 62	**Parsnips** – GI 52
Couscous – GI 65	**Mango** – GI 56	**Whole-wheat bread** – GI 69	**Brown rice** – GI 68

High Glycemic Index (GI 70+)

These foods rapidly raise blood sugar levels and are best enjoyed sparingly or balanced with low-GI foods and fiber.

White bread – GI 75	**Popcorn** – GI 72	**Instant oatmeal** – GI 79	**White rice (short-grain)** – GI 72
Rice cakes – GI 82	**Pumpkin** – GI 75	**French fries** – GI 75	**Glucose (for comparison)** – GI 100
Cornflakes – GI 81	**Pretzels** – GI 83	**Pineapple juice** – GI 70	**Gatorade/sports drinks** – GI 78
Doughnuts – GI 76	**Bagel** – GI 72	**Potatoes (baked)** – GI 85	**Crackers (saltine)** – GI 74
Watermelon – GI 76	**Soda** – GI 75	**Rice pasta** – GI 75	**Puffed wheat cereal** – GI 80

Common Foods and Recommended Alternatives for Diabetics

For individuals managing diabetes, food choices play a vital role in controlling blood sugar levels, boosting energy, and maintaining overall health. Replacing high-carb, high-sugar items with diabetes-friendly alternatives can help achieve steady blood glucose levels.

Common foods	Diabetes-friendly alternatives	Reasons for substitute
White Bread	Whole Grain Bread or Low-Carb Wraps	Whole-grain bread and low-carb wraps contain more fiber, which slows sugar absorption and helps regulate blood sugar levels.
White Rice	Cauliflower Rice or Quinoa	Cauliflower rice is low in carbs and calories, while quinoa has protein and fiber, which support stable blood sugar levels.
Potatoes	Sweet Potatoes or Cauliflower	Sweet potatoes have a lower glycemic index, providing a slower release of glucose. Cauliflower offers a low-carb, versatile substitute.
Pasta	Zucchini Noodles or Shirataki Noodles	Zucchini noodles are nutrient-dense and low in carbohydrates, while shirataki noodles are almost carb-free, making them ideal for blood sugar management.
Sugary Cereals	Steel-cut oats or Chia Seed Pudding	Steel-cut oats have more fiber and lower glycemic impact, while chia seed pudding offers fiber and healthy fats for stable energy.
White Flour	Almond Flour or Coconut Flour	Almond and coconut flour are lower in carbs, high in fiber, and have a milder impact on blood glucose.
Fried Foods	Air-Fried Vegetables or Lean Proteins	Air frying reduces added fats and calories, making it a heart-healthy, low-carb option that's easier on blood sugar levels.
Sugary Yogurt	Unsweetened Greek Yogurt	Greek yogurt has more protein, which can keep blood sugar levels steady and prevent spikes compared to sweetened versions.
Fruit Juice	Whole Fruits (Berries, Apples)	Whole fruits have fiber that helps moderate blood sugar, while juice can lead to rapid spikes.
Soda	Sparkling Water with Lemon or Lime	Sparkling water is free of sugar and carbs, making it a great alternative to blood-sugar-spiking sodas.
Regular Milk	Almond Milk or Coconut Milk	Unsweetened almond and coconut milk are lower in carbs, offering a diabetes-friendly option for cereals and beverages.
High-Sugar Snacks	Nuts and Seeds	Nuts and seeds provide protein and healthy fats, which help to stabilize blood sugar and provide lasting energy.
Ice Cream	Greek Yogurt with Berries or Coconut Ice Cream	Greek yogurt with berries is high in fiber and low in sugar. Coconut ice cream (unsweetened) is a low-carb, healthy-fat option.
Sugar	Stevia or Monk Fruit	These natural sweeteners have no calories and do not impact blood glucose levels, providing a suitable sweetener alternative.
White Tortillas	Lettuce Wraps or Low-Carb Tortillas	Lettuce wraps and low-carb tortillas have fewer carbs and add fiber, making them suitable for controlled glucose levels.
High-sugar sauces (e.g., ketchup)	Homemade Salsa or Sugar-Free Ketchup	Salsa and sugar-free ketchup are low-carb options, making them ideal for adding flavor without spiking blood sugar.
Chips	Kale Chips or Air-Fried Veggie Chips	Kale and veggie chips are nutrient-dense and lower in carbs, offering a healthier, diabetes-friendly snack.
High-Fat Cheese	Low-Fat Cottage Cheese or Ricotta	These cheeses are protein-rich with lower fat content, making them beneficial for weight and blood sugar management.
Cream-Based Dressings	Olive Oil and Vinegar or Greek Yogurt Dressings	Olive oil and vinegar are low-carb with healthy fats, while Greek yogurt dressings offer added protein and fewer carbs.
Canned Soup	Homemade Vegetable Soup	Homemade soup is free from added sugars and preservatives, offering a nutritious, fiber-rich alternative.
Energy Bars	Homemade Nut and Seed Bars	Homemade bars with nuts and seeds are lower in sugar and higher in fiber, making them suitable snacks for people with diabetes.

HOW TO USE YOUR AIR FRYER EFFECTIVELY

The air fryer is a powerful tool for preparing quick, healthy meals. When used effectively, it can help you easily create diabetes-friendly dishes. In this chapter, we'll cover everything you need to know to get started with your air fryer, from basic setup to maximizing its benefits. You'll also find helpful tips for getting perfect results every time and learn how to avoid common mistakes many beginners make.

Getting Started with Your Air Fryer

If you're new to air frying, don't worry—it's easier. Air fryers use rapid air circulation to cook food evenly and quickly, creating a crispy texture similar to traditional frying but with much less oil. Here are the basic steps to get started:

Read the Manual: Each air fryer model has unique features, so reading the user manual before you begin is essential. Familiarize yourself with the various functions, such as temperature control, cooking presets, and the timer.

Essential Functions and Settings: Most air fryers have a simple interface with temperature and timer dials or digital controls. The temperature typically ranges from 180°F to 400°F, and cooking times can vary depending on the food. Many air fryers also have preset programs for common foods like fries, chicken, or vegetables, which can take the guesswork out of cooking.

Preheat Your Air Fryer: Just like an oven, preheating your air fryer before adding food can help ensure even cooking. Most air fryers take just 3-5 minutes to preheat.

Cleaning and Maintenance: To keep your air fryer in good working order, clean it regularly. Most parts, like the basket and tray, are dishwasher-safe, but always refer to the manual for cleaning instructions. Regular maintenance will prevent the buildup of grease and food particles, which can affect performance and taste.

By mastering the basics, you'll be ready to tackle a wide range of recipes, from crispy veggies to tender proteins.

Air Fryer vs. Traditional Cooking

One of the most significant advantages of using an air fryer is its health benefits compared to traditional cooking methods like frying, baking, or grilling. Here's a look at why air frying is a game-changer, especially for those managing diabetes:

Less Oil, Fewer Calories: Traditional frying methods require a lot of oil, which adds unnecessary fat and calories to your meals. In contrast, air frying uses little to no oil, making it a healthier option. For people with diabetes, this fat reduction can help with weight management and heart health, which are crucial for controlling blood sugar.

Faster Cooking: Air fryers cook food much quicker than conventional ovens or stovetops. The rapid air circulation ensures that your food is cooked evenly and quickly, often cutting cooking times in half. This means less time in the kitchen and more time enjoying your meals.

Crispy Results Without the Guilt: The crispiness achieved through air frying is similar to deep-fried foods but without the added grease. This means you can still enjoy "fried" textures in your meals, whether chicken wings or zucchini fries, without spiking your blood sugar or increasing your fat intake.

Retention of Nutrients: Air frying at lower temperatures helps retain more nutrients in your food than other high-heat cooking methods like grilling. This is particularly important for people with diabetes, who need nutrient-dense meals to support overall health and energy levels.

By switching to air frying, you can enjoy the flavors and textures you love while making smarter health choices.

Tips for Perfect Air Fryer Recipes

To get the most out of your air fryer, it's essential to follow a few simple tips to ensure even cooking and achieve that perfect crispy finish with minimal oil:

Avoid Overcrowding: Air fryers circulate hot air around the food. Overcrowding the basket can block the airflow, leading to uneven cooking. Arrange food in a single layer, and if you're cooking a large batch, it's better to cook in batches to ensure everything gets crispy.

Use Minimal Oil: While air fryers don't require much oil, a light oil spray can help achieve a golden, crispy texture. Avoid pouring oil directly onto the food, as this can lead to soggy results. Instead, use a spray bottle or brush to coat the surface lightly.

Shake or Flip Food Halfway: For even cooking, shake the basket or flip the food halfway through the cooking time. This ensures all sides are exposed to the hot air, resulting in a consistent texture.

Adjust Cooking Times and Temperatures: Each air fryer model cooks slightly differently, so monitoring your food the first few times you try a new recipe is essential. You may need to adjust the temperature or time based on the specific ingredients and size of the food.

Add Seasoning Before Cooking: Seasoning your food before it goes into the air fryer allows the spices to adhere better and enhances the flavor during cooking. Dry rubs, marinades, and a touch of oil can help the seasoning stick.

These tips will help you get perfect results every time, whether cooking vegetables, proteins, or snacks.

Common Mistakes to Avoid

Even with the best intentions, making a few mistakes when using an air fryer is easy. Here's how to avoid some of the most common pitfalls:

Not Preheating: Skipping the preheating step can lead to uneven cooking, especially for recipes that require crispy textures. Always preheat your air fryer for a few minutes before adding food.

Using Too Much Oil: While air fryers use significantly less oil than frying, using too much oil can lead to greasy, soggy results. Stick to a light spray or brush of oil for best results.

Overcrowding the Basket: Trying to cook too much food at once will prevent proper air circulation and result in uneven cooking. It's always better to cook in batches than to overcrowd the basket.

Ignoring the Shake or Flip: Air fryers cook from the top down, so the food at the bottom of the basket may not crisp up unless you shake or flip it halfway through. Make sure to give your food a good shake for even results.

Using Wet Batters: Foods with a wet batter, like tempura or beer-battered fish, don't work well in the air fryer. The batter tends to drip off and create a mess. Instead, use a dry breading or coating for air-fried dishes.

Learning from these common mistakes will help you make the most of your air fryer and avoid frustrating results.

BREAKFAST

Breakfast is often called the most important meal of the day, and for those managing diabetes, this couldn't be more accurate. A well-balanced breakfast sets the tone for the rest of the day, stabilizing blood sugar levels and providing the energy needed for daily activities. Skipping breakfast or making poor choices can lead to blood sugar spikes or crashes, disrupting your energy levels, mood, and overall health.

For people with diabetes, focusing on a combination of protein, healthy fats, and low-glycemic carbohydrates in the morning is crucial. This balance helps slow the absorption of sugar into the bloodstream, keeping glucose levels steady and preventing the post-meal spikes common with high-carb, sugary breakfasts. With an air fryer, preparing a nutritious breakfast is quick and easy, allowing you to enjoy delicious meals that fit your dietary needs without spending too much time in the kitchen.

Air frying is particularly beneficial for breakfast because it uses minimal oil, reduces cooking time, and retains more nutrients. From crispy egg bites and veggie-packed frittatas to whole grain toasts and low-carb pancake bites, an air fryer offers versatility and speed—perfect for busy mornings. By starting your day with a diabetes-friendly breakfast cooked in the air fryer, you set yourself up for better blood sugar control, increased energy, and improved overall health.

CRISPY BACON and EGGS CUPS

Crispy bacon is wrapped around a whole egg and cooked in the air fryer until perfectly set

Ingredients:
- 4 slices of bacon
- 4 large eggs
- Salt and black pepper to taste
- Cooking spray

Directions:
1. Preheat the air fryer to 375°F (190°C). Spray a muffin tin with cooking spray. Wrap each slice of bacon around the edge of the muffin cups to create a "nest."
2. Crack one egg into each bacon-lined cup, then season with salt and black pepper.
3. Place the muffin tin in the air fryer and cook for 8-10 minutes, or until the eggs are set and the bacon is crispy to your liking.
4. Carefully remove the bacon and egg cups from the tin and serve warm.

 2 servings   5 minutes   10 minutes

Nutritional information (per serving):
200 calories, 12 g protein, 1 g carbohydrates, 16 g fat, 0 g fiber, 225 mg cholesterol, 430 mg sodium, 160 mg potassium.

FRENCH TOAST STICKS

Classic French toast slices with cinnamon, and vanilla air fried to golden perfection

Ingredients:
- 4 slices of bread (preferably thick-cut)
- 2 large eggs
- 1/4 cup (60 ml) milk (dairy or non-dairy)
- 1/2 tsp vanilla extract
- 1/2 tsp ground cinnamon
- 1 tbsp butter, melted
- Cooking spray

Directions:
1. Cut each slice of bread into 3 sticks. In a shallow bowl, whisk together the eggs, milk, vanilla extract, cinnamon, and melted butter.
2. Dip each bread stick into the egg mixture, making sure all sides are coated. Shake off excess.
3. Spray the air fryer basket with cooking spray and arrange the coated bread sticks in a single layer. Air fry at 375°F (190°C) for 6-8 minutes, flipping halfway through, until golden and crispy.
4. Serve warm with your choice of syrup or toppings.

 2 servings   5 minutes   8 minutes

Nutritional information (per serving):
240 calories, 9 g protein, 28 g carbohydrates, 10 g fat, 2 g fiber, 140 mg cholesterol, 310 mg sodium, 120 mg potassium.

VEGGIE OMELETTE CUPS

Perfectly portioned, protein-packed omelette cups with bell peppers, spinach, and tomatoes

Ingredients:

- 4 large eggs
- 1/4 cup (60 ml) milk (use low-fat or almond milk for a lighter option)
- 1/4 cup (30 g) diced bell peppers (any color)
- 1/4 cup (30 g) diced tomatoes
- 1/4 cup (30 g) chopped spinach
- 1/4 cup (30 g) shredded cheddar cheese
- Salt and black pepper to taste
- Cooking spray

Directions:

1. In a bowl, whisk the eggs and milk until fully combined. Add the diced bell peppers, tomatoes, chopped spinach, shredded cheese, salt, and black pepper, mixing well.
2. Spray a silicone muffin mold with cooking spray and pour the mixture evenly into the cups.
3. Place the mold in the air fryer basket and cook at 350°F (175°C) for 10-12 minutes or until the omelette cups are set and lightly golden on top.
4. Let the omelette cups cool for a minute before removing them from the mold. Serve warm.

 2 servings   5 minutes 12 minutes

Nutritional information (per serving):
145 calories, 10 g protein, 3 g carbohydrates, 10 g fat, 1 g fiber, 190 mg cholesterol, 220 mg sodium, 150 mg potassium.

CRISPY SAUSAGE PATTIES

Low-fat turkey sausage patties cooked to perfection with minimal oil

Ingredients:

- 1/2 lb (225 g) ground turkey (93% lean)
- 1/2 tsp garlic powder
- 1/2 tsp onion powder
- 1/4 tsp smoked paprika
- 1/4 tsp dried sage
- 1/4 tsp salt
- 1/8 tsp black pepper
- Cooking spray

Directions:

1. In a bowl, mix the ground turkey with garlic powder, onion powder, smoked paprika, dried sage, salt, and black pepper until evenly combined.
2. Divide the mixture into 4 equal portions and shape them into patties about 1/2 inch thick.
3. Spray the air fryer basket with cooking spray and place the patties inside. Air fry at 375°F (190°C) for 8-10 minutes, flipping halfway through, until the patties are cooked through and crispy.
4. Remove from the air fryer and serve warm.

 2 servings   5 minutes 12 minutes

Nutritional information (per serving):
160 calories, 18 g protein, 1 g carbohydrates, 9 g fat, 0 g fiber, 70 mg cholesterol, 350 mg sodium, 300 mg potassium.

LOW CARB EGG and CHEESE MUFFINS

Fluffy egg muffins with cheese and your choice of low-carb vegetables

Ingredients:

- 4 large eggs
- 1/4 cup (30 g) shredded cheddar cheese
- 1/4 cup (30 g) diced bell peppers (any color)
- 1/4 cup (30 g) chopped spinach
- 1/8 tsp salt
- 1/8 tsp black pepper
- Cooking spray

Directions:

1. In a bowl, whisk the eggs, then mix in the shredded cheddar cheese, diced bell peppers, chopped spinach, salt, and black pepper until thoroughly combined.
2. Spray a silicone muffin mold with cooking spray and pour the mixture evenly into the cups.
3. Place the mold in the air fryer basket and cook at 350°F (175°C) for 10-12 minutes or until the muffins are set and golden.
4. Let the muffins cool for a minute before removing them from the mold. Serve warm.

 2 servings   5 minutes 12 minutes

Nutritional information (per serving):
160 calories, 12 g protein, 2 g carbohydrates, 11 g fat, 1 g fiber, 220 mg cholesterol, 300 mg sodium, 180 mg potassium.

CINNAMON CHIA BREAKFAST BITES

A sweet, fiber-rich option made with almond flour, chia seeds, and a hint of cinnamon

Ingredients:

- Ingredients:
- 1/2 cup (60 g) almond flour
- 1 tbsp chia seeds
- 1 large egg
- 1/4 tsp ground cinnamon
- 1 tbsp unsweetened almond milk
- 1 tbsp erythritol (or other low-carb sweetener)
- 1/2 tsp baking powder
- 1/8 tsp salt
- Cooking spray

Directions:

1. In a bowl, mix almond flour, chia seeds, cinnamon, erythritol, baking powder, and salt. Add the egg and almond milk, stirring until a dough forms.
2. Spray a silicone muffin mold with cooking spray and spoon the mixture evenly into the cups.
3. Place the mold in the air fryer basket and cook at 350°F (175°C) for 8-10 minutes or until golden brown and set.
4. Let the bites cool for a minute before serving.

 2 servings 5 minutes 10 minutes

Nutritional information (per serving):
130 calories, 6 g protein, 6 g carbohydrates, 10 g fat, 3 g fiber, 55 mg cholesterol, 150 mg sodium, 130 mg potassium.

AVOCADO TOAST with a TWIST

Whole grain toast topped with mashed avocado and a perfectly air-fried egg

Ingredients:

- 2 slices whole grain bread
- 1 ripe avocado
- 2 large eggs
- 1/4 tsp red pepper flakes (optional)
- 1/4 tsp lemon juice
- Salt and black pepper to taste
- Cooking spray

Directions:

1. Toast the whole grain bread slices in the air fryer at 350°F (175°C) for 3-4 minutes until crispy.
2. While the bread is toasting, mash the avocado in a bowl with lemon juice, salt, and black pepper.
3. Lightly spray the air fryer basket with cooking spray and air fry the eggs at 350°F (175°C) for 4-5 minutes or until they reach your desired doneness.
4. Spread the mashed avocado onto the toasted bread, top each with an egg, and sprinkle with red pepper flakes if desired. Serve immediately.

 2 servings 5 minutes 5 minutes

Nutritional information (per serving):
290 calories, 11 g protein, 23 g carbohydrates, 18 g fat, 8 g fiber, 185 mg cholesterol, 300 mg sodium, 450 mg potassium.

ZUCCHINI and MUSHROOM FRITTATA SLICES

A light, veggie-filled frittata, great for meal prepping in advance

Ingredients:

- 4 large eggs
- 1/2 cup (60 g) diced zucchini
- 1/2 cup (50 g) sliced mushrooms
- 1/4 cup (30 g) shredded mozzarella cheese
- 1/4 tsp garlic powder
- Salt and black pepper to taste
- Cooking spray

Directions:

1. In a bowl, whisk the eggs, then stir in the diced zucchini, sliced mushrooms, shredded mozzarella, garlic powder, salt, and black pepper until well combined.
2. Spray a small oven-safe dish or silicone mold with cooking spray and pour the mixture into the dish.
3. Place the dish in the air fryer basket and cook at 350°F (175°C) for 10-12 minutes or until the frittata is set and golden.
4. Let the frittata cool slightly, slice, and serve warm.

 2 servings 7 minutes 12 minutes

Nutritional information (per serving):
190 calories, 14 g protein, 5 g carbohydrates, 13 g fat, 1 g fiber, 280 mg cholesterol, 350 mg sodium, 330 mg potassium.

BLUEBERRY PROTEIN PANCAKE BITES

Low-carb pancake bites made with almond flour and packed with fresh blueberries

Ingredients:

- 1/2 cup (60 g) almond flour
- 1/4 cup (30 g) vanilla protein powder
- 1/2 tsp baking powder
- 1/4 cup (60 ml) unsweetened almond milk
- 1 large egg
- 1/4 cup (40 g) fresh blueberries
- 1/2 tsp vanilla extract
- Cooking spray

Directions:

1. In a bowl, mix the almond flour, protein powder, and baking powder. Add the almond milk, egg, and vanilla extract, stirring until a smooth batter forms. Gently fold in the blueberries.
2. Spray a silicone muffin mold with cooking spray and spoon the batter evenly into the cups.
3. Place the mold in the air fryer basket and cook at 350°F (175°C) for 6-8 minutes or until the pancake bites are golden and set.
4. Let the pancake bites cool for a minute before removing them from the mold. Serve warm.

 2 servings 5 minutes 8 minutes

Nutritional information (per serving):
180 calories, 12 g protein, 10 g carbohydrates, 10 g fat, 3 g fiber, 70 mg cholesterol, 220 mg sodium, 200 mg potassium.

CHEESY CAULIFLOWER HASH BROWNS

Crispy, low-carb hash browns made from cauliflower rice and shredded cheese

Ingredients:

- 1 1/2 cups (150 g) riced cauliflower (fresh or frozen, thawed)
- 1/4 cup (30 g) shredded cheddar cheese
- 1 large egg
- 1/4 tsp garlic powder
- 1/4 tsp onion powder
- 1/8 tsp salt
- 1/8 tsp black pepper
- Cooking spray

Directions:

1. In a bowl, combine the riced cauliflower, shredded cheddar cheese, egg, garlic powder, onion powder, salt, and black pepper. Mix until well combined.
2. Form the mixture into small patties about 1/2 inch thick.
3. Spray the air fryer basket with cooking spray and place the patties in a single layer. Air fry at 375°F (190°C) for 10-12 minutes, flipping halfway through, until golden and crispy.
4. Let cool for a minute before serving.

 2 servings 8 minutes 12 minutes

Nutritional information (per serving):
120 calories, 8 g protein, 5 g carbohydrates, 8 g fat, 2 g fiber, 75 mg cholesterol, 230 mg sodium, 220 mg potassium.

STUFFED BELL PEPPERS with EGGS

Bell peppers stuffed with eggs, spinach, and a sprinkle of cheese for a colorful, nutritious breakfast

Ingredients:

- 2 large bell peppers (any color)
- 2 large eggs
- 1/4 cup (30 g) shredded mozzarella cheese
- 1/4 tsp garlic powder
- 1/4 tsp black pepper
- 1/8 tsp salt
- Cooking spray

Directions:

1. Cut the tops off the bell peppers and remove the seeds and membranes inside.
2. Crack one egg into each bell pepper, then sprinkle with garlic powder, salt, and black pepper. Top with shredded mozzarella cheese.
3. Lightly spray the air fryer basket with cooking spray and place the stuffed bell peppers inside. Air fry at 350°F (175°C) for 10-12 minutes, or until the eggs are set and the cheese is melted and golden.
4. Let cool for a minute before serving.

 2 servings 5 minutes 12 minutes

Nutritional information (per serving):
190 calories, 13 g protein, 9 g carbohydrates, 11 g fat, 2 g fiber, 220 mg cholesterol, 270 mg sodium, 300 mg potassium.

SPINACH and FETA BREAKFAST WRAPS

Whole wheat tortilla wraps filled with spinach, feta, and scrambled eggs, lightly crisped in the air fryer

Ingredients:

- 2 whole wheat tortillas (8-inch)
- 1/2 cup (30 g) fresh spinach, chopped
- 1/4 cup (30 g) crumbled feta cheese
- 2 large eggs
- 1/4 tsp garlic powder
- 1/4 tsp black pepper
- Cooking spray

Directions:

1. In a bowl, whisk the eggs with garlic powder and black pepper. Heat a small skillet and scramble the eggs until fully cooked.
2. Divide the scrambled eggs, spinach, and crumbled feta evenly between the two tortillas.
3. Roll each tortilla into a wrap, folding the sides in. Lightly spray the air fryer basket with cooking spray, and place the wraps inside seam-side down.
4. Air fry at 350°F (175°C) for 6-8 minutes or until the wraps are crispy and golden. Serve warm.

 2 servings 5 minutes 8 minutes

Nutritional information (per serving):
220 calories, 13 g protein, 22 g carbohydrates, 10 g fat, 4 g fiber, 180 mg cholesterol, 450 mg sodium, 350 mg potassium.

SWEET POTATO BREAKFAST HASH

A healthy, hearty hash lightly seasoned and air fried until crispy

Ingredients:

- 1 medium sweet potato (about 8 oz / 225 g), peeled and diced
- 1/2 medium onion, diced
- 1/2 bell pepper (any color), diced
- 1 tbsp olive oil
- 1/2 tsp garlic powder
- 1/2 tsp paprika
- Salt and black pepper to taste
- Cooking spray

Directions:

1. In a large bowl, toss the diced sweet potato, onion, and bell pepper with olive oil, garlic powder, paprika, salt, and black pepper until well coated.
2. Spray the air fryer basket with cooking spray and spread the seasoned mixture in an even layer.
3. Air fry at 375°F (190°C) for 12-15 minutes, shaking the basket halfway through until the sweet potatoes are crispy and tender.
4. Serve warm and enjoy!

 2 servings 10 minutes 15 minutes

Nutritional information (per serving):
180 calories, 2 g protein, 30 g carbohydrates, 7 g fat, 4 g fiber, 0 mg cholesterol, 140 mg sodium, 350 mg potassium.

EASY BREAKFAST BURRITOS

Whole wheat tortillas filled with scrambled eggs, cheese, and veggies, rolled into burritos, and crisped in the air fryer

Ingredients:

- 2 whole wheat tortillas (8-inch)
- 3 large eggs
- 1/4 cup (30 g) shredded cheddar cheese
- 1/4 cup (30 g) diced bell peppers
- 1/4 cup (30 g) diced onions
- 1 tbsp olive oil or butter (for cooking eggs)
- Salt and black pepper to taste
- Cooking spray

Directions:

1. heat olive oil or butter over medium heat in a skillet. Add the diced bell peppers and onions, cooking for 3-4 minutes until softened. Scramble the eggs, season with salt and pepper, and cook until just set. Stir in the shredded cheese.
2. Divide the scrambled egg mixture evenly between the two tortillas. Fold in the sides of each tortilla, then roll them into burritos.
3. Spray the air fryer basket with cooking spray and place the burritos seam-side down. Air fry at 375°F (190°C) for 6-8 minutes or until the tortillas are crispy and golden.
4. Let cool for a minute before serving.

 2 servings 7 minutes 8 minutes

Nutritional information (per serving):
280 calories, 14 g protein, 24 g carbohydrates, 14 g fat, 4 g fiber, 210 mg cholesterol, 430 mg sodium, 220 mg potassium.

BREAKFAST QUESADILLA

Toasted quesadilla stuffed with scrambled eggs, cheese, and your favorite fillings

Ingredients:

- 2 whole wheat tortillas (8-inch)
- 3 large eggs
- 1/4 cup (30 g) shredced cheddar cheese
- 1/4 cup (30 g) diced bell peppers (optional)
- 1/4 cup (30 g) cooked sausage or bacon bits (optional)
- 1 tbsp olive oil or butter (for cooking eggs)
- Salt and black pepper to taste
- Cooking spray

Directions:

1. Heat olive oil or butter in a skillet over medium heat. Scramble the eggs until fully cooked, then mix in the diced bell peppers, cooked sausage or bacon, and shredded cheddar cheese—season with salt and pepper.
2. Place one tortilla on a flat surface, spread the egg mixture evenly on top, and cover with the second tortilla.
3. Spray the air fryer basket with cooking spray and place the quesadilla inside. Air fry at 375°F (190°C) for 6-8 minutes, flipping halfway through, until the tortillas are golden and crispy.
4. Slice and serve warm.

 2 servings   5 minutes   8 minutes

Nutritional information (per serving):
310 calories, 18 g protein, 25 g carbohydrates, 16 g fat, 4 g fiber, 245 mg cholesterol, 480 mg sodium, 280 mg potassium.

ENGLISH MUFFIN BREAKFAST SANDWICHES

English muffins filled with scrambled eggs, cheese, and your choice of sausage or bacon

Ingredients:

- 2 whole wheat English muffins, split
- 2 large eggs
- 2 slices of cheddar cheese
- 2 sausage patties or 4 slices of cooked bacon
- 1 tbsp butter or olive oil (for scrambling eggs)
- Salt and black pepper to taste
- Cooking spray

Directions:

1. In a skillet, heat butter or olive oil over medium heat and scramble the eggs. Season with salt and black pepper.
2. Toast the English muffin halves in the air fryer at 350°F (175°C) for 2-3 minutes until lightly crispy.
3. Assemble the sandwiches by layering scrambled eggs, a slice of cheese, and a sausage patty or bacon on each toasted muffin half. Top with the other muffin half to form a sandwich.
4. Place the assembled sandwiches in the air fryer and cook at 350°F (175°C) for 4-5 minutes until the cheese is melted and the sandwich is warmed through.
5. Serve warm.

 2 servings   5 minutes   8 minutes

Nutritional information (per serving):
390 calories, 20 g protein, 30 g carbohydrates, 20 g fat, 4 g fiber, 230 mg cholesterol, 700 mg sodium, 350 mg potassium.

CRISPY TURKEY BACON STRIPS

Healthier turkey bacon strips air fried to crispy perfection

Ingredients:

- 6 slices of turkey bacon
- Cooking spray (optional)

Directions:

1. Preheat the air fryer to 375°F (190°C).
2. Lightly spray the air fryer basket with cooking spray if desired, then arrange the turkey bacon strips in a single layer without overlapping.
3. Air fry for 6-8 minutes, flipping halfway through, until the turkey bacon is crispy to your liking.
4. Remove and serve warm.

 2 servings   1 minutes   8 minutes

Nutritional information (per serving):
80 calories, 6 g protein, 1 g carbohydrates, 6 g fat, 0 g fiber, 30 mg cholesterol, 400 mg sodium, 100 mg potassium.

MINI BREAKFAST PIZZA

Mini pizzas made with whole wheat English muffins, topped with scrambled eggs, veggies, and cheese

Ingredients:

- 2 whole wheat English muffins, split
- 2 large eggs
- 1/4 cup (30 g) diced bell peppers
- 1/4 cup (30 g) shredded mozzarella cheese
- 1 tbsp olive oil or butter (for cooking eggs)
- Salt and black pepper to taste
- Cooking spray

Directions:

1. In a skillet, heat olive oil or butter over medium heat and scramble the eggs with the diced bell peppers. Season with salt and black pepper.
2. Toast the English muffin halves in the air fryer at 350°F (175°C) for 2-3 minutes until slightly crispy.
3. Top each toasted muffin with the scrambled eggs and bell pepper mixture, then sprinkle with shredded mozzarella cheese.
4. Place the topped muffins back in the air fryer and cook at 350°F (175°C) for 4-5 minutes, until the cheese is melted and bubbly.
5. Serve warm.

 2 servings   5 minutes   8 minutes

Nutritional information (per serving):
280 calories, 16 g protein, 30 g carbohydrates, 11 g fat, 5 g fiber, 210 mg cholesterol, 450 mg sodium, 230 mg potassium.

BANANA PANCAKE BITES

Banana pancakes are made with a simple batter, air fried, and served warm with a drizzle of honey or syrup

Ingredients:

- 1 ripe banana, mashed
- 1/4 cup (30 g) all-purpose flour
- 1 large egg
- 1/4 tsp baking powder
- 1/4 tsp vanilla extract
- 1/8 tsp ground cinnamon (optional)
- Cooking spray
- Honey or syrup for drizzling (optional)

Directions:

1. In a bowl, mix the mashed banana, flour, egg, baking powder, vanilla extract, and cinnamon (if using) until smooth.
2. Lightly spray the air fryer basket with cooking spray. Scoop small spoonfuls of the batter into the basket, forming bite-sized rounds.
3. Air fry at 350°F (175°C) for 6-8 minutes, flipping halfway through, until the pancake bites are golden and cooked through.
4. Serve warm with a drizzle of honey or syrup, if desired.

 2 servings   5 minutes 8 minutes

Nutritional information (per serving):
180 calories, 5 g protein, 30 g carbohydrates, 4 g fat, 2 g fiber, 55 mg cholesterol, 120 mg sodium, 250 mg potassium.

APPLE CINNAMON OATMEAL BITES

A delicious small Oatmeal bites crispy on the outside and soft on the inside

Ingredients:

- 1/2 cup (40 g) rolled oats
- 1/4 cup (60 ml) unsweetened applesauce
- 1/4 cup (30 g) diced apple
- 1 tbsp honey or maple syrup
- 1/2 tsp ground cinnamon
- 1/4 tsp vanilla extract
- 1/8 tsp salt
- Cooking spray

Directions:

1. In a bowl, mix together the oats, applesauce, diced apple, honey, cinnamon, vanilla extract, and salt until well combined.
2. Form the mixture into small bite-sized balls (about 1 inch in diameter).
3. Spray the air fryer basket with cooking spray and place the oatmeal bites in a single layer. Air fry at 350°F (175°C) for 8-10 minutes, until golden and crispy on the outside.
4. Let cool slightly before serving.

 2 servings   5 minutes 10 minutes

Nutritional information (per serving):
140 calories, 3 g protein, 30 g carbohydrates, 2 g fat, 4 g fiber, 0 mg cholesterol, 40 mg sodium, 140 mg potassium.

GRAINS AND LEGUMES

Whole grains and legumes are packed with dietary fiber, which helps slow down the absorption of sugars into the bloodstream. This means fewer blood sugar spikes after meals. High-fiber foods also contribute to better digestion and long-lasting satiety, which can aid in weight management—a crucial factor for Type 2 diabetics.

Whole grains like quinoa, barley, bulgur, and legumes such as lentils and chickpeas have a low glycemic index (GI). Foods with a low GI are digested and absorbed more slowly, leading to more gradual increases in blood sugar levels. This makes them great options for people with diabetes aiming to manage their glucose levels. Grains and legumes provide essential nutrients like potassium, magnesium, and antioxidants, all contributing to better heart health by regulating blood pressure and cholesterol levels.

Beyond fiber, grains, and legumes are nutrient powerhouses. They are rich in B vitamins, iron, and protein—vital for energy production and maintaining muscle mass. For those following a low-carb, low-sugar diet, grains and legumes offer a satisfying, nutrient-dense carbohydrate option without relying on processed foods.

RED LENTIL CRACKERS
Thin, crispy red lentil crackers, perfect for dipping or snacking

Ingredients:
- 1/2 cup (100 g) red lentils, soaked for 2-3 hours and drained
- 1/4 cup (30 g) whole wheat flour
- 1/2 tsp garlic powder
- 1/4 tsp cumin
- Salt to taste
- 2 tbsp water (as needed)
- Cooking spray

Directions:
1. In a blender or food processor, blend the soaked red lentils until smooth. Transfer to a bowl and mix in the whole wheat flour, garlic powder, cumin, and salt. Add water as needed to form a smooth, spreadable batter.
2. Spread the batter thinly onto parchment paper-lined air fryer racks or trays, making sure to create an even layer.
3. Lightly spray the top with cooking spray and air fry at 350°F (175°C) for 10-12 minutes, or until crispy and golden.
4. Break into pieces and serve as crackers, perfect for dipping or snacking.

 2 servings 10 minutes 12 minutes

Nutritional information (per serving):
150 calories, 8 g protein, 28 g carbohydrates, 1.5 g fat, 8 g fiber, 0 mg cholesterol, 180 mg sodium, 320 mg potassium.

QUINOA-STUFFED BELL PEPPERS
Bell peppers stuffed with quinoa, veggies, and herbs, air-fried for a hearty, low-carb meal

Ingredients:
- 2 large bell peppers, tops cut off and seeds removed
- 1/2 cup (90 g) cooked quinoa
- 1/4 cup (30 g) diced zucchini
- 1/4 cup (30 g) diced tomatoes
- 1 tbsp chopped fresh parsley (or 1 tsp dried parsley)
- 1/4 tsp garlic powder
- 1/4 tsp onion powder
- Salt and black pepper to taste
- 1/4 cup (30 g) shredded mozzarella or cheddar cheese
- Cooking spray

Directions:
1. In a bowl, mix the cooked quinoa, zucchini, tomatoes, parsley, garlic powder, onion powder, salt, and black pepper until well combined.
2. Stuff each bell pepper with the quinoa mixture, pressing down gently. Top with shredded cheese.
3. Spray the air fryer basket with cooking spray and place the stuffed peppers inside. Air fry at 350°F (175°C) for 10-12 minutes, or until the peppers are tender and the cheese is melted and golden.
4. Let cool for a minute before serving.

 2 servings 10 minutes 12 minutes

Nutritional information (per serving):
210 calories, 8 g protein, 30 g carbohydrates, 8 g fat, 6 g fiber, 15 mg cholesterol, 320 mg sodium, 450 mg potassium.

BLACK BEAN TACOS

Crispy taco shells filled with seasoned black beans and veggies, air-fried for extra crunch

Ingredients:

- 4 small corn tortillas
- 1/2 cup (120 g) cooked black beans, drained and rinsed
- 1/4 cup (30 g) diced bell peppers
- 1/4 cup (30 g) diced tomatoes
- 1/4 cup (30 g) shredded lettuce
- 1/4 tsp cumin
- 1/4 tsp chili powder
- Salt and black pepper to taste
- 1/4 cup (30 g) shredded cheddar cheese (optional)
- Cooking spray

Directions:

1. In a bowl, combine the black beans, bell peppers, cumin, chili powder, salt, and black pepper. Stir until well mixed.
2. Warm the tortillas slightly to make them more pliable. Divide the black bean mixture between the tortillas, top with diced tomatoes and shredded cheese (if using), and fold each tortilla in half to form a taco.
3. Lightly spray the air fryer basket with cooking spray and place the tacos inside. Air fry at 375°F (190°C) for 6-8 minutes, flipping halfway through, until the tortillas are crispy and golden.
4. Remove from the air fryer and serve with shredded lettuce and your favorite salsa.

 2 servings   10 minutes   8 minutes

Nutritional information (per serving):
240 calories, 9 g protein, 35 g carbohydrates, 7 g fat, 9 g fiber, 10 mg cholesterol, 380 mg sodium, 420 mg potassium.

CHICKPEA SNACKS

Roasted chickpeas with a crispy exterior, flavored with your favorite spices for a healthy, crunchy snack

Ingredients:

- 1 can (15 oz / 425 g) chickpeas, drained and rinsed
- 1 tbsp olive oil
- 1/2 tsp garlic powder
- 1/2 tsp smoked paprika
- 1/4 tsp cumin (optional)
- Salt and black pepper to taste
- Cooking spray

Directions:

1. Pat the chickpeas dry with a paper towel to remove excess moisture. In a bowl, toss the chickpeas with olive oil, garlic powder, smoked paprika, cumin (if using), salt, and black pepper until well coated.
2. Spray the air fryer basket with cooking spray and spread the chickpeas in a single layer.
3. Air fry at 400°F (200°C) for 12-15 minutes, shaking the basket halfway through, until the chickpeas are crispy and golden brown.
4. Let cool slightly before serving as a crunchy snack.

 2 servings   5 minutes   15 minutes

Nutritional information (per serving):
190 calories, 8 g protein, 25 g carbohydrates, 7 g fat, 6 g fiber, 0 mg cholesterol, 290 mg sodium, 300 mg potassium.

MILLET VEGGIE NUGGETS

Millet and mixed vegetables shaped into nuggets, perfect for a healthy, crispy snack

Ingredients:

- 1/2 cup (100 g) cooked millet
- 1/4 cup (30 g) grated carrots
- 1/4 cup (30 g) diced zucchini
- 1/4 cup (30 g) breadcrumbs (whole wheat preferred)
- 1 egg, beaten
- 1/2 tsp garlic powder
- Salt and black pepper to taste
- Cooking spray

Directions:

1. In a bowl, combine the cooked millet, grated carrots, diced zucchini, breadcrumbs, beaten egg, garlic powder, salt, and black pepper until well mixed.
2. Form the mixture into small nugget shapes.
3. Spray the air fryer basket with cooking spray and place the nuggets inside in a single layer. Lightly spray the tops of the nuggets with cooking spray.
4. Air fry at 375°F (190°C) for 10-12 minutes, flipping halfway through, until golden and crispy.
5. Serve warm with your favorite dipping sauce.

 2 servings   10 minutes   12 minutes

Nutritional information (per serving):
210 calories, 7 g protein, 32 g carbohydrates, 5 g fat, 4 g fiber, 55 mg cholesterol, 320 mg sodium, 250 mg potassium.

CRISPY LENTIL FRITTERS

Crunchy lentil fritters seasoned with spices, perfect as a snack or side dish

Ingredients:

- 1/2 cup (100 g) dried lentils, soaked for 4 hours and drained
- 1/4 cup (30 g) diced onion
- 1 garlic clove, minced
- 1/4 cup (30 g) diced carrot
- 1 tbsp chopped fresh cilantro (or 1 tsp dried)
- 1/2 tsp ground cumin
- 1/4 tsp ground coriander
- 1/4 tsp chili powder (optional)
- Salt and black pepper to taste
- 1 tbsp olive oil
- Cooking spray

Directions:

1. In a food processor, combine the soaked lentils, onion, garlic, carrot, cilantro, cumin, coriander, chili powder, salt, and black pepper. Pulse until the mixture is combined but still slightly chunky. Add olive oil and pulse again.
2. Form the mixture into small patties or balls, about 1 inch thick.
3. Spray the air fryer basket with cooking spray and place the lentil fritters inside in a single layer. Air fry at 375°F (190°C) for 10-12 minutes, flipping halfway through, until golden and crispy.
4. Serve warm as a snack or side dish.

 2 servings 10 minutes 12 minutes

Nutritional information (per serving):
180 calories, 9 g protein, 22 g carbohydrates, 7 g fat, 7 g fiber, 0 mg cholesterol, 300 mg sodium, 400 mg potassium.

POLENTA FRIES

Polenta cut into sticks and air-fried for a healthier take on fries with a crispy outside and soft inside

Ingredients:

- 1 cup (240 g) cooked polenta (pre-cooked or homemade, cooled)
- 1 tbsp olive oil
- 1/2 tsp garlic powder
- 1/2 tsp paprika
- Salt and black pepper to taste
- Cooking spray

Directions:

1. Cut the cooled polenta into fry-shaped sticks, about 1/2 inch thick.
2. In a bowl, toss the polenta sticks with olive oil, garlic powder, paprika, salt, and black pepper until well coated.
3. Spray the air fryer basket with cooking spray and arrange the polenta fries in a single layer.
4. Air fry at 400°F (200°C) for 12-15 minutes, flipping halfway through, until the fries are crispy on the outside and soft inside.
5. Serve warm with your favorite dipping sauce.

 2 servings 10 minutes 15 minutes

Nutritional information (per serving):
180 calories, 3 g protein, 30 g carbohydrates, 6 g fat, 3 g fiber, 0 mg cholesterol, 200 mg sodium, 150 mg potassium.

FRYER FARRO SALADAS BITES

Farro mixed with herbs and veggies, shaped into bite-sized salad cakes and air-fried to perfection

Ingredients:

- 1/2 cup (100 g) cooked farro
- 1/4 cup (30 g) diced bell peppers
- 1/4 cup (30 g) diced zucchini
- 1 tbsp chopped fresh parsley (or 1 tsp dried parsley)
- 1 egg, beaten
- 1/4 cup (30 g) breadcrumbs (whole wheat preferred)
- 1/4 tsp garlic powder
- Salt and black pepper to taste
- Cooking spray

Directions:

1. In a bowl, mix the cooked farro, bell peppers, zucchini, parsley, egg, breadcrumbs, garlic powder, salt, and black pepper until well combined.
2. Shape the mixture into small, bite-sized cakes or balls.
3. Spray the air fryer basket with cooking spray and place the farro bites inside in a single layer. Air fry at 375°F (190°C) for 10-12 minutes, flipping halfway through, until golden and crispy.
4. Serve warm as a snack or side dish with your favorite dipping sauce.

 2 servings 10 minutes 12 minutes

Nutritional information (per serving):
210 calories, 7 g protein, 34 g carbohydrates, 5 g fat, 5 g fiber, 55 mg cholesterol, 320 mg sodium, 300 mg potassium.

BROWN RICE and VEGGIE BALLS

Brown rice combined with vegetables and cheese, rolled into balls, and air-fried for a crispy outer layer

Ingredients:

- 1/2 cup (100 g) cooked brown rice
- 1/4 cup (30 g) shredded carrots
- 1/4 cup (30 g) diced bell peppers
- 1/4 cup (30 g) shredded mozzarella or cheddar cheese
- 1 egg, beaten
- 1/4 cup (30 g) breadcrumbs (whole wheat preferred)
- 1/4 tsp garlic powder
- Salt and black pepper to taste
- Cooking spray

Directions:

1. In a bowl, mix the cooked brown rice, shredded carrots, diced bell peppers, cheese, egg, breadcrumbs, garlic powder, salt, and black pepper until well combined.
2. Form the mixture into small balls, about 1 inch in diameter.
3. Spray the air fryer basket with cooking spray and place the rice balls inside in a single layer. Air fry at 375°F (190°C) for 10-12 minutes, flipping halfway through, until golden and crispy.
4. Serve warm as a snack or side dish.

 2 servings 10 minutes 12 minutes

Nutritional information (per serving):
220 calories, 9 g protein, 30 g carbohydrates, 7 g fat, 4 g fiber, 55 mg cholesterol, 340 mg sodium, 280 mg potassium.

BUCKWHEAT and SWEET POTATO CAKES

Nutty buckwheat combined with sweet potatoes, air-fried into savory cakes

Ingredients:

- 1/2 cup (100 g) cooked buckwheat
- 1/2 cup (90 g) mashed sweet potato (cooked)
- 1/4 cup (30 g) breadcrumbs (whole wheat preferred)
- 1 egg, beaten
- 1/4 tsp ground cumin
- 1/4 tsp garlic powder
- Salt and black pepper to taste
- Cooking spray

Directions:

1. In a bowl, mix the cooked buckwheat, mashed sweet potato, breadcrumbs, beaten egg, cumin, garlic powder, salt, and black pepper until well combined.
2. Form the mixture into small cakes, about 1 inch thick.
3. Spray the air fryer basket with cooking spray and place the cakes inside in a single layer. Lightly spray the tops of the cakes with cooking spray.
4. Air fry at 375°F (190°C) for 10-12 minutes, flipping halfway through, until the cakes are golden and crispy on the outside.
5. Serve warm with a dipping sauce or as a side dish.

 2 servings 10 minutes 12 minutes

Nutritional information (per serving):
210 calories, 7 g protein, 36 g carbohydrates, 5 g fat, 5 g fiber, 55 mg cholesterol, 300 mg sodium, 450 mg potassium.

QUINOA-CRUSTED CHICKEN TENDERS

Chicken tenders coated in a quinoa crust, air-fried for a crunchy, protein-packed meal

Ingredients:

- 6 oz (170 g) chicken tenders
- 1/2 cup (90 g) cooked quinoa
- 1/4 cup (30 g) breadcrumbs (whole wheat preferred)
- 1/2 tsp garlic powder
- 1/2 tsp paprika
- Salt and black pepper to taste
- 1 egg, beaten
- Cooking spray

Directions:

1. In a shallow bowl, combine the cooked quinoa, breadcrumbs, garlic powder, paprika, salt, and black pepper.
2. Dip each chicken tender into the beaten egg, allowing excess to drip off, then coat each tender in the quinoa mixture, pressing gently to adhere.
3. Spray the air fryer basket with cooking spray and place the chicken tenders inside in a single layer. Lightly spray the tops of the tenders with cooking spray.
4. Air fry at 375°F (190°C) for 10-12 minutes, flipping halfway through, until the chicken is golden and cooked through (internal temperature should reach 165°F/75°C).
5. Serve warm with your favorite dipping sauce.

 2 servings 10 minutes 12 minutes

Nutritional information (per serving):
280 calories, 27 g protein, 20 g carbohydrates, 10 g fat, 2 g fiber, 130 mg cholesterol, 380 mg sodium, 350 mg potassium.

BULGUR WHEAT FALAFEL

Classic falafel made with bulgur wheat and chickpeas, air-fried for a healthier, crispy version

Ingredients:

- 1/4 cup (45 g) bulgur wheat, cooked
- 1/2 cup (85 g) canned chickpeas, drained and rinsed
- 1/4 cup (30 g) diced onion
- 1 garlic clove, minced
- 2 tbsp chopped fresh parsley (or 1 tsp dried parsley), 1 tbsp olive oil
- 1/2 tsp ground cumin
- 1/4 tsp ground coriander
- Salt and black pepper to taste
- 1/4 cup (30 g) breadcrumbs (optional for binding), Cooking spray

Directions:

1. In a food processor, combine the cooked bulgur wheat, chickpeas, onion, garlic, parsley, cumin, coriander, salt, and black pepper. Pulse until the mixture is well combined but still slightly chunky. Add breadcrumbs if needed for binding.
2. Form the mixture into small balls or patties, about 1 inch thick.
3. Spray the air fryer basket with cooking spray and place the falafel inside. Lightly spray the tops with cooking spray as well.
4. Air fry at 375°F (190°C) for 8-10 minutes, flipping halfway through, until golden and crispy.
5. Serve warm with your favorite dipping sauce or in a pita wrap.

 2 servings **15** minutes **10** minutes

Nutritional information (per serving):
220 calories, 8 g protein, 35 g carbohydrates, 7 g fat, 9 g fiber, 0 mg cholesterol, 320 mg sodium, 300 mg potassium.

KIDNEY BEAN and CORN PATTIES

Kidney beans and corn formed into flavorful patties, air-fried to crispy perfection

Ingredients:

- 1/2 cup (120 g) canned kidney beans, drained and rinsed
- 1/4 cup (40 g) canned corn, drained
- 1/4 cup (30 g) breadcrumbs (whole wheat preferred)
- 1/4 cup (30 g) diced bell peppers
- 1 egg, beaten
- 1/2 tsp ground cumin
- Salt and black pepper to taste
- Cooking spray

Directions:

1. In a bowl, mash the kidney beans with a fork, leaving some chunks for texture. Stir in the corn, breadcrumbs, diced bell peppers, beaten egg, cumin, salt, and black pepper until well combined.
2. Form the mixture into small patties, about 1 inch thick.
3. Spray the air fryer basket with cooking spray and place the patties inside in a single layer. Lightly spray the tops of the patties with cooking spray.
4. Air fry at 375°F (190°C) for 10-12 minutes, flipping halfway through, until the patties are crispy and golden.
5. Serve warm with your favorite dipping sauce or as a side dish.

 2 servings **10** minutes **12** minutes

Nutritional information (per serving):
220 calories, 9 g protein, 35 g carbohydrates, 5 g fat, 7 g fiber, 55 mg cholesterol, 340 mg sodium, 380 mg potassium.

BARLEY-STUFFED MUSHROOMS

Mushrooms stuffed with a hearty barley mixture and air-fried until tender and golden

Ingredients:

- 6 large mushrooms, stems removed
- 1/2 cup (100 g) cooked barley
- 1/4 cup (30 g) diced bell peppers
- 1 garlic clove, minced
- 1 tbsp olive oil
- 1 tbsp chopped fresh parsley (or 1 tsp dried)
- Salt and black pepper to taste
- 2 tbsp grated Parmesan cheese
- Cooking spray

Directions:

1. In a bowl, mix the cooked barley, diced bell peppers, minced garlic, olive oil, parsley, salt, black pepper, and Parmesan cheese until well combined.
2. Stuff each mushroom cap with the barley mixture, pressing gently to fill.
3. Spray the air fryer basket with cooking spray and place the stuffed mushrooms inside in a single layer.
4. Air fry at 375°F (190°C) for 10-12 minutes, until the mushrooms are tender and the tops are golden.
5. Serve warm as an appetizer or side dish.

 2 servings **10** minutes **12** minutes

Nutritional information (per serving):
190 calories, 6 g protein, 24 g carbohydrates, 8 g fat, 4 g fiber, 5 mg cholesterol, 220 mg sodium, 300 mg potassium.

BARLEY and VEGGIE PATTIES

Nutritious barley and mixed veggies formed into patties and crisped in the air fryer

Ingredients:

- 1/2 cup (100 g) cooked barley
- 1/4 cup (30 g) grated carrots
- 1/4 cup (30 g) diced zucchini
- 1/4 cup (30 g) finely chopped spinach
- 1 egg, beaten
- 1/4 cup (30 g) breadcrumbs (use whole wheat for a healthier option)
- 1 tbsp chopped fresh parsley (or 1 tsp dried parsley)
- 1/2 tsp garlic powder
- Salt and black pepper to taste
- Cooking spray

Directions:

1. In a bowl, combine the cooked barley, grated carrots, diced zucchini, chopped spinach, egg, breadcrumbs, parsley, garlic powder, salt, and black pepper. Mix well until all ingredients are evenly combined.
2. Form the mixture into small patties, about 1 inch thick.
3. Spray the air fryer basket with cooking spray and place the patties inside in a single layer. Air fry at 375°F (190°C) for 10-12 minutes, flipping halfway through, until the patties are golden and crispy.
4. Let cool for a minute before serving.

 2 servings 10 minutes 12 minutes

Nutritional information (per serving):
200 calories, 7 g protein, 30 g carbohydrates, 6 g fat, 5 g fiber, 55 mg cholesterol, 300 mg sodium, 300 mg potassium.

LENTIL and SPINACH PATTIES

Flavorful lentil and spinach patties that are crisp on the outside and tender inside

Ingredients:

- 1/2 cup (100 g) cooked lentils
- 1/2 cup (30 g) fresh spinach, chopped
- 1/4 cup (30 g) breadcrumbs (whole wheat preferred)
- 1 egg, beaten
- 1 garlic clove, minced
- 1 tbsp chopped fresh parsley (or 1 tsp dried parsley)
- 1/2 tsp ground cumin
- Salt and black pepper to taste
- Cooking spray

Directions:

1. In a bowl, mix the cooked lentils, chopped spinach, breadcrumbs, beaten egg, garlic, parsley, cumin, salt, and black pepper until well combined.
2. Form the mixture into small patties, about 1 inch thick.
3. Spray the air fryer basket with cooking spray and place the patties inside in a single layer. Lightly spray the tops of the patties with cooking spray.
4. Air fry at 375°F (190°C) for 10-12 minutes, flipping halfway through, until the patties are crispy on the outside and tender inside.
5. Serve warm with a side of your favorite dipping sauce or in a pita.

 2 servings 10 minutes 12 minutes

Nutritional information (per serving):
180 calories, 10 g protein, 23 g carbohydrates, 5 g fat, 6 g fiber, 55 mg cholesterol, 310 mg sodium, 420 mg potassium.

OATMEAL and RAISIN BARS

Soft, chewy oatmeal bars with raisins, air-fried for a lightly crispy texture

Ingredients:

- 1/2 cup (45 g) rolled oats
- 1/4 cup (30 g) whole wheat flour
- 2 tbsp (30 g) raisins
- 2 tbsp (30 g) honey or maple syrup
- 1/4 tsp cinnamon
- 1/4 tsp vanilla extract
- 1 tbsp (15 g) melted butter or coconut oil
- 1 egg, beaten
- Cooking spray

Directions:

1. In a bowl, mix together the oats, whole wheat flour, raisins, cinnamon, and a pinch of salt. Stir in the honey, vanilla extract, melted butter, and the beaten egg until fully combined.
2. Press the mixture evenly into a parchment-lined, small oven-safe dish or tray that fits in your air fryer.
3. Air fry at 350°F (175°C) for 10-12 minutes, or until the bars are golden and slightly crispy on top.
4. Let cool before cutting into bars. Serve as a snack or breakfast treat.

 2 servings 10 minutes 12 minutes

Nutritional information (per serving):
230 calories, 5 g protein, 40 g carbohydrates, 7 g fat, 4 g fiber, 45 mg cholesterol, 85 mg sodium, 200 mg potassium.

CHICKPEA and KALE FRITTERS

Nutritious chickpeas and kale blended into fritters and air-fried until golden and crisp

Ingredients:

- 1/2 cup (85 g) canned chickpeas, drained and rinsed
- 1/2 cup (30 g) fresh kale, finely chopped
- 1/4 cup (30 g) breadcrumbs (whole wheat preferred)
- 1 egg, beaten
- 1 garlic clove, minced
- 1 tbsp olive oil
- 1/4 tsp cumin
- Salt and black pepper to taste, Cooking spray

Directions:

1. In a food processor, blend the chickpeas, garlic, cumin, salt, and black pepper until coarsely combined. Add the chopped kale, breadcrumbs, and egg, mixing until a thick mixture forms.
2. Form the mixture into small patties or fritters, about 1 inch thick.
3. Spray the air fryer basket with cooking spray and place the fritters inside in a single layer. Lightly spray the tops of the fritters with cooking spray.
4. Air fry at 375°F (190°C) for 10-12 minutes, flipping halfway through, until golden and crisp.
5. Serve warm with your favorite dipping sauce.

 2 servings 10 minutes 12 minutes

Nutritional information (per serving):
200 calories, 8 g protein, 24 g carbohydrates, 9 g fat, 5 g fiber, 55 mg cholesterol, 280 mg sodium, 300 mg potassium.

CRISPY WILD RICE CAKES

Wild rice and vegetables shaped into cakes and air-fried for a crispy, wholesome snack

Ingredients:

- 1/2 cup (100 g) cooked wild rice
- 1/4 cup (30 g) shredded carrots
- 1/4 cup (30 g) diced bell peppers
- 1/4 cup (30 g) breadcrumbs (whole wheat preferred)
- 1 egg, beaten
- 1 tbsp chopped fresh parsley (or 1 tsp dried parsley)
- 1/4 tsp garlic powder
- Salt and black pepper to taste
- Cooking spray

Directions:

1. In a bowl, combine the cooked wild rice, shredded carrots, diced bell peppers, breadcrumbs, beaten egg, parsley, garlic powder, salt, and black pepper until well mixed.
2. Form the mixture into small patties, about 1 inch thick.
3. Spray the air fryer basket with cooking spray and place the wild rice cakes inside in a single layer. Lightly spray the tops of the cakes with cooking spray.
4. Air fry at 375°F (190°C) for 10-12 minutes, flipping halfway through, until the cakes are golden and crispy.
5. Serve warm as a snack or side dish.

 2 servings 10 minutes 12 minutes

Nutritional information (per serving):
210 calories, 7 g protein, 30 g carbohydrates, 6 g fat, 4 g fiber, 55 mg cholesterol, 320 mg sodium, 250 mg potassium.

SPICED BLACK BEANS and RICE

Black beans and rice seasoned with spices, air-fried into a satisfying, crispy dish

Ingredients:

- 1/2 cup (100 g) cooked black beans, drained and rinsed
- 1/2 cup (100 g) cooked rice (brown or white)
- 1/4 cup (30 g) diced bell peppers
- 1/4 cup (30 g) diced onions
- 1 tbsp olive oil
- 1/2 tsp ground cumin
- 1/2 tsp smoked paprika
- Salt and black pepper to taste, Cooking spray

Directions:

1. In a bowl, combine the cooked black beans, cooked rice, diced bell peppers, diced onions, olive oil, cumin, smoked paprika, salt, and black pepper. Mix well.
2. Form the mixture into small patties or spread it in a thin layer if you prefer a crispy rice mixture.
3. Spray the air fryer basket with cooking spray and place the bean and rice mixture inside in a single layer.
4. Air fry at 375°F (190°C) for 10-12 minutes, flipping halfway through, until crispy and golden.
5. Serve warm as a side dish or a filling for tacos or wraps.

 2 servings 10 minutes 12 minutes

Nutritional information (per serving):
250 calories, 8 g protein, 40 g carbohydrates, 7 g fat, 8 g fiber, 0 mg cholesterol, 320 mg sodium, 350 mg potassium.

SALADS

For anyone managing diabetes, eating nutrient-dense, low-carb meals is essential to maintain stable blood sugar levels. Salads, when prepared thoughtfully, are a fantastic way to incorporate a variety of vegetables, lean proteins, and healthy fats into your diet. They offer a range of benefits that make them ideal for people with Type 1, Type 2, or prediabetes.

Low in Carbohydrates: Salads primarily consist of leafy greens, non-starchy vegetables, and healthy proteins, making them naturally low in carbohydrates. This helps prevent the blood sugar spikes resulting from more carb-heavy meals.

High in Fiber: Many salad ingredients, such as leafy greens, cucumbers, peppers, and beans, are high in fiber. Fiber plays a critical role in slowing down the absorption of sugar into the bloodstream, stabilizing glucose levels, and promoting digestive health.

Rich in Nutrients: Salads are packed with essential vitamins and minerals. Leafy greens like spinach and kale are rich in iron, magnesium, and antioxidants. At the same time, other vegetables and healthy fats, like avocado and olive oil, contribute to heart health and support weight management.

Customizable for Healthy Fats and Protein: Salads can easily be enhanced with proteins like grilled chicken, fish, or legumes, making them more satisfying and balanced. Adding healthy fats, such as olive oil, avocado, or nuts, can further support heart health and improve satiety without raising blood sugar levels.

Supports Weight Management: Salads are low in calories yet high in fiber and nutrients, so they help with weight control—a key factor for managing Type 2 diabetes and reducing the risk of complications.

With an air fryer, you can create salads that taste delicious and have the added texture and crispiness that make them even more satisfying. Air-frying ingredients like vegetables, proteins, and croutons add a fun, crispy twist to your salad recipes while keeping them diabetes-friendly.

FALAFEL SALAD

Crispy air-fried falafel served over a fresh salad of cucumbers, tomatoes, and greens, topped with a drizzle of tahini

Ingredients:

- 1 cup (170 g) canned chickpeas, drained and rinsed
- 1/4 cup (30 g) chopped onion
- 2 garlic cloves, minced
- 2 tbsp fresh parsley, chopped (or 1 tsp dried parsley)
- 1 tbsp olive oil
- 1/2 tsp ground cumin
- 1/2 tsp ground coriander
- Salt and black pepper to taste
- 1/4 cup (30 g) breadcrumbs (whole wheat preferred)
- 4 cups (120 g) mixed greens
- 1/2 cup (75 g) chopped cucumber
- 1/2 cup (75 g) chopped tomatoes

For the Tahini Drizzle:

- 2 tbsp tahini
- 1 tbsp lemon juice
- 1 tbsp water (adjust as needed for consistency)
- Salt to taste

Directions:

1. Preheat the air fryer to 375°F (190°C). In a food processor, combine the chickpeas, onion, garlic, parsley, olive oil, cumin, coriander, salt, black pepper, and breadcrumbs. Pulse until the mixture is well combined but slightly chunky.
2. Form the mixture into small falafel balls or patties. Spray the air fryer basket with cooking spray and place the falafel inside in a single layer. Air fry for 10-12 minutes, flipping halfway through, until crispy and golden.
3. In a small bowl, whisk together the tahini, lemon juice, water, and salt to create the tahini drizzle.
4. Divide the mixed greens, cucumbers, and tomatoes between two plates. Top with the crispy falafel and drizzle with the tahini sauce.
5. Serve immediately and enjoy!

 2 servings   15 minutes   12 minutes

Nutritional information (per serving):
350 calories, 12 g protein, 42 g carbohydrates, 17 g fat, 10 g fiber, 0 mg cholesterol, 400 mg sodium, 700 mg potassium.

CRISPY TOFU and SPINACH SALAD

Air-fried tofu bites add a crunchy, protein-packed topping to fresh spinach, cucumbers, and sesame dressing

Ingredients:

- 8 oz (225 g) firm tofu, pressed and cubed
- 1 tbsp olive oil
- 1/2 tsp garlic powder
- 1/2 tsp soy sauce
- Salt and black pepper to taste
- 4 cups (120 g) fresh spinach
- 1/2 cup (60 g) sliced cucumbers
- 1 tbsp sesame seeds (optional)

For the Sesame Dressing:

- 1 tbsp sesame oil
- 1 tbsp rice vinegar
- 1 tsp soy sauce
- 1/2 tsp honey (optional)
- 1/2 tsp grated ginger

Directions:

1. Preheat the air fryer to 375°F (190°C). Toss the tofu cubes with olive oil, garlic powder, soy sauce, salt, and black pepper. Place the tofu in the air fryer basket and cook for 10-12 minutes, shaking halfway through, until crispy.

2. In a small bowl, whisk together the sesame oil, rice vinegar, soy sauce, honey (if using), and grated ginger to make the sesame dressing.

3. Divide the spinach and sliced cucumbers between two plates. Top with the crispy tofu bites and drizzle with the sesame dressing.

4. Sprinkle with sesame seeds (optional) and serve immediately.

 2 servings   **10** minutes   **12** minutes

Nutritional information (per serving):
280 calories, 14 g protein, 12 g carbohydrates, 20 g fat, 3 g fiber, 0 mg cholesterol, 380 mg sodium, 650 mg potassium.

SHRIMP and QUINOA SALAD

Delicious air-fried shrimp served over a quinoa and arugula salad with a zesty lime dressing

Ingredients:

- 8 oz (225 g) shrimp, peeled and deveined
- 1 tbsp olive oil
- 1/2 tsp garlic powder
- 1/2 tsp paprika
- Salt and black pepper to taste
- 1/2 cup (90 g) cooked quinoa
- 2 cups (60 g) arugula
- 1/2 avocado, sliced

For the Lime Dressing:

- 1 tbsp olive oil
- 1 tbsp fresh lime juice
- 1/2 tsp honey (optional)
- Salt and black pepper to taste

Directions:

1. Preheat the air fryer to 375°F (190°C). Toss the shrimp with olive oil, garlic powder, paprika, salt, and black pepper. Place the shrimp in the air fryer basket and cook for 6-8 minutes, flipping halfway through, until the shrimp are pink and cooked through.

2. In a small bowl, whisk together the olive oil, lime juice, honey (if using), salt, and black pepper to make the dressing.

3. Divide the cooked quinoa and arugula between two plates. Top with the air-fried shrimp and avocado slices.

4. Drizzle the salad with the lime dressing and serve immediately.

 2 servings   **10** minutes   **8** minutes

Nutritional information (per serving):
360 calories, 24 g protein, 20 g carbohydrates, 22 g fat, 6 g fiber, 165 mg cholesterol, 460 mg sodium, 700 mg potassium.

CHICKEN CAESAR SALAD

Crispy air-fried chicken breast served over a bed of romaine lettuce and topped with Parmesan and a light dressing

Ingredients:

- 2 small chicken breasts (about 6 oz/170 g each)
- 1 tbsp olive oil
- 1/2 tsp garlic powder
- 1/2 tsp paprika
- Salt and black pepper to taste
- 4 cups (180 g) chopped romaine lettuce
- 2 tbsp grated Parmesan cheese
- 2 tbsp light Caesar dressing
- Optional: 1/4 cup (30 g) air-fried croutons

Directions:

1. Preheat the air fryer to 375°F (190°C). Rub the chicken breasts with olive oil, garlic powder, paprika, salt, and black pepper.
2. Place the chicken breasts in the air fryer basket and cook for 10-12 minutes, flipping halfway through, until the internal temperature reaches 165°F (75°C). Let rest for a few minutes before slicing.
3. Arrange the chopped romaine lettuce on two plates and top with sliced chicken, grated Parmesan cheese, and a drizzle of light Caesar dressing.
4. Optional: Add air-fried croutons for extra crunch.
5. Serve immediately and enjoy!

 2 servings   10 minutes   12 minutes

Nutritional information (per serving):
320 calories, 32 g protein, 6 g carbohydrates, 18 g fat, 2 g fiber, 85 mg cholesterol, 540 mg sodium, 500 mg potassium.

KALE and SWEET POTATO SALAD

Tender, roasted sweet potato cubes and air-fried crispy kale combined for a hearty and nutrient-rich salad

Ingredients:

- 1 medium sweet potato, peeled and diced (about 8 oz/225 g)
- 1 tbsp olive oil, divided
- 1/4 tsp garlic powder
- 1/4 tsp paprika
- 2 cups (60 g) kale, stems removed and torn into bite-sized pieces
- 1 tbsp lemon juice
- Salt and black pepper to taste
- 1 tbsp grated Parmesan cheese (optional)

Directions:

1. Preheat the air fryer to 375°F (190°C). Toss the diced sweet potatoes with 1/2 tbsp olive oil, garlic powder, paprika, salt, and pepper. Place the sweet potatoes in the air fryer basket and cook for 12-15 minutes, shaking halfway through, until tender and golden.
2. While the sweet potatoes cook, massage the kale with olive oil, lemon juice, and a pinch of salt. Add the kale to the air fryer in the last 3-5 minutes of cooking until crispy.
3. Combine the roasted sweet potatoes and crispy kale in a bowl. Toss with Parmesan cheese if desired.
4. Serve the salad warm or at room temperature for a hearty, nutrient-rich meal.

 2 servings   10 minutes   15 minutes

Nutritional information (per serving):
180 calories, 4 g protein, 27 g carbohydrates, 7 g fat, 6 g fiber, 0 mg cholesterol, 160 mg sodium, 600 mg potassium.

SALMON SALAD with AVOCADO

Perfectly cooked, flaky air-fried salmon on a bed of mixed greens with avocado and a light lemon vinaigrette

Ingredients:

- 2 salmon fillets (4 oz/115 g each)
- 1 tbsp olive oil
- 1/2 tsp garlic powder
- Salt and black pepper to taste
- 4 cups (160 g) mixed greens
- 1 ripe avocado, sliced
- 1 tbsp lemon juice
- 1 tbsp olive oil (for dressing)
- 1/2 tsp Dijon mustard
- 1/4 tsp honey (optional)
- Salt and black pepper to taste (for dressing)

Directions:

1. Preheat the air fryer to 400°F (200°C). Rub the salmon fillets with olive oil, garlic powder, salt, and black pepper. Place the salmon in the air fryer basket and cook for 8-10 minutes, until cooked through and flaky.

2. To make the vinaigrette, whisk together the lemon juice, olive oil, Dijon mustard, honey (if using), salt, and pepper in a small bowl.

3. Arrange the mixed greens on two plates. Top each plate with avocado slices and the cooked salmon.

4. Drizzle the salad with the lemon vinaigrette and serve immediately.

 2 servings   10 minutes   10 minutes

Nutritional information (per serving):
370 calories, 25 g protein, 10 g carbohydrates, 28 g fat, 7 g fiber, 55 mg cholesterol, 260 mg sodium, 820 mg potassium.

ROASTED VEGETABLE SALAD

A medley of air-fried zucchini, bell peppers, and cherry tomatoes over mixed greens, tossed with balsamic vinaigrette

Ingredients:

- 1 small zucchini, diced (about 4 oz / 115 g)
- 1/2 bell pepper, diced (about 3 oz / 85 g)
- 1/2 cup (75 g) cherry tomatoes
- 1 tbsp olive oil
- Salt and black pepper to taste
- 4 cups (160 g) mixed greens

For the Balsamic Vinaigrette:

- 1 tbsp balsamic vinegar
- 1 tbsp olive oil
- 1/2 tsp Dijon mustard
- 1/2 tsp honey (optional)
- Salt and black pepper to taste

Directions:

1. Preheat the air fryer to 375°F (190°C). Toss the zucchini, bell peppers, and cherry tomatoes with olive oil, salt, and black pepper. Place the vegetables in the air fryer basket and cook for 8-10 minutes, shaking halfway through, until tender and slightly caramelized.

2. To make the vinaigrette, whisk together the balsamic vinegar, olive oil, Dijon mustard, honey (if using), salt, and black pepper in a small bowl.

3. Divide the mixed greens between two plates, top with the roasted vegetables, and drizzle with the balsamic vinaigrette.

4. Serve immediately and enjoy.

 2 servings   10 minutes   10 minutes

Nutritional information (per serving):
180 calories, 4 g protein, 15 g carbohydrates, 12 g fat, 4 g fiber, 0 mg cholesterol, 180 mg sodium, 450 mg potassium.

SOUPS

Soup can be essential to a diabetic-friendly diet, offering both nutrition and versatility. For those managing Type 1, Type 2, or prediabetes, well-prepared soups provide a low-carb, high-nutrient, easy-to-digest, and flavorful option. As a main course or a comforting side, soup can help regulate blood sugar levels while offering a satisfying, balanced meal.

Low in Carbohydrates: Soups made with non-starchy vegetables, lean proteins, and healthy fats are naturally low in carbohydrates. This helps people with diabetes maintain stable blood sugar levels, preventing spikes that could result from more carb-heavy meals.

High in Fiber: Many soup ingredients, such as vegetables, legumes, and beans, are high in dietary fiber. Fiber helps slow digestion, leading to a gradual rise in blood sugar rather than sudden spikes. This can be particularly helpful in controlling blood glucose levels throughout the day.

Packed with Nutrients: Soups can easily incorporate nutrient-dense ingredients into your diet. They often feature multiple vegetables, lean proteins, and healthy fats, delivering vitamins, minerals, and antioxidants essential for overall health.

Hydration and Satiety: Soups naturally hydrate and fill due to their high water content. This helps promote satiety, meaning you feel fuller for longer without consuming excessive calories or carbohydrates. Soups can help with weight management, an essential factor in managing diabetes.

Customizable for Diabetic Needs: Soup's beauty is its versatility. You can easily adjust the ingredients to suit your dietary needs, incorporating more protein, adding heart-healthy fats, or focusing on low-glycemic vegetables.

Although using an air fryer for soups may sound unconventional, it's a fantastic way to roast and crisp vegetables, proteins, and other ingredients before blending them into a hearty stew. The air fryer helps retain nutrients and intensify flavors while using minimal oil.

RED PEPPER and LENTIL SOUP

Roasted red bell peppers and lentils come together for a protein-packed, fiber-rich soup with smoky flavors

Ingredients:

- 2 red bell peppers, halved and seeds removed
- 1/2 cup (100 g) dried red lentils, rinsed
- 1 small onion, diced
- 2 garlic cloves, minced
- 1 tbsp olive oil
- 1/2 tsp smoked paprika
- 1/4 tsp ground cumin
- Salt and black pepper to taste
- 2 cups (480 ml) low-sodium vegetable broth
- 1 tbsp fresh parsley, chopped (optional for garnish)

Directions:

1. Preheat the air fryer to 375°F (190°C). Toss the red bell pepper halves with 1/2 tbsp olive oil, salt, and pepper. Air fry for 12-15 minutes until charred and tender. Set aside to cool slightly, then chop into smaller pieces.
2. In a pot, sauté the diced onion and minced garlic with the remaining olive oil for 3-4 minutes until softened. Add the smoked paprika, cumin, red lentils, and chopped roasted red peppers. Stir to combine.
3. Add the vegetable broth and bring to a boil. Reduce the heat and simmer for 10-12 minutes until the lentils are tender.
4. Blend the soup until smooth (or leave it slightly chunky if preferred), and season with salt and pepper to taste.
5. Serve warm, garnished with chopped parsley if desired.

 2 servings   **10** minutes   **20** minutes

Nutritional information (per serving):
250 calories, 12 g protein, 35 g carbohydrates, 7 g fat, 10 g fiber, 0 mg cholesterol, 380 mg sodium, 780 mg potassium.

MUSHROOM SOUP

Rich, creamy soup made from air-fried mushrooms and onions, blended with vegetable broth and coconut milk

Ingredients:

- 1 cup (100 g) mushrooms, sliced
- 1 small onion, diced
- 2 garlic cloves, minced
- 1 tbsp olive oil
- 2 cups (480 ml) low-sodium vegetable broth
- 1/4 cup (60 ml) coconut milk (optional for creaminess)
- 1/2 tsp thyme
- Salt and black pepper to taste

Directions:

1. Toss mushrooms, onion, and garlic with olive oil and season with thyme, salt, and pepper. Air fry at 375°F (190°C) for 10 minutes, stirring halfway through.
2. Transfer the roasted mushrooms and onion to a pot, add the vegetable broth, and simmer for 5 minutes.
3. Blend the soup until smooth (add coconut milk for a creamy texture).
4. Serve warm and garnish with extra thyme if desired.

 2 servings   10 minutes   12 minutes

Nutritional information (per serving):
160 calories, 4 g protein, 14 g carbohydrates, 10 g fat, 3 g fiber, 0 mg cholesterol, 220 mg sodium, 380 mg potassium.

SWEET POTATO and LENTIL SOUP

Hearty, nutritious soup made with roasted sweet potatoes, red lentils, and warm spices

Ingredients:

- 1 medium sweet potato, diced
- 1/2 cup (100 g) red lentils, rinsed
- 1 tbsp olive oil
- 1/2 tsp cumin
- 1/4 tsp smoked paprika
- 2 cups (480 ml) low-sodium vegetable broth
- Salt and black pepper to taste

Directions:

1. Toss diced sweet potatoes with olive oil, cumin, paprika, salt, and pepper. Air fry at 375°F (190°C) for 12-15 minutes until tender.
2. Combine air-fried sweet potatoes, lentils, and vegetable broth in a pot. Simmer for 10-12 minutes until lentils are tender.
3. Blend part of the soup for a creamy texture, leaving some chunks for added heartiness.
4. Serve warm with a drizzle of olive oil if desired.

 2 servings   10 minutes   15 minutes

Nutritional information (per serving):
290 calories, 11 g protein, 48 g carbohydrates, 8 g fat, 10 g fiber, 0 mg cholesterol, 360 mg sodium, 720 mg potassium.

ROASTED TOMATO BASIL SOUP

Flavorful, creamy tomato soup made from air-fried tomatoes and fresh basil

Ingredients:

- 4 medium tomatoes, halved (about 16 oz / 450 g)
- 1 small onion, quartered
- 2 garlic cloves
- 1 tbsp olive oil
- Salt and black pepper to taste
- 1 cup (240 ml) low-sodium vegetable broth
- 1/4 cup (60 ml) coconut milk or cream (optional for creaminess)
- 1/4 cup fresh basil leaves, chopped
- 1/4 tsp dried oregano (optional)

Directions:

1. Preheat the air fryer to 375°F (190°C). Toss the tomatoes, onion, and garlic with olive oil, salt, and pepper. Place the vegetables in the air fryer basket and roast for 12-15 minutes until tender and slightly caramelized.
2. Transfer the roasted vegetables to a blender. Add vegetable broth, coconut milk or cream (if using), fresh basil, and oregano. Blend until smooth and creamy.
3. Pour the soup into a pot and heat over low for 2-3 minutes to combine the flavors.
4. Serve warm, garnished with extra basil if desired.

 2 servings   10 minutes   15 minutes

Nutritional information (per serving):
180 calories, 4 g protein, 18 g carbohydrates, 10 g fat, 4 g fiber, 0 mg cholesterol, 350 mg sodium, 550 mg potassium.

BUTTERNUT SQUASH SOUP

Roasted butternut squash blended into a smooth, rich soup, seasoned with cinnamon and nutmeg for warmth

Ingredients:

- 2 cups (about 10 oz / 280 g) butternut squash, peeled and diced
- 1 small onion, quartered
- 2 garlic cloves
- 1 tbsp olive oil
- 1/4 tsp cinnamon
- 1/8 tsp ground nutmeg
- Salt and black pepper to taste
- 1 cup (240 ml) low-sodium vegetable broth
- 1/4 cup (60 ml) coconut milk or cream (optional for added creaminess)

Directions:

1. Preheat the air fryer to 375°F (190°C). Toss the diced butternut squash, onion, and garlic with olive oil, cinnamon, nutmeg, salt, and pepper. Place the vegetables in the air fryer basket and roast for 12-15 minutes until tender and caramelized.
2. Transfer the roasted vegetables to a blender, add the vegetable broth and coconut milk (if using), and blend until smooth and creamy.
3. Pour the blended soup into a pot and heat over low for 2-3 minutes to combine the flavors.
4. Serve warm, garnished with a sprinkle of cinnamon if desired.

 2 servings   10 minutes   15 minutes

Nutritional information (per serving):
210 calories, 3 g protein, 28 g carbohydrates, 10 g fat, 5 g fiber, 0 mg cholesterol, 250 mg sodium, 600 mg potassium.

ZUCCHINI and LEEK SOUP

Light and velvety soup made from air-fried zucchini and leeks, blended with vegetable broth and seasoned with thyme

Ingredients:

- 1 medium zucchini, diced
- 1 leek, cleaned and sliced
- 1 tbsp olive oil
- 1 garlic clove, minced
- 2 cups (480 ml) low-sodium vegetable broth
- 1/4 tsp thyme
- Salt and black pepper to taste

Directions:

1. Toss zucchini, leek, and garlic with olive oil, thyme, salt, and pepper. Air fry at 375°F (190°C) for 10-12 minutes until softened.
2. Combine the air-fried vegetables with vegetable broth in a pot and simmer for 5 minutes.
3. Blend until smooth and creamy.
4. Serve warm, garnished with olive oil or extra thyme.

 2 servings   5 minutes   8 minutes

Nutritional information (per serving):
140 calories, 4 g protein, 16 g carbohydrates, 8 g fat, 3 g fiber, 0 mg cholesterol, 210 mg sodium, 460 mg potassium

BROCCOLI and CHEDDAR SOUP

Crispy air-fried broccoli turned into a creamy, cheesy soup that's both comforting and diabetes-friendly

Ingredients:

- 2 cups (200 g) broccoli florets
- 1 tbsp olive oil
- Salt and black pepper to taste
- 1/2 small onion, diced
- 1 garlic clove, minced
- 1 cup (240 ml) low-sodium vegetable broth
- 1/2 cup (120 ml) milk or unsweetened almond milk
- 1/2 cup (60 g) shredded cheddar cheese
- 1/4 tsp ground mustard (optional)

Directions:

1. Preheat the air fryer to 375°F (190°C). Toss the broccoli florets with olive oil, salt, and pepper. Air fry for 10-12 minutes until crispy and tender, shaking the basket halfway through.
2. In a small pot, sauté the diced onion and minced garlic for 2-3 minutes until softened. Add the roasted broccoli, vegetable broth, and milk, and simmer for 5 minutes.
3. Blend the soup until smooth, then stir in the shredded cheddar cheese and ground mustard (if using). Heat gently until the cheese is melted and fully incorporated.
4. Serve warm, garnished with extra cheese if desired.

 2 servings   10 minutes 15 minutes

Nutritional information (per serving):
240 calories, 10 g protein, 12 g carbohydrates, 18 g fat, 3 g fiber, 30 mg cholesterol, 450 mg sodium, 400 mg potassium.

CARROT and GINGER SOUP

Sweet, roasted carrots with a spicy kick from fresh ginger, blended into a healthy, low-carb soup

Ingredients:

- 3 medium carrots, pee ed and chopped (about 10 oz / 280 g)
- 1 tbsp olive oil
- 1 tbsp fresh ginger, minced
- 1 garlic clove, minced
- 1/2 tsp ground cumin (optional)
- Salt and black pepper to taste
- 2 cups (480 ml) low-sodium vegetable broth
- 1/4 cup (60 ml) coconut milk (optional for creaminess)

Directions:

1. Preheat the air fryer to 375°F (190°C). Toss the chopped carrots with olive oil, salt, and pepper. Place in the air fryer basket and roast for 12-15 minutes until tender and slightly caramelized.
2. In a small pot, sauté the minced ginger and garlic for 2-3 minutes. Add the roasted carrots, cumin (if using), and vegetable broth, and simmer for 5 minutes.
3. Blend the mixture until smooth and creamy. If using coconut milk, stir in it and heat for another 2 minutes.
4. Serve warm, garnished with a drizzle of coconut milk or fresh herbs if desired.

 2 servings 10 minutes 15 minutes

Nutritional information (per serving):
190 calories, 4 g protein, 22 g carbohydrates, 10 g fat, 5 g fiber, 0 mg cholesterol, 300 mg sodium, 600 mg potassium.

CHICKEN and VEGETABLE SOUP

Tender air-fried chicken combined with roasted vegetables in a light broth, perfect for a hearty yet healthy meal

Ingredients:

- 1 small chicken breast (6 oz / 170 g), diced
- 1 tbsp olive oil, divided
- 1 carrot, peeled and chopped
- 1 zucchini, diced
- 1/2 onion, diced
- 1 garlic clove, minced
- 1/2 tsp dried thyme
- Salt and black pepper to taste
- 2 cups (480 ml) low-sodium chicken broth
- 1/2 cup (60 g) spinach (optional)

Directions:

1. Preheat the air fryer to 375°F (190°C). Toss the diced chicken with 1/2 tbsp olive oil, salt, and pepper. Air fry for 10-12 minutes until cooked through, flipping halfway.
2. In the same air fryer, toss the carrots, zucchini, onion, and garlic with the remaining olive oil, thyme, salt, and pepper. Air fry for 10 minutes until tender.
3. Combine the air-fried chicken, roasted vegetables, and chicken broth in a pot. Bring to a simmer and cook for 5 minutes. Add spinach if using and cook for an additional 2 minutes.
4. Serve warm and enjoy your hearty and healthy chicken and vegetable soup.

 2 servings 10 minutes 20 minutes

Nutritional information (per serving):
260 calories, 28 g protein, 18 g carbohydrates, 9 g fat, 4 g fiber, 65 mg cholesterol, 380 mg sodium, 650 mg potassium

CAULIFLOWER SOUP

Roasted cauliflower pureed into a velvety soup, with hints of garlic and herbs for a light, filling dish

Ingredients:

- 2 cups (200 g) cauliflower florets
- 1 tbsp olive oil
- 1 garlic clove, minced
- 1/2 small onion, diced
- 1/2 tsp dried thyme
- Salt and black pepper to taste
- 1 cup (240 ml) low-sodium vegetable broth
- 1/2 cup (120 ml) milk or unsweetened almond milk

Directions:

1. Preheat the air fryer to 375°F (190°C). Toss the cauliflower florets with olive oil, salt, and black pepper. Air fry for 12-15 minutes until golden and tender, shaking the basket halfway through.
2. In a small pot, sauté the diced onion and minced garlic for 2-3 minutes until softened. Add the roasted cauliflower, dried thyme, vegetable broth, and milk. Simmer for 5 minutes.
3. Blend the mixture until smooth and creamy.
4. Serve warm, garnished with a sprinkle of thyme or a drizzle of olive oil if desired.

 2 servings 10 minutes 15 minutes

Nutritional information (per serving):
160 calories, 4 g protein, 14 g carbohydrates, 10 g fat, 3 g fiber, 0 mg cholesterol, 300 mg sodium, 450 mg potassium.

SIDES AND VEGETABLES

For people managing Type 1, Type 2, or prediabetes, vegetables and well-prepared side dishes can be crucial to maintaining balanced blood sugar levels. Vegetables are naturally low in carbohydrates and high in fiber, making them an excellent choice for those looking to keep blood glucose in check. Moreover, sides and vegetables can provide essential vitamins, minerals, and antioxidants that contribute to overall health and well-being.

Low-Carb and Nutrient-Dense: Vegetables like broccoli, cauliflower, zucchini, and bell peppers are low in carbohydrates and rich in essential nutrients, which help regulate blood sugar levels without causing spikes. Sides based on whole grains or legumes, such as quinoa or lentils, can also be diabetes-friendly when consumed in moderation.

High in Fiber: Fiber is vital for people with diabetes because it slows down the digestion of carbohydrates, helping prevent quick rises in blood sugar. Vegetables and whole grains are packed with fiber, aiding digestion and keeping you full for longer, which supports weight management—key to managing Type 2 diabetes.

Packed with Essential Vitamins and Minerals: Vegetables provide vital nutrients like potassium, magnesium, and antioxidants, all of which help reduce inflammation, support heart health, and stabilize blood pressure—common concerns for people with diabetes.

Versatile and Satisfying: When prepared well, vegetables and side dishes can be delicious and satisfying, ensuring that meals remain exciting. Using an air fryer allows you to achieve crispy, flavorful vegetables without excessive oil, making it a healthier way to enjoy your favorite sides.

Supports a Low-Glycemic Diet: Choosing low-glycemic index (GI) vegetables and sides helps stabilize blood sugar levels. Many non-starchy vegetables have a low GI, meaning they don't cause a rapid rise in glucose, making them ideal for people with diabetes.

CRISPY BRUSSELS SPROUTS

Perfectly crisp Brussels sprouts with a slight char, seasoned with garlic and balsamic vinegar

Ingredients:

- 2 cups (about 8 oz / 225 g) Brussels sprouts, halved
- 1 tbsp olive oil
- 1 tsp garlic powder
- 1 tbsp balsamic vinegar
- Salt and black pepper to taste
- Cooking spray

Directions:

1. Preheat the air fryer to 375°F (190°C). Toss the halved Brussels sprouts with olive oil, garlic powder, salt, and black pepper.
2. Lightly spray the air fryer basket with cooking spray. Place the Brussels sprouts in a single layer in the basket.
3. Air fry for 10-12 minutes, shaking the basket halfway through until the Brussels sprouts are crispy and slightly charred.
4. Remove the Brussels sprouts from the air fryer and drizzle with balsamic vinegar. Toss to combine and serve warm.

 2 servings   5 minutes   12 minutes

Nutritional information (per serving):
120 calories, 4 g protein, 14 g carbohydrates, 7 g fat, 6 g fiber, 0 mg cholesterol, 120 mg sodium, 450 mg potassium.

ROASTED CAULIFLOWER

Tender cauliflower florets, roasted to perfection with olive oil and a sprinkle of paprika

Ingredients:

- 2 cups (about 8 oz / 225 g) cauliflower florets
- 1 tbsp olive oil
- 1/2 tsp paprika
- Salt and black pepper to taste
- Cooking spray

Directions:

1. Preheat the air fryer to 375°F (190°C). Toss the cauliflower florets with olive oil, paprika, salt, and black pepper until evenly coated.
2. Lightly spray the air fryer basket with cooking spray. Place the cauliflower florets in a single layer in the basket.
3. Air fry for 10-12 minutes, shaking the basket halfway through until the cauliflower is tender and golden brown.
4. Serve warm as a side dish or snack.

 2 servings 5 minutes 12 minutes

Nutritional information (per serving):
110 calories, 3 g protein, 8 g carbohydrates, 8 g fat, 3 g fiber, 0 mg cholesterol, 150 mg sodium, 400 mg potassium.

GARLIC GREEN BEANS

Fresh green beans lightly tossed with olive oil and garlic, air-fried until crisp-tender

Ingredients:

- 2 cups (about 6 oz / 170 g) fresh green beans, trimmed
- 1 tbsp olive oil
- 1 tsp garlic powder
- Salt and black pepper to taste
- Cooking spray

Directions:

1. Preheat the air fryer to 375°F (190°C). Toss the green beans with olive oil, garlic powder, salt, and black pepper until evenly coated.
2. Lightly spray the air fryer basket with cooking spray. Place the green beans in a single layer of the basket.
3. Air fry for 6-8 minutes, shaking the basket halfway through until the green beans are crisp-tender and slightly browning.
4. Serve warm as a healthy side dish.

 2 servings 5 minutes 8 minutes

Nutritional information (per serving):
100 calories, 2 g protein, 8 g carbohydrates, 7 g fat, 3 g fiber, 0 mg cholesterol, 160 mg sodium, 230 mg potassium.

ZUCCHINI FRIES

Crispy, low-carb zucchini fries with a Parmesan coating, ideal for a guilt-free side or snack

Ingredients:

- 1 medium zucchini (about 8 oz / 225 g), cut into fry-sized sticks
- 1/4 cup (30 g) grated Parmesan cheese
- 1/4 cup (30 g) breadcrumbs (whole wheat preferred)
- 1/2 tsp garlic powder
- 1/2 tsp paprika
- 1 egg, beaten
- Salt and black pepper to taste
- Cooking spray

Directions:

1. Preheat the air fryer to 400°F (200°C). Combine the Parmesan, breadcrumbs, garlic powder, paprika, salt, and black pepper in a bowl.
2. Dip each zucchini stick into the beaten egg, then coat with the Parmesan-breadcrumb mixture.
3. Lightly spray the air fryer basket with cooking spray and place the zucchini fries in a single layer. Air fry for 8-10 minutes, shaking halfway through, until crispy and golden brown.
4. Serve warm as a side or snack with your favorite dipping sauce.

 2 servings 10 minutes 10 minutes

Nutritional information (per serving):
170 calories, 9 g protein, 14 g carbohydrates, 9 g fat, 2 g fiber, 55 mg cholesterol, 300 mg sodium, 350 mg potassium.

SWEET POTATO WEDGES

Seasoned sweet potato wedges air-fried for a crispy outside and soft, tender inside

Ingredients:

- 1 medium sweet potato (about 8 oz / 225 g), cut into wedges
- 1 tbsp olive oil
- 1/2 tsp paprika
- 1/2 tsp garlic powder
- Salt and black pepper to taste
- Cooking spray

Directions:

1. Preheat the air fryer to 400°F (200°C). Toss the sweet potato wedges with olive oil, paprika, garlic powder, salt, and black pepper.
2. Lightly spray the air fryer basket with cooking spray. Place the sweet potato wedges in a single layer in the basket.
3. Air fry for 12-15 minutes, shaking the basket halfway through until the wedges are crispy on the outside and tender inside.
4. Serve warm as a side dish or snack.

 2 servings 5 minutes 15 minutes

Nutritional information (per serving):
180 calories, 2 g protein, 26 g carbohydrates, 7 g fat, 4 g fiber, 0 mg cholesterol, 220 mg sodium, 450 mg potassium.

BROCCOLI with LEMON

Crunchy air-fried broccoli florets with a zesty lemon dressing for a fresh and tangy side

Ingredients:

- 2 cups (about 6 oz / 170 g) broccoli florets
- 1 tbsp olive oil
- 1 tsp garlic powder
- Salt and black pepper to taste
- 1 tbsp fresh lemon juice
- 1/2 tsp lemon zest

Directions:

1. Preheat the air fryer to 375°F (190°C). Toss the broccoli florets with olive oil, garlic powder, salt, and black pepper.
2. Place the broccoli in the air fryer basket in a single layer and air fry for 8-10 minutes, shaking halfway through, until crisp-tender and slightly browned.
3. Remove the broccoli from the air fryer and toss with lemon juice and lemon zest.
4. Serve immediately as a fresh and tangy side dish.

 2 servings 5 minutes 10 minutes

Nutritional information (per serving):
120 calories, 4 g protein, 10 g carbohydrates, 9 g fat, 4 g fiber, 0 mg cholesterol, 160 mg sodium, 400 mg potassium.

ASPARAGUS with PARMESAN

Tender asparagus spears topped with melted Parmesan cheese and roasted to perfection

Ingredients:

- 1 bunch (about 8 oz / 225 g) asparagus, trimmed
- 1 tbsp olive oil
- 1/4 tsp garlic powder
- Salt and black pepper to taste
- 2 tbsp grated Parmesan cheese

Directions:

1. Preheat the air fryer to 375°F (190°C). Toss the asparagus spears with olive oil, garlic powder, salt, and black pepper until evenly coated.
2. Place the asparagus in the air fryer basket in a single layer and air fry for 6-8 minutes, shaking halfway through, until tender.
3. Sprinkle the grated Parmesan cheese over the asparagus during the last 1-2 minutes of cooking to melt the cheese.
4. Serve warm as a savory, cheesy side dish.

 2 servings 5 minutes 8 minutes

Nutritional information (per serving):
150 calories, 5 g protein, 8 g carbohydrates, 11 g fat, 3 g fiber, 5 mg cholesterol, 240 mg sodium, 400 mg potassium.

BUTTERNUT SQUASH CUBES

Sweet and savory roasted butternut squash cubes with a hint of cinnamon

Ingredients:

- 2 cups (about 10 oz / 280 g) butternut squash, peeled and cubed
- 1 tbsp olive oil
- 1/2 tsp cinnamon
- Salt and black pepper to taste

Directions:

1. Preheat the air fryer to 375°F (190°C). Toss the butternut squash cubes with olive oil, cinnamon, salt, and black pepper until evenly coated.
2. Place the squash cubes in the air fryer basket in a single layer.
3. Air fry for 12-15 minutes, shaking the basket halfway through until the squash is tender and golden brown.
4. Serve warm as a sweet and savory side dish.

 2 servings 5 minutes 15 minutes

Nutritional information (per serving):
160 calories, 2 g protein, 22 g carbohydrates, 8 g fat, 4 g fiber, 0 mg cholesterol, 200 mg sodium, 580 mg potassium.

CARROT FRIES

Slightly sweet carrot sticks air-fried to a crispy finish, with a sprinkle of cumin

Ingredients:

- 4 medium carrots (about 8 oz / 225 g), peeled and cut into sticks
- 1 tbsp olive oil
- 1/2 tsp ground cumin
- Salt and black pepper to taste

Directions:

1. Preheat the air fryer to 375°F (190°C). Toss the carrot sticks with olive oil, cumin, salt, and black pepper until evenly coated.
2. Place the carrot sticks in the air fryer basket in a single layer.
3. Air fry for 10-12 minutes, shaking halfway through until the carrots are crispy on the outside and tender inside.
4. Serve warm as a slightly sweet, crispy side dish or snack.

 2 servings 5 minutes 12 minutes

Nutritional information (per serving):
130 calories, 1 g protein, 12 g carbohydrates, 9 g fat, 4 g fiber, 0 mg cholesterol, 200 mg sodium, 500 mg potassium.

ROASTED BELL PEPPERS

Vibrant bell peppers air-fried for a smoky, caramelized flavor, perfect as a side or topping

Ingredients:

- 2 medium bell peppers (about 8 oz / 225 g), cut into strips
- 1 tbsp olive oil
- Salt and black pepper to taste

Directions:

1. Preheat the air fryer to 375°F (190°C). Toss the bell pepper strips with olive oil, salt, and black pepper until evenly coated.
2. Place the pepper strips in the air fryer basket in a single layer.
3. Air fry for 8-10 minutes, shaking halfway through until the peppers are soft and slightly charred with a smoky, caramelized flavor.
4. Serve warm as a side dish or topping for sandwiches, salads, or other dishes.

2 servings 5 minutes 10 minutes

Nutritional information (per serving):
110 calories, 1 g protein, 8 g carbohydrates, 9 g fat, 2 g fiber, 0 mg cholesterol, 200 mg sodium, 300 mg potassium.

EGGPLANT CHIPS

Thinly sliced eggplant rounds seasoned with herbs and air-fried until crispy

Ingredients:

- 1 small eggplant (about 8 oz / 225 g), thinly sliced into rounds
- 1 tbsp olive oil
- 1/2 tsp garlic powder
- 1/2 tsp dried oregano
- Salt and black pepper to taste
- Cooking spray

Directions:

1. Preheat the air fryer to 375°F (190°C). Toss the eggplant slices with olive oil, garlic powder, oregano, salt, and black pepper until evenly coated.
2. Lightly spray the air fryer basket with cooking spray and arrange the eggplant slices in a single layer.
3. Air fry for 10-12 minutes, flipping halfway through until the eggplant rounds are crispy and golden.
4. Serve warm as a crispy, healthy snack or side dish.

 2 servings 5 minutes 12 minutes

Nutritional information (per serving):
120 calories, 1 g protein, 8 g carbohydrates, 9 g fat, 4 g fiber, 0 mg cholesterol, 210 mg sodium, 320 mg potassium.

CRISPY KALE CHIPS

Crunchy kale chips seasoned with sea salt, offering a nutritious and low-calorie snack

Ingredients:

- 2 cups (about 2 oz / 60 g) kale leaves, stems removed and torn into bite-sized pieces
- 1 tbsp olive oil
- 1/4 tsp sea salt (or to taste)
- Cooking spray

Directions:

1. Preheat the air fryer to 350°F (175°C). Toss the kale leaves with olive oil and sea salt until evenly coated.
2. Lightly spray the air fryer basket with cooking spray and arrange the kale in a single layer.
3. Air fry for 5-6 minutes, shaking the basket halfway through until the kale chips are crispy and lightly browned.
4. Serve immediately as a crunchy, nutritious snack.

 2 servings 5 minutes 6 minutes

Nutritional information (per serving):
80 calories, 2 g protein, 7 g carbohydrates, 6 g fat, 2 g fiber, 0 mg cholesterol, 150 mg sodium, 400 mg potassium.

SPAGHETTI SQUASH

Spaghetti squash roasted and shredded into pasta-like strands, perfect as a low-carb side

Ingredients:

- 1 small spaghetti squash (about 1.5 lbs / 680 g), halved and seeds removed
- 1 tbsp olive oil
- Salt and black pepper to taste

Directions:

1. Preheat the air fryer to 375°F (190°C). Rub the cut sides of the spaghetti squash halves with olive oil and season with salt and black pepper.
2. Place the squash halves, cut side up, in the air fryer basket. Air fry for 20-25 minutes until the squash is tender and easily pierced with a fork.
3. Once cooked, use a fork to scrape the inside of the squash, creating spaghetti-like strands.
4. Serve as a low-carb side dish or use as a base for your favorite toppings or sauces.

 2 servings 5 minutes 25 minutes

Nutritional information (per serving):
100 calories, 2 g protein, 20 g carbohydrates, 4 g fat, 4 g fiber, 0 mg cholesterol, 200 mg sodium, 300 mg potassium.

BALSAMIC MUSHROOMS

Juicy mushrooms roasted in balsamic vinegar and garlic for a rich, earthy side dish

Ingredients:

- 8 oz (225 g) mushrooms, halved or quartered
- 1 tbsp balsamic vinegar
- 1 tbsp olive oil
- 1 garlic clove, minced
- Salt and black pepper to taste

Directions:

1. Preheat the air fryer to 375°F (190°C). Toss the mushrooms with balsamic vinegar, olive oil, garlic, salt, and black pepper until well coated.
2. Place the mushrooms in a single layer in the air fryer basket.
3. Air fry for 8-10 minutes, shaking the basket halfway through until the mushrooms are tender and slightly caramelized.
4. Serve warm as a rich, earthy side dish.

 2 servings   5 minutes   10 minutes

Nutritional information (per serving):
110 calories, 2 g protein, 5 g carbohydrates, 9 g fat, 1 g fiber, 0 mg cholesterol, 150 mg sodium, 300 mg potassium.

STUFFED MINI PEPPERS

Mini bell peppers stuffed with a savory quinoa and vegetable filling, air-fried until tender

Ingredients:

- 8-10 mini bell peppers (about 8 oz / 225 g)
- 1/2 cup (90 g) cooked quinoa
- 1/4 cup (30 g) diced zucchini
- 1/4 cup (30 g) diced tomatoes
- 1 tbsp olive oil
- 1/2 tsp garlic powder
- Salt and black pepper to taste
- 2 tbsp grated Parmesan cheese (optional)

Directions:

1. Preheat the air fryer to 375°F (190°C). Cut the tops off the mini bell peppers and remove the seeds.
2. In a bowl, mix the cooked quinoa, diced zucchini, diced tomatoes, olive oil, garlic powder, salt, and black pepper until well combined.
3. Stuff each mini bell pepper with the quinoa mixture and place them in the air fryer basket. If using, sprinkle the tops with Parmesan cheese.
4. Air fry for 8-10 minutes until the peppers are tender and the filling is heated.
5. Serve warm as a delicious side or appetizer.

 2 servings   10 minutes   10 minutes

Nutritional information (per serving):
180 calories, 6 g protein, 24 g carbohydrates, 7 g fat, 4 g fiber, 0 mg cholesterol, 160 mg sodium, 450 mg potassium.

PARMESAN CRUSTED CAULIFLOWER

Crispy Parmesan-crusted cauliflower florets, perfect as a crunchy side or snack

Ingredients:

- 2 cups (about 8 oz / 225 g) cauliflower florets
- 1/4 cup (30 g) grated Parmesan cheese
- 1/4 cup (30 g) breadcrumbs (whole wheat preferred)
- 1 tbsp olive oil
- 1/2 tsp garlic powder
- Salt and black pepper to taste
- Cooking spray

Directions:

1. Preheat the air fryer to 375°F (190°C). Toss the cauliflower florets in a bowl with olive oil, garlic powder, salt, and black pepper.
2. In a separate bowl, mix the Parmesan cheese and breadcrumbs. Coat each cauliflower floret with the Parmesan-breadcrumb mixture.
3. Lightly spray the air fryer basket with cooking spray and place the cauliflower in a single layer.
4. Air fry for 10-12 minutes, shaking halfway through until the cauliflower is crispy and golden brown.
5. Serve warm as a crunchy side or snack.

 2 servings   5 minutes   12 minutes

Nutritional information (per serving):
190 calories, 7 g protein, 16 g carbohydrates, 10 g fat, 4 g fiber, 10 mg cholesterol, 320 mg sodium, 400 mg potassium.

ROASTED BEETS

Sweet, tender beets roasted in the air fryer, great for salads or as a standalone side

Ingredients:

- 2 medium beets (about 8 oz / 225 g), peeled and diced
- 1 tbsp olive oil
- Salt and black pepper to taste
- Cooking spray

Directions:

1. Preheat the air fryer to 375°F (190°C). Toss the diced beets with olive oil, salt, and black pepper.
2. Lightly spray the air fryer basket with cooking spray and place the beets in a single layer.
3. Air fry for 20-25 minutes, shaking the basket halfway through until the beets are tender and slightly caramelized.
4. Serve warm as a side dish or add to salads for extra flavor and color.

 2 servings | 5 minutes | 25 minutes

Nutritional information (per serving):
120 calories, 3 g protein, 16 g carbohydrates, 7 g fat, 4 g fiber, 0 mg cholesterol, 150 mg sodium, 400 mg potassium.

CHICKPEAS

Crispy roasted chickpeas seasoned with smoked paprika and garlic, ideal for snacking or salads

Ingredients:

- 1 cup (170 g) canned chickpeas, drained and rinsed
- 1 tbsp olive oil
- 1/2 tsp smoked paprika
- 1/2 tsp garlic powder
- Salt and black pepper to taste
- Cooking spray

Directions:

1. Preheat the air fryer to 375°F (190°C). Pat the chickpeas dry with a paper towel to remove excess moisture.
2. In a bowl, toss the chickpeas with olive oil, smoked paprika, garlic powder, salt, and black pepper until evenly coated.
3. Lightly spray the air fryer basket with cooking spray and add the chickpeas in a single layer.
4. Air fry for 12-15 minutes, shaking the basket halfway through until the chickpeas are crispy and golden brown.
5. Serve as a snack or sprinkle over salads for added crunch.

 2 servings | 5 minutes | 15 minutes

Nutritional information (per serving):
180 calories, 6 g protein, 20 g carbohydrates, 8 g fat, 6 g fiber, 0 mg cholesterol, 280 mg sodium, 220 mg potassium.

CORN on the COB

Sweet corn roasted to perfection with a light seasoning of butter and herbs

Ingredients:

- 2 ears of corn, husked
- 1 tbsp butter, melted
- 1/2 tsp garlic powder
- 1/2 tsp dried parsley or fresh parsley (optional)
- Salt and black pepper to taste
- Cooking spray

Directions:

1. Preheat the air fryer to 375°F (190°C). Brush the corn on the cob with melted butter, then season with garlic powder, parsley, salt, and black pepper.
2. Lightly spray the air fryer basket with cooking spray and place the corn in a single layer.
3. Air fry for 10-12 minutes, turning the corn halfway through until the kernels are golden and slightly charred.
4. Serve warm, with an optional drizzle of extra butter if desired.

 2 servings | 5 minutes | 12 minutes

Nutritional information (per serving):
140 calories, 3 g protein, 22 g carbohydrates, 7 g fat, 2 g fiber, 15 mg cholesterol, 75 mg sodium, 270 mg potassium.

GREEN PEAS

Crispy air-fried green peas with a hint of garlic and salt, perfect for snacking or salads

Ingredients:

- 1 cup (150 g) frozen green peas, thawed and patted dry
- 1 tbsp olive oil
- 1/2 tsp garlic powder
- Salt to taste
- Cooking spray

Directions:

1. Preheat the air fryer to 375°F (190°C). Toss the green peas with olive oil, garlic powder, and salt until evenly coated.
2. Lightly spray the air fryer basket with cooking spray and spread the peas in a single layer.
3. Air fry for 10-12 minutes, shaking the basket halfway through until the peas are crispy and golden.
4. Serve as a crunchy snack or sprinkle over salads for added texture.

 2 servings   5 minutes   12 minutes

Nutritional information (per serving):
130 calories, 4 g protein, 12 g carbohydrates, 8 g fat, 4 g fiber, 0 mg cholesterol, 200 mg sodium, 240 mg potassium.

BABY POTATOES

Golden baby potatoes with a crispy exterior, seasoned with rosemary and olive oil

Ingredients:

- 12 oz (340 g) baby potatoes, halved
- 1 tbsp olive oil
- 1/2 tsp dried rosemary
- Salt and black pepper to taste
- Cooking spray

Directions:

1. Preheat the air fryer to 375°F (190°C). Toss the baby potatoes with olive oil, rosemary, salt, and black pepper until evenly coated.
2. Lightly spray the air fryer basket with cooking spray and place the potatoes in a single layer.
3. Air fry for 12-15 minutes, shaking the basket halfway through until the potatoes are golden and crispy on the outside and tender on the inside.
4. Serve warm as a crispy, flavorful side dish.

 2 servings   5 minutes   15 minutes

Nutritional information (per serving):
190 calories, 3 g protein, 32 g carbohydrates, 7 g fat, 4 g fiber, 0 mg cholesterol, 180 mg sodium, 600 mg potassium.

CABBAGE STEAKS

Thick slices of cabbage seasoned with garlic and roasted to tender, crispy perfection

Ingredients:

- 1 small cabbage (about 12 oz / 340 g), cut into thick slices (steaks)
- 1 tbsp olive oil
- 1 tsp garlic powder
- Salt and black pepper to taste
- Cooking spray

Directions:

1. Preheat the air fryer to 375°F (190°C). Brush both sides of the cabbage steaks with olive oil and season with garlic powder, salt, and black pepper.
2. Lightly spray the air fryer basket with cooking spray and place the cabbage steaks in a single layer.
3. Air fry for 10-12 minutes, flipping halfway through until the cabbage is crispy on the edges and tender in the center.
4. Serve warm as a flavorful and healthy side dish.

 2 servings   5 minutes   12 minutes

Nutritional information (per serving):
130 calories, 3 g protein, 12 g carbohydrates, 9 g fat, 6 g fiber, 0 mg cholesterol, 180 mg sodium, 400 mg potassium.

ARTICHOKE HEARTS

Crispy artichoke hearts seasoned with herbs and olive oil, great as an appetizer or side

Ingredients:

- 1 can (14 oz / 400 g) artichoke hearts, drained and patted dry
- 1 tbsp olive oil
- 1/2 tsp garlic powder
- 1/2 tsp dried oregano or thyme
- Salt and black pepper to taste
- Cooking spray

Directions:

1. Preheat the air fryer to 375°F (190°C). Toss the artichoke hearts with olive oil, garlic powder, oregano (or thyme), salt, and black pepper until evenly coated.
2. Lightly spray the air fryer basket with cooking spray and place the artichoke hearts in a single layer.
3. Air fry for 8-10 minutes, shaking the basket halfway through until the artichoke hearts are crispy and golden.
4. Serve warm as a delicious appetizer or side dish.

 2 servings 5 minutes 10 minutes

Nutritional information (per serving):
140 calories, 4 g protein, 12 g carbohydrates, 9 g fat, 6 g fiber, 0 mg cholesterol, 280 mg sodium, 250 mg potassium.

SPINACH STUFFED MUSHROOMS

Mushrooms stuffed with a cheesy spinach filling and air-fried until golden

Ingredients:

- 8 large mushrooms, stems removed
- 1/2 cup (30 g) fresh spinach, chopped
- 1/4 cup (30 g) cream cheese, softened
- 2 tbsp grated Parmesan cheese
- 1 garlic clove, minced
- Salt and black pepper to taste
- Cooking spray

Directions:

1. Preheat the air fryer to 375°F (190°C). Mix the chopped spinach, cream cheese, Parmesan, garlic, salt, and black pepper in a small bowl until well combined.
2. Stuff each mushroom cap with the spinach mixture and place them in a single layer in the air fryer basket.
3. Lightly spray the stuffed mushrooms with cooking spray.
4. Air fry for 8-10 minutes until the mushrooms are tender and the filling is golden and bubbly.
5. Serve warm as a tasty appetizer or side dish.

 2 servings 10 minutes 10 minutes

Nutritional information (per serving):
160 calories, 7 g protein, 8 g carbohydrates, 11 g fat, 2 g fiber, 25 mg cholesterol, 270 mg sodium, 350 mg potassium.

OKRA FRIES

Crunchy okra fries seasoned with salt and spices, perfect as a diabetes-friendly snack or side

Ingredients:

- 1 cup (about 6 oz / 170 g) fresh okra, sliced lengthwise
- 1 tbsp olive oil
- 1/2 tsp paprika
- 1/2 tsp garlic powder
- Salt and black pepper to taste
- Cooking spray

Directions:

1. Preheat the air fryer to 375°F (190°C). Toss the sliced okra with olive oil, paprika, garlic powder, salt, and black pepper until evenly coated.
2. Lightly spray the air fryer basket with cooking spray and arrange the okra in a single layer.
3. Air fry for 8-10 minutes, shaking the basket halfway through until the okra is crispy and golden.
4. Serve warm as a crunchy snack or side dish.

 2 servings 5 minutes 10 minutes

Nutritional information (per serving):
110 calories, 2 g protein, 10 g carbohydrates, 7 g fat, 4 g fiber, 0 mg cholesterol, 220 mg sodium, 270 mg potassium.

POULTRY

Poultry, such as chicken, turkey, and duck, plays a vital role in a balanced and healthy diet, especially for individuals managing Type 1, Type 2, or prediabetes. Poultry is naturally lean, rich in protein, and low in carbohydrates, making it an excellent option for those following a low-carb, low-sugar eating plan. Including poultry in your diet helps manage blood sugar levels, promotes muscle health, and provides a variety of essential nutrients.

High in Lean Protein: Poultry provides a high-quality source of lean protein, which helps build and repair muscles and keeps you feeling full longer without spiking blood sugar levels. This helps manage weight, which is critical for controlling Type 2 diabetes.

Low in Carbohydrates: Poultry contains few carbohydrates, making it ideal for diabetes patients. Consuming low-carb meals helps prevent blood sugar spikes, leading to more stable daily glucose levels.

Versatile in Meal Planning: Poultry can be cooked in numerous ways and seasoned with herbs and spices to fit into nearly any meal plan. From roasted chicken to crispy air-fried turkey, poultry offers flexibility in creating diabetes-friendly meals.

Rich in Essential Nutrients: Poultry provides vitamins and minerals such as B vitamins (especially niacin and B6), zinc, and selenium, which support energy metabolism, immune function, and heart health. This is important for individuals managing diabetes, as they are at a higher risk of heart disease and related complications.

Low in Saturated Fat: Poultry is a low-fat protein option when skinless or prepared without excess fats. Maintaining a diet low in saturated fats helps manage cholesterol levels and reduce the risk of cardiovascular disease, a common concern for people with diabetes.

Using an air fryer to cook poultry is a great way to enjoy crispy, flavorful dishes without deep frying or excess oil. Air-fried poultry is a healthier alternative, using minimal oil while maintaining the desired texture and flavor. The air fryer also helps preserve the nutrients in poultry while giving it a delicious crispness that's perfect for various recipes.

TURKEY and VEGGIE PATTIES

Patties made with ground turkey and mixed vegetables, air-fried for a crunchy, healthy bite

Ingredients:

- 8 oz (225 g) ground turkey
- 1/4 cup (30 g) finely diced zucchini
- 1/4 cup (30 g) finely diced bell pepper
- 1/4 cup (30 g) grated carrot
- 1 egg, beaten
- 1/4 cup (30 g) breadcrumbs (whole wheat preferred)
- 1 tsp garlic powder
- Salt and black pepper to taste
- Cooking spray

Directions:

1. In a bowl, combine the ground turkey, zucchini, bell pepper, grated carrot, egg, breadcrumbs, garlic powder, salt, and black pepper. Mix until well combined.
2. Form the mixture into small patties (about 4 patties).
3. Preheat the air fryer to 375°F (190°C). Lightly spray the air fryer basket with cooking spray and place the patties in a single layer.
4. Air fry for 10-12 minutes, flipping halfway through until the patties are golden brown and the internal temperature reaches 165°F (75°C).
5. Serve warm as a healthy meal or snack.

 2 servings   **10** minutes   **12** minutes

Nutritional information (per serving):
220 calories, 25 g protein, 12 g carbohydrates, 8 g fat, 2 g fiber, 105 mg cholesterol, 300 mg sodium, 400 mg potassium.

HERB-CRUSTED TURKEY CUTLETS

Features tender turkey cutlets coated in a flavorful herb and breadcrumb crust

Ingredients:

- 8 oz (225 g) turkey cutlets
- 1/4 cup (30 g) breadcrumbs (whole wheat preferred)
- 1 tbsp fresh parsley, chopped (or 1 tsp dried)
- 1/2 tsp dried thyme
- 1/2 tsp garlic powder
- 1/2 tsp onion powder
- 1 tbsp olive oil
- Salt and black pepper to taste
- Cooking spray

Directions:

1. Preheat the air fryer to 375°F (190°C). Mix breadcrumbs, parsley, thyme, garlic powder, onion powder, salt, and black pepper in a bowl.
2. Rub the turkey cutlets with olive oil and coat them evenly with the breadcrumb mixture.
3. Lightly spray the air fryer basket with cooking spray and place the cutlets in a single layer.
4. Air fry for 10-12 minutes, flipping halfway through until the cutlets are golden brown and cooked to an internal temperature of 165°F (75°C).
5. Let rest for a few minutes before serving.

 2 servings 10 minutes 12 minutes

Nutritional information (per serving):
280 calories, 28 g protein, 12 g carbohydrates, 12 g fat, 1 g fiber, 75 mg cholesterol, 320 mg sodium, 400 mg potassium.

TURKEY MEATBALLS

Juicy turkey meatballs seasoned with garlic and herbs, perfect as a protein-packed snack or main dish

Ingredients:

- 8 oz (225 g) ground turkey
- 1/4 cup (30 g) breadcrumbs (whole wheat preferred)
- 1 egg
- 1 garlic clove, minced
- 1 tsp dried oregano
- 1 tsp dried parsley
- Salt and black pepper to taste
- Cooking spray

Directions:

1. In a bowl, mix the ground turkey, breadcrumbs, egg, minced garlic, oregano, parsley, salt, and black pepper until well combined.
2. Form the mixture into small meatballs (about 1 inch in diameter).
3. Preheat the air fryer to 375°F (190°C). Lightly spray the basket with cooking spray, then place the meatballs in a single layer.
4. Air fry for 10-12 minutes, shaking the basket halfway through until the meatballs are golden brown and cooked.
5. Serve warm as a protein-packed snack or main dish.

 2 servings 10 minutes 12 minutes

Nutritional information (per serving):
180 calories, 23 g protein, 8 g carbohydrates, 7 g fat, 1 g fiber, 95 mg cholesterol, 280 mg sodium, 320 mg potassium.

TURKEY TENDERLOIN

A tender, marinated turkey tenderloin air-fried for a juicy and flavorful meal

Ingredients:

- 1 turkey tenderloin (about 8 oz / 225 g)
- 1 tbsp olive oil
- 1 tbsp lemon juice
- 2 garlic cloves, minced
- 1 tsp dried thyme
- 1/2 tsp paprika
- Salt and black pepper to taste
- Cooking spray

Directions:

1. In a bowl, mix olive oil, lemon juice, minced garlic, thyme, paprika, salt, and black pepper to create the marinade. Coat the turkey tenderloin in the marinade and refrigerate for at least 30 minutes.
2. Preheat the air fryer to 375°F (190°C). Lightly spray the air fryer basket with cooking spray.
3. Place the marinated turkey tenderloin in the air fryer basket and air fry for 18-20 minutes, flipping halfway through, until the internal temperature reaches 165°F (75°C).
4. Let the turkey rest for 5 minutes before slicing and serving.

 2 servings 10 minutes 20 minutes

Nutritional information (per serving):
220 calories, 35 g protein, 1 g carbohydrates, 8 g fat, 0 g fiber, 90 mg cholesterol, 250 mg sodium, 450 mg potassium.

TURKEY KEBABS

Skewered turkey pieces marinated and air-fried for a flavorful, low-carb meal

Ingredients:

- 8 oz (225 g) turkey breast, cut into bite-sized pieces
- 1 tbsp olive oil
- 1 tbsp lemon juice
- 1 garlic clove, minced
- 1 tsp paprika
- 1/2 tsp dried oregano
- Salt and black pepper to taste
- Wooden or metal skewers (if wooden, soak in water for 30 minutes)

Directions:

1. In a bowl, mix olive oil, lemon juice, garlic, paprika, oregano, salt, and black pepper. Add the turkey pieces and coat them with the marinade. Cover and refrigerate for at least 30 minutes.
2. Preheat the air fryer to 375°F (190°C). Thread the marinated turkey pieces onto skewers.
3. Lightly spray the air fryer basket with cooking spray and place the skewers in a single layer.
4. Air fry for 10-12 minutes, turning halfway through until the turkey is cooked and the internal temperature reaches 165°F (75°C).
5. Serve warm with a side of your choice for a low-carb meal.

 2 servings   40 minutes   12 minutes

Nutritional information (per serving):
220 calories, 28 g protein, 2 g carbohydrates, 10 g fat, 0 g fiber, 75 mg cholesterol, 250 mg sodium, 400 mg potassium.

TURKEY SAUSAGE PATTIES

Homemade turkey sausage patties seasoned with spices and cooked to a crispy golden brown

Ingredients:

- 8 oz (225 g) ground turkey
- 1/2 tsp garlic powder
- 1/2 tsp onion powder
- 1/2 tsp smoked paprika
- 1/4 tsp dried sage
- 1/4 tsp dried thyme
- Salt and black pepper to taste
- Cooking spray

Directions:

1. In a bowl, combine the ground turkey with garlic powder, onion powder, smoked paprika, sage, thyme, salt, and black pepper. Mix until well combined.
2. Shape the mixture into 4 small patties.
3. Preheat the air fryer to 375°F (190°C). Lightly spray the air fryer basket with cooking spray and place the patties in a single layer.
4. Air fry for 8-10 minutes, flipping halfway through, until the patties are golden brown and reach an internal temperature of 165°F (75°C).
5. Serve warm as a protein-packed breakfast or snack.

 2 servings   5 minutes 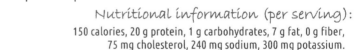 10 minutes

Nutritional information (per serving):
150 calories, 20 g protein, 1 g carbohydrates, 7 g fat, 0 g fiber, 75 mg cholesterol, 240 mg sodium, 300 mg potassium.

TURKEY BREAST

Tender turkey breast roasted to perfection with rosemary and garlic

Ingredients:

- 1 lb (450 g) boneless, skinless turkey breast
- 1 tbsp olive oil
- 2 garlic cloves, minced
- 1 tsp dried rosemary
- 1/2 tsp dried thyme
- Salt and black pepper to taste
- Cooking spray

Directions:

1. Preheat the air fryer to 375°F (190°C). Rub the turkey breast with olive oil, garlic, rosemary, thyme, salt, and black pepper until well coated.
2. Lightly spray the air fryer basket with cooking spray. Place the seasoned turkey breast in the air fryer basket.
3. Air fry for 20-25 minutes, turning halfway through until the turkey reaches an internal temperature of 165°F (75°C).
4. Let the turkey rest for 5 minutes before slicing and serving.

 2 servings   5 minutes   25 minutes

Nutritional information (per serving):
230 calories, 45 g protein, 1 g carbohydrates, 6 g fat, 0 g fiber, 110 mg cholesterol, 240 mg sodium, 700 mg potassium.

TURKEY WINGS

Crispy, seasoned turkey wings cooked to perfection without deep frying

Ingredients:

- 2 turkey wings (about 1 lb / 450 g)
- 1 tbsp olive oil
- 1 tsp paprika
- 1/2 tsp garlic powder
- 1/2 tsp onion powder
- 1/2 tsp dried thyme
- Salt and black pepper to taste
- Cooking spray

Directions:

1. Preheat the air fryer to 380°F (195°C). In a bowl, coat the turkey wings with olive oil, paprika, garlic powder, onion powder, thyme, salt, and black pepper.
2. Lightly spray the air fryer basket with cooking spray and place the seasoned turkey wings in a single layer.
3. Air fry for 25-30 minutes, flipping halfway through, until the wings are golden brown and crispy, with an internal temperature of 165°F (75°C).
4. Serve warm as a delicious, crispy main dish or snack.

 2 servings 10 minutes 25 minutes

Nutritional information (per serving):
370 calories, 32 g protein, 0 g carbohydrates, 25 g fat, 0 g fiber, 130 mg cholesterol, 300 mg sodium, 350 mg potassium.

TURKEY BURGERS

Flavorful and healthy turkey burgers with a crispy exterior, ideal for a low-carb meal

Ingredients:

- 8 oz (225 g) ground turkey
- 1/4 cup (30 g) breadcrumbs (whole wheat preferred)
- 1 garlic clove, minced
- 1 tsp onion powder
- 1 tsp dried parsley
- 1 egg
- Salt and black pepper to taste
- Cooking spray

Directions:

1. In a bowl, mix the ground turkey, breadcrumbs, minced garlic, onion powder, parsley, egg, salt, and black pepper until well combined.
2. Shape the mixture into two equal-sized patties.
3. Preheat the air fryer to 375°F (190°C). Lightly spray the air fryer basket with cooking spray and place the turkey patties in a single layer.
4. Air fry for 10-12 minutes, flipping halfway through, until the internal temperature of the patties reaches 165°F (75°C).
5. Serve on a low-carb bun or lettuce wrap for a healthy, low-carb meal.

 2 servings 10 minutes 12 minutes

Nutritional information (per serving):
220 calories, 28 g protein, 10 g carbohydrates, 8 g fat, 1 g fiber, 100 mg cholesterol, 280 mg sodium, 380 mg potassium.

TURKEY STUFFED PEPPERS

Bell peppers stuffed with turkey, quinoa, and vegetables, air-fried until tender

Ingredients:

- 2 medium bell peppers, tops removed and seeds cleaned out
- 4 oz (115 g) ground turkey
- 1/4 cup (45 g) cooked quinoa
- 1/4 cup (30 g) diced tomatoes
- 1/4 cup (30 g) diced zucchini
- 1 garlic clove, minced
- 1/2 tsp cumin
- 1/2 tsp paprika
- Salt and black pepper to taste
- Cooking spray

Directions:

1. Preheat the air fryer to 360°F (180°C). In a bowl, combine the ground turkey, cooked quinoa, diced tomatoes, zucchini, minced garlic, cumin, paprika, salt, and black pepper.
2. Stuff the bell peppers with the turkey mixture.
3. Lightly spray the air fryer basket with cooking spray and place the stuffed peppers in the basket.
4. Air fry for 10-12 minutes, until the peppers are tender and the turkey is fully cooked through, with an internal temperature of 165°F (75°C).
5. Serve warm as a nutritious main dish.

 2 servings 15 minutes 12 minutes

Nutritional information (per serving):
230 calories, 20 g protein, 25 g carbohydrates, 6 g fat, 5 g fiber, 50 mg cholesterol, 320 mg sodium, 500 mg potassium.

TURKEY DRUMSTICKS

Large, juicy drumsticks with a crispy skin, seasoned with herbs and spices

Ingredients:

- 2 turkey drumsticks (about 1.5 lbs / 680 g)
- 1 tbsp olive oil
- 1 tsp paprika
- 1/2 tsp garlic powder
- 1/2 tsp onion powder
- 1/2 tsp dried rosemary
- Salt and black pepper to taste
- Cooking spray

Directions:

1. Preheat the air fryer to 375°F (190°C). In a small bowl, mix olive oil, paprika, garlic powder, onion powder, rosemary, salt, and black pepper.
2. Rub the turkey drumsticks with the seasoning mixture until well coated.
3. Lightly spray the air fryer basket with cooking spray and place the drumsticks in a single layer.
4. Air fry for 25-30 minutes, turning halfway through, until the drumsticks are golden and crispy, with an internal temperature of 165°F (75°C).
5. Let rest for a few minutes before serving.

 2 servings   10 minutes   30 minutes

Nutritional information (per serving):
400 calories, 45 g protein, 0 g carbohydrates, 22 g fat, 0 g fiber, 130 mg cholesterol, 350 mg sodium, 400 mg potassium.

TURKEY CUTLETS

Breaded turkey cutlets with a crispy coating, great as a light and healthy meal

Ingredients:

- 2 turkey cutlets (about 8 oz / 225 g total)
- 1/4 cup (30 g) breadcrumbs (whole wheat preferred)
- 2 tbsp grated Parmesan cheese
- 1 egg, beaten
- 1/2 tsp garlic powder
- 1/2 tsp paprika
- Salt and black pepper to taste
- Cooking spray

Directions:

1. Preheat the air fryer to 375°F (190°C). In a shallow dish, mix the breadcrumbs, Parmesan cheese, garlic powder, paprika, salt, and black pepper.
2. Dip each turkey cutlet in the beaten egg, then coat in the breadcrumb mixture, pressing gently to adhere.
3. Lightly spray the air fryer basket with cooking spray and place the cutlets in a single layer.
4. Air fry for 10-12 minutes, flipping halfway through, until the cutlets are golden brown and reach an internal temperature of 165°F (75°C).
5. Serve warm with your favorite side dish for a light and healthy meal.

 2 servings   10 minutes   12 minutes

Nutritional information (per serving):
230 calories, 32 g protein, 10 g carbohydrates, 8 g fat, 1 g fiber, 90 mg cholesterol, 300 mg sodium, 400 mg potassium.

GROUND TURKEY TACOS

Ground turkey seasoned and air-fried, served in taco shells with fresh toppings

Ingredients:

- 8 oz (225 g) ground turkey
- 1 tsp chili powder
- 1/2 tsp cumin
- 1/2 tsp paprika
- 1/2 tsp garlic powder
- Salt and black pepper to taste
- 4 small taco shells
- Fresh toppings (e.g., diced tomatoes, lettuce, shredded cheese, salsa)

Directions:

1. Preheat the air fryer to 375°F (190°C). In a bowl, mix the ground turkey with chili powder, cumin, paprika, garlic powder, salt, and black pepper.
2. Place the seasoned turkey in the air fryer basket, breaking it up into small pieces, and air fry for 8-10 minutes, stirring halfway through, until fully cooked.
3. Warm the taco shells in the air fryer for 1-2 minutes, if desired.
4. Serve the cooked turkey in taco shells and top with fresh toppings like diced tomatoes, lettuce, shredded cheese, and salsa.

 2 servings   10 minutes   10 minutes

Nutritional information (per serving):
300 calories, 30 g protein, 25 g carbohydrates, 10 g fat, 4 g fiber, 90 mg cholesterol, 350 mg sodium, 450 mg potassium.

TURKEY NUGGETS

Bite-sized turkey nuggets coated in breadcrumbs and cooked until crispy

Ingredients:

- 8 oz (225 g) ground turkey
- 1/4 cup (30 g) breadcrumbs (whole wheat preferred)
- 1 egg, beaten
- 1/4 cup (30 g) flour
- 1/2 tsp garlic powder
- 1/2 tsp onion powder
- Salt and black pepper to taste
- Cooking spray

Directions:

1. Preheat the air fryer to 375°F (190°C). Season the ground turkey with garlic powder, onion powder, salt, and black pepper, then shape into small bite-sized nuggets.
2. Coat each nugget in flour, then dip into the beaten egg, and finally roll in breadcrumbs to fully coat.
3. Lightly spray the air fryer basket with cooking spray. Place the nuggets in a single layer in the basket.
4. Air fry for 8-10 minutes, flipping halfway through, until the nuggets are golden brown and the internal temperature reaches 165°F (75°C).
5. Serve warm with your favorite dipping sauce.

 2 servings   10 minutes   10 minutes

Nutritional information (per serving):
280 calories, 26 g protein, 20 g carbohydrates, 10 g fat, 1 g fiber, 105 mg cholesterol, 320 mg sodium, 400 mg potassium.

TURKEY MEATLOAF

A healthy take on classic meatloaf, made with lean ground turkey and air-fried to perfection

Ingredients:

- 8 oz (225 g) lean ground turkey
- 1/4 cup (30 g) breadcrumbs (whole wheat preferred)
- 1 egg, beaten
- 1/4 cup (60 ml) ketchup (plus extra for topping)
- 1/2 small onion, finely diced
- 1 garlic clove, minced
- 1 tsp dried thyme
- 1/2 tsp paprika
- Salt and black pepper to taste
- Cooking spray

Directions:

1. Preheat the air fryer to 350°F (175°C). In a bowl, combine the ground turkey, breadcrumbs, egg, ketchup, onion, garlic, thyme, paprika, salt, and black pepper. Mix until well combined.
2. Shape the mixture into a small loaf and place it on a piece of parchment paper.
3. Lightly spray the air fryer basket with cooking spray and carefully place the meatloaf in the basket.
4. Air fry for 20-25 minutes, brushing the top with extra ketchup during the last 5 minutes of cooking, until the internal temperature reaches 165°F (75°C).
5. Let the meatloaf rest for a few minutes before slicing and serving.

 2 servings   10 minutes  25 minutes

Nutritional information (per serving):
250 calories, 28 g protein, 16 g carbohydrates, 8 g fat, 1 g fiber, 120 mg cholesterol, 400 mg sodium, 400 mg potassium.

TURKEY BACON

Crispy turkey bacon strips, a lighter alternative to traditional bacon

Ingredients:

- 6 slices turkey bacon

Directions:

1. Preheat the air fryer to 375°F (190°C). Arrange the turkey bacon slices in a single layer in the air fryer basket.
2. Air fry the turkey bacon for 6-8 minutes, flipping halfway through, until crispy and golden.
3. Remove the bacon from the air fryer and place it on a paper towel to absorb any excess grease.
4. Serve as a lighter, crispy alternative to traditional bacon.

 2 servings   2 minutes   8 minutes

Nutritional information (per serving):
70 calories, 6 g protein, 1 g carbohydrates, 5 g fat, 0 g fiber, 20 mg cholesterol, 300 mg sodium, 100 mg potassium.

CRISPY CHICKEN WINGS

Crispy chicken wings seasoned with garlic and paprika, air-fried without added oil

Ingredients:

- 1 lb (450 g) chicken wings
- 1 tsp garlic powder
- 1 tsp paprika
- 1/2 tsp salt
- 1/4 tsp black pepper
- Cooking spray

Directions:

1. Preheat the air fryer to 400°F (200°C). Pat the chicken wings dry with a paper towel.
2. In a bowl, toss the wings with garlic powder, paprika, salt, and black pepper until evenly coated.
3. Lightly spray the air fryer basket with cooking spray. Arrange the wings in a single layer in the basket.
4. Air fry for 18-20 minutes, flipping halfway through, until the wings are crispy and golden brown with an internal temperature of 165°F (75°C).
5. Serve hot as a crispy snack or main dish.

 2 servings   5 minutes   20 minutes

Nutritional information (per serving):
350 calories, 30 g protein, 0 g carbohydrates, 24 g fat, 0 g fiber, 150 mg cholesterol, 700 mg sodium, 270 mg potassium.

CHICKEN BREAST

A tender and juicy chicken breast cooked with minimal oil, perfect for salads or main courses

Ingredients:

- 2 boneless, skinless chicken breasts (about 8 oz / 225 g each)
- 1 tbsp olive oil
- 1/2 tsp garlic powder
- 1/2 tsp paprika
- 1/2 tsp dried oregano
- Salt and black pepper to taste
- Cooking spray

Directions:

1. Preheat the air fryer to 375°F (190°C). Rub the chicken breasts with olive oil and season with garlic powder, paprika, oregano, salt, and black pepper.
2. Lightly spray the air fryer basket with cooking spray and place the seasoned chicken breasts in the basket.
3. Air fry for 12-15 minutes, flipping halfway through, until the internal temperature reaches 165°F (75°C).
4. Let the chicken rest for 5 minutes before slicing. Serve as part of a salad or main course.

 2 servings   5 minutes   15 minutes

Nutritional information (per serving):
220 calories, 35 g protein, 1 g carbohydrates, 9 g fat, 0 g fiber, 100 mg cholesterol, 300 mg sodium, 450 mg potassium.

CHICKEN PARMESAN

A lighter version of the classic, with breaded chicken and melted Parmesan cheese

Ingredients:

- 2 boneless, skinless chicken breasts (about 8 oz / 225 g each)
- 1/4 cup (30 g) whole wheat breadcrumbs
- 1/4 cup (30 g) grated Parmesan cheese (plus extra for topping)
- 1 egg, beaten
- 1/2 tsp garlic powder
- 1/2 tsp dried oregano
- 1/2 cup (120 ml) marinara sauce
- Cooking spray

Directions:

1. Preheat the air fryer to 375°F (190°C). In a shallow dish, combine breadcrumbs, Parmesan, garlic powder, and oregano.
2. Dip each chicken breast into the beaten egg, then coat with the breadcrumb mixture, pressing gently to adhere.
3. Lightly spray the air fryer basket with cooking spray and place the breaded chicken breasts in a single layer. Air fry for 10-12 minutes, flipping halfway through, until golden brown and the internal temperature reaches 165°F (75°C).
4. During the last 2 minutes of cooking, top each chicken breast with marinara sauce and a sprinkle of Parmesan cheese. Continue cooking until the cheese is melted.
5. Serve warm, garnished with extra Parmesan if desired.

2 servings   10 minutes   12 minutes

Nutritional information (per serving):
350 calories, 40 g protein, 18 g carbohydrates, 12 g fat, 2 g fiber, 130 mg cholesterol, 600 mg sodium, 500 mg potassium.

CHICKEN THIGHS

Juicy chicken thighs seasoned and roasted to perfection with a crispy skin

Ingredients:

- 4 bone-in, skin-on chicken thighs (about 1 lb / 450 g)
- 1 tbsp olive oil
- 1 tsp garlic powder
- 1 tsp paprika
- 1/2 tsp dried thyme
- Salt and black pepper to taste
- Cooking spray

Directions:

1. Preheat the air fryer to 375°F (190°C). Pat the chicken thighs dry with a paper towel.
2. In a small bowl, mix the olive oil, garlic powder, paprika, thyme, salt, and black pepper. Rub the seasoning mixture all over the chicken thighs.
3. Lightly spray the air fryer basket with cooking spray and place the chicken thighs skin-side up in the basket.
4. Air fry for 18-20 minutes, flipping halfway through, until the skin is crispy and the internal temperature reaches 165°F (75°C).
5. Let the chicken rest for 5 minutes before serving.

 2 servings 5 minutes 20 minutes

Nutritional information (per serving):
310 calories, 28 g protein, 1 g carbohydrates, 21 g fat, 0 g fiber, 120 mg cholesterol, 380 mg sodium, 400 mg potassium.

LEMON GARLIC CHICKEN

Chicken pieces marinated in lemon juice and garlic, air-fried to golden perfection

Ingredients:

- 2 boneless, skinless chicken breasts (about 8 oz / 225 g each), cut into bite-sized pieces
- 2 tbsp lemon juice
- 1 tbsp olive oil
- 2 garlic cloves, minced
- 1/2 tsp dried oregano
- Salt and black pepper to taste
- Cooking spray

Directions:

1. In a bowl, combine the lemon juice, olive oil, minced garlic, oregano, salt, and black pepper. Add the chicken pieces and toss to coat. Marinate in the refrigerator for at least 30 minutes.
2. Preheat the air fryer to 375°F (190°C). Lightly spray the air fryer basket with cooking spray.
3. Place the marinated chicken pieces in the air fryer basket in a single layer.
4. Air fry for 12-15 minutes, flipping halfway through, until the chicken is golden brown and reaches an internal temperature of 165°F (75°C).
5. Serve hot with a side of your choice or over a salad.

 2 servings 40 minutes 15 minutes

Nutritional information (per serving):
230 calories, 35 g protein, 1 g carbohydrates, 9 g fat, 0 g fiber, 100 mg cholesterol, 300 mg sodium, 450 mg potassium.

CHICKEN TENDERS

Breaded chicken tenders made with whole wheat breadcrumbs for a healthy, crispy snack or meal

Ingredients:

- 8 oz (225 g) chicken tenders
- 1/4 cup (30 g) whole wheat breadcrumbs
- 2 tbsp grated Parmesan cheese
- 1 egg, beaten
- 1/2 tsp garlic powder
- 1/2 tsp paprika
- Salt and black pepper to taste
- Cooking spray

Directions:

1. Preheat the air fryer to 375°F (190°C). In a shallow dish, mix the breadcrumbs, Parmesan, garlic powder, paprika, salt, and black pepper.
2. Dip each chicken tender into the beaten egg, then coat it in the breadcrumb mixture.
3. Lightly spray the air fryer basket with cooking spray and place the breaded tenders in a single layer.
4. Air fry for 10-12 minutes, flipping halfway through, until the tenders are golden brown and reach an internal temperature of 165°F (75°C).
5. Serve warm as a healthy snack or meal with your favorite dipping sauce.

 2 servings 10 minutes 12 minutes

Nutritional information (per serving):
250 calories, 28 g protein, 12 g carbohydrates, 9 g fat, 2 g fiber, 120 mg cholesterol, 350 mg sodium, 400 mg potassium.

BUFFALO CHICKEN BITES
Spicy buffalo chicken bites, perfect as a low-carb appetizer or snack

Ingredients:

- 8 oz (225 g) boneless, skinless chicken breasts, cut into bite-sized pieces
- 1/4 cup (60 ml) buffalo sauce
- 1 tbsp olive oil
- 1/2 tsp garlic powder
- 1/2 tsp paprika
- Salt and black pepper to taste
- Cooking spray

Directions:

1. Preheat the air fryer to 375°F (190°C). In a bowl, toss the chicken pieces with olive oil, garlic powder, paprika, salt, and black pepper.
2. Lightly spray the air fryer basket with cooking spray and place the chicken bites in a single layer in the basket.
3. Air fry for 10-12 minutes, shaking the basket halfway through, until the chicken is cooked through and golden brown.
4. Toss the cooked chicken bites with buffalo sauce, coating evenly. Serve warm with your favorite dipping sauce.

 2 servings 10 minutes 12 minutes

Nutritional information (per serving):
220 calories, 28 g protein, 3 g carbohydrates, 10 g fat, 0 g fiber, 85 mg cholesterol, 700 mg sodium, 350 mg potassium.

CHICKEN MEATBALLS
Tender chicken meatballs, seasoned and air-fried for a healthy snack or main dish

Ingredients:

- 8 oz (225 g) ground chicken
- 1/4 cup (30 g) breadcrumbs (whole wheat preferred)
- 1 egg, beaten
- 1 garlic clove, minced
- 1/4 cup (30 g) grated Parmesan cheese
- 1 tsp dried oregano
- 1/2 tsp garlic powder
- Salt and black pepper to taste
- Cooking spray

Directions:

1. Preheat the air fryer to 375°F (190°C). In a bowl, combine the ground chicken, breadcrumbs, egg, minced garlic, Parmesan cheese, oregano, garlic powder, salt, and black pepper. Mix until well combined.
2. Form the mixture into small meatballs (about 8-10 meatballs).
3. Lightly spray the air fryer basket with cooking spray and place the meatballs in a single layer.
4. Air fry for 10-12 minutes, shaking the basket halfway through, until the meatballs are golden brown and reach an internal temperature of 165°F (75°C).
5. Serve as a healthy snack or main dish.

 2 servings 10 minutes 12 minutes

Nutritional information (per serving):
220 calories, 26 g protein, 10 g carbohydrates, 9 g fat, 1 g fiber, 110 mg cholesterol, 350 mg sodium, 300 mg potassium.

CHICKEN and BROCCOLI
A simple, healthy chicken and broccoli stir-fry made in the air fryer

Ingredients:

- 8 oz (225 g) boneless, skinless chicken breast, cut into bite-sized pieces
- 2 cups (200 g) broccoli florets
- 1 tbsp olive oil
- 1 tbsp soy sauce (low sodium)
- 1 tsp garlic powder
- 1 tsp onion powder
- 1/2 tsp paprika
- Salt and black pepper to taste
- Cooking spray

Directions:

1. Preheat the air fryer to 375°F (190°C). In a bowl, toss the chicken and broccoli with olive oil, soy sauce, garlic powder, onion powder, paprika, salt, and black pepper.
2. Lightly spray the air fryer basket with cooking spray. Place the chicken and broccoli in the basket in a single layer.
3. Air fry for 12-15 minutes, shaking the basket halfway through, until the chicken is cooked through and the broccoli is tender.
4. Serve hot as a simple, healthy stir-fry, perfect for a quick meal.

 2 servings 10 minutes 15 minutes

Nutritional information (per serving):
260 calories, 30 g protein, 8 g carbohydrates, 12 g fat, 3 g fiber, 85 mg cholesterol, 480 mg sodium, 600 mg potassium.

CHICKEN FAJITAS

Chicken strips cooked with bell peppers and onions, served with a side of tortillas or lettuce wraps

Ingredients:

- 8 oz (225 g) boneless, skinless chicken breasts, cut into thin strips
- 1/2 red bell pepper, sliced
- 1/2 green bell pepper, sliced
- 1/2 onion, sliced
- 1 tbsp olive oil
- 1 tsp chili powder
- 1/2 tsp cumin
- 1/2 tsp garlic powder
- Salt and black pepper to taste
- Tortillas or lettuce wraps for serving
- Optional: fresh cilantro, lime wedges, sour cream for garnish

Directions:

1. Preheat the air fryer to 375°F (190°C). In a bowl, toss the chicken strips, bell peppers, and onions with olive oil, chili powder, cumin, garlic powder, salt, and black pepper until well coated.
2. Lightly spray the air fryer basket with cooking spray and place the chicken and vegetables in a single layer in the basket.
3. Air fry for 10-12 minutes, shaking the basket halfway through, until the chicken is cooked through and the vegetables are tender.
4. Serve the chicken and vegetables in tortillas or lettuce wraps, garnished with fresh cilantro and lime wedges if desired.

 2 servings 10 minutes 12 minutes

Nutritional information (per serving):
290 calories, 28 g protein, 15 g carbohydrates, 12 g fat, 3 g fiber, 85 mg cholesterol, 400 mg sodium, 450 mg potassium.

CHICKEN DRUMSTICKS

Crispy drumsticks coated in herbs and spices, air-fried to a perfect golden brown

Ingredients:

- 4 chicken drumsticks (about 1 lb / 450 g)
- 1 tbsp olive oil
- 1 tsp garlic powder
- 1 tsp paprika
- 1/2 tsp dried thyme
- Salt and black pepper to taste
- Cooking spray

Directions:

1. Preheat the air fryer to 375°F (190°C). Pat the chicken drumsticks dry with a paper towel.
2. In a bowl, toss the drumsticks with olive oil, garlic powder, paprika, thyme, salt, and black pepper until evenly coated.
3. Lightly spray the air fryer basket with cooking spray and place the drumsticks in a single layer.
4. Air fry for 22-25 minutes, turning halfway through, until the drumsticks are crispy and golden brown, with an internal temperature of 165°F (75°C).
5. Let the drumsticks rest for a few minutes before serving.

 2 servings 5 minutes 25 minutes

Nutritional information (per serving):
320 calories, 30 g protein, 1 g carbohydrates, 22 g fat, 0 g fiber, 140 mg cholesterol, 400 mg sodium, 300 mg potassium.

CHICKEN WINGS with HONEY MUSTARD GLAZE

Sweet and tangy wings, air-fried and brushed with a light honey mustard glaze

Ingredients:

- 1 lb (450 g) chicken wings
- 1 tbsp olive oil
- 1/2 tsp garlic powder
- Salt and black pepper to taste
- 2 tbsp honey
- 1 tbsp Dijon mustard
- 1 tsp apple cider vinegar

Directions:

1. Preheat the air fryer to 400°F (200°C). Toss the chicken wings with olive oil, garlic powder, salt, and black pepper.
2. Place the wings in a single layer in the air fryer basket. Air fry for 18-20 minutes, flipping halfway through, until crispy and golden.
3. While the wings are cooking, mix honey, Dijon mustard, and apple cider vinegar in a small bowl to make the glaze.
4. When the wings are done, brush them with the honey mustard glaze and serve immediately.

 2 servings  5 minutes 20 minutes

Nutritional information (per serving):
320 calories, 26 g protein, 12 g carbohydrates, 19 g fat, 0 g fiber, 120 mg cholesterol, 400 mg sodium, 300 mg potassium.

BBQ CHICKEN THIGHS

Chicken thighs slathered in a diabetic-friendly BBQ sauce and air-fried until crispy

Ingredients:

- 4 bone-in, skin-on chicken thighs (about 1 lb / 450 g)
- 1/4 cup (60 ml) diabetic-friendly BBQ sauce
- 1 tbsp olive oil
- 1 tsp garlic powder
- Salt and black pepper to taste
- Cooking spray

Directions:

1. Preheat the air fryer to 375°F (190°C). Pat the chicken thighs dry with a paper towel. Rub the thighs with olive oil, garlic powder, salt, and black pepper.
2. Lightly spray the air fryer basket with cooking spray. Place the chicken thighs skin-side up in the basket.
3. Air fry for 18 minutes, flipping halfway through. After flipping, brush the chicken thighs with BBQ sauce and continue cooking until the internal temperature reaches 165°F (75°C).
4. Serve warm with an extra drizzle of BBQ sauce if desired.

 2 servings 5 minutes 🕐 20 minutes

Nutritional information (per serving):
320 calories, 30 g protein, 5 g carbohydrates, 22 g fat, 0 g fiber, 140 mg cholesterol, 450 mg sodium, 300 mg potassium.

CHICKEN PATTIES

Ground chicken patties with herbs and spices, a delicious alternative to burgers

Ingredients:

- 8 oz (225 g) ground chicken
- 1/4 cup (30 g) breadcrumbs (whole wheat preferred)
- 1 egg, beaten
- 1 garlic clove, minced
- 1/2 tsp onion powder
- 1/2 tsp dried oregano
- Salt and black pepper to taste
- Cooking spray

Directions:

1. Preheat the air fryer to 375°F (190°C). In a bowl, mix the ground chicken, breadcrumbs, egg, garlic, onion powder, oregano, salt, and black pepper until well combined.
2. Form the mixture into 2 to 4 patties, depending on the size you prefer.
3. Lightly spray the air fryer basket with cooking spray and place the patties in a single layer in the basket.
4. Air fry for 10-12 minutes, flipping halfway through, until the patties are golden brown and reach an internal temperature of 165°F (75°C).
5. Serve the patties with your favorite toppings or as a sandwich alternative.

 2 servings 10 minutes 12 minutes

Nutritional information (per serving):
240 calories, 25 g protein, 12 g carbohydrates, 10 g fat, 1 g fiber, 110 mg cholesterol, 350 mg sodium, 300 mg potassium.

CHICKEN QUESADILLAS

Whole wheat tortillas filled with air-fried chicken, cheese, and veggies, crisped in the air fryer

Ingredients:

- 1/2 lb (225 g) cooked, air-fried chicken breast, shredded
- 1/2 cup (60 g) shredded cheddar cheese
- 1/4 cup (30 g) diced bell peppers
- 1/4 cup (30 g) diced onions
- 2 whole wheat tortillas
- 1 tbsp olive oil
- Cooking spray

Directions:

1. Preheat the air fryer to 375°F (190°C). Lightly spray the air fryer basket with cooking spray.
2. Place one tortilla on a clean surface. Spread half of the shredded chicken, cheese, bell peppers, and onions on one side of the tortilla. Fold the tortilla in half to create a quesadilla.
3. Brush the outside of the tortilla with olive oil and place it in the air fryer basket. Repeat with the second tortilla.
4. Air fry for 5-6 minutes, flipping halfway through, until the tortillas are crispy and golden brown, and the cheese is melted.
5. Slice the quesadillas into wedges and serve warm.

 2 servings 10 minutes 🕐 10 minutes

Nutritional information (per serving):
380 calories, 30 g protein, 32 g carbohydrates, 15 g fat, 6 g fiber, 70 mg cholesterol, 600 mg sodium, 400 mg potassium.

DUCK BREAST

Perfectly cooked duck breast with crispy skin, seasoned with herbs and garlic

Ingredients:

- 2 duck breasts (about 8 oz / 225 g each)
- 1 tsp olive oil
- 1 tsp garlic powder
- 1/2 tsp dried thyme
- 1/2 tsp dried rosemary
- Salt and black pepper to taste
- Cooking spray

Directions:

1. Preheat the air fryer to 375°F (190°C). Score the duck skin with a sharp knife, making cross-hatch marks, being careful not to cut into the meat. Pat dry with a paper towel.
2. Rub the duck breasts with olive oil, then season with garlic powder, thyme, rosemary, salt, and black pepper.
3. Lightly spray the air fryer basket with cooking spray. Place the duck breasts skin-side down in the basket.
4. Air fry for 12-15 minutes, flipping halfway through, until the skin is crispy and the internal temperature reaches 135°F (57°C) for medium-rare or 145°F (63°C) for medium.
5. Let the duck breasts rest for 5 minutes before slicing and serving.

 2 servings 10 minutes 15 minutes

Nutritional information (per serving):
370 calories, 32 g protein, 0 g carbohydrates, 26 g fat, 0 g fiber, 120 mg cholesterol, 200 mg sodium, 300 mg potassium.

DUCK LEGS

Crispy duck legs cooked with a savory blend of spices, perfect for a hearty meal

Ingredients:

- 2 duck legs (about 10 oz / 280 g each)
- 1 tbsp olive oil
- 1 tsp garlic powder
- 1/2 tsp dried thyme
- 1/2 tsp smoked paprika
- Salt and black pepper to taste
- Cooking spray

Directions:

1. Preheat the air fryer to 375°F (190°C). Pat the duck legs dry with a paper towel.
2. Rub the duck legs with olive oil, then season with garlic powder, thyme, smoked paprika, salt, and black pepper.
3. Lightly spray the air fryer basket with cooking spray. Place the duck legs skin-side down in the basket.
4. Air fry for 20-25 minutes, flipping halfway through, until the skin is crispy and the internal temperature reaches 165°F (75°C).
5. Let the duck legs rest for 5 minutes before serving.

 2 servings 10 minutes 25 minutes

Nutritional information (per serving):
450 calories, 30 g protein, 0 g carbohydrates, 36 g fat, 0 g fiber, 150 mg cholesterol, 350 mg sodium, 400 mg potassium.

DUCK NUGGETS

Bite-sized duck pieces breaded and air-fried for a unique, crispy snack or appetizer

Ingredients:

- 8 oz (225 g) duck breast or leg meat, cut into bite-sized pieces
- 1/4 cup (30 g) breadcrumbs (whole wheat preferred)
- 1/4 cup (30 g) flour
- 1 egg, beaten
- 1/2 tsp garlic powder
- 1/2 tsp smoked paprika
- Salt and black pepper to taste
- Cooking spray

Directions:

1. Preheat the air fryer to 375°F (190°C). Pat the duck pieces dry with a paper towel.
2. In three separate bowls, place flour, beaten egg, and breadcrumbs mixed with garlic powder, smoked paprika, salt, and black pepper.
3. Dredge each duck piece in flour, then dip in the egg, and coat with the breadcrumb mixture.
4. Lightly spray the air fryer basket with cooking spray and place the duck nuggets in a single layer.
5. Air fry for 10-12 minutes, flipping halfway through, until the nuggets are golden and crispy, with an internal temperature of 165°F (75°C).

 2 servings 10 minutes 12 minutes

Nutritional information (per serving):
320 calories, 28 g protein, 12 g carbohydrates, 18 g fat, 1 g fiber, 120 mg cholesterol, 350 mg sodium, 300 mg potassium.

DUCK WINGS

Tender and flavorful duck wings, air-fried to golden crispness

Ingredients:

- 1 lb (450 g) duck wings
- 1 tbsp olive oil
- 1 tsp garlic powder
- 1/2 tsp smoked paprika
- 1/2 tsp dried thyme
- Salt and black pepper to taste
- Cooking spray

Directions:

1. Preheat the air fryer to 375°F (190°C). Pat the duck wings dry with a paper towel.
2. Toss the wings in a bowl with olive oil, garlic powder, smoked paprika, thyme, salt, and black pepper until evenly coated.
3. Lightly spray the air fryer basket with cooking spray and place the wings in a single layer.
4. Air fry for 22-25 minutes, flipping halfway through, until the wings are crispy and golden brown, with an internal temperature of 165°F (75°C).
5. Serve hot with your favorite dipping sauce or side.

 2 servings   5 minutes   25 minutes

Nutritional information (per serving):
400 calories, 28 g protein, 0 g carbohydrates, 32 g fat, 0 g fiber, 150 mg cholesterol, 350 mg sodium, 300 mg potassium.

DUCK with ORANGE GLAZE

A flavorful duck breast cooked in the air fryer and topped with a citrusy orange glaze

Ingredients:

- 2 duck breasts (about 8 oz / 225 g each)
- 1 tbsp olive oil
- Salt and black pepper to taste
- 1/4 cup (60 ml) fresh orange juice
- 1 tbsp honey
- 1 tsp orange zest
- 1/2 tsp soy sauce (low sodium)
- 1/2 tsp garlic powder

Directions:

1. Preheat the air fryer to 375°F (190°C). Score the skin of the duck breasts in a crosshatch pattern, being careful not to cut into the meat. Pat the duck breasts dry and rub with olive oil, salt, and black pepper.
2. Place the duck breasts skin-side down in the air fryer basket. Air fry for 12-15 minutes, flipping halfway through, until the internal temperature reaches 135°F (57°C) for medium-rare or 145°F (63°C) for medium.
3. While the duck is cooking, prepare the orange glaze: In a small saucepan, combine the orange juice, honey, orange zest, soy sauce, and garlic powder. Simmer over low heat for 5-7 minutes until the glaze thickens.
4. Once the duck breasts are done, let them rest for 5 minutes. Slice the duck and drizzle with the orange glaze before serving.

 2 servings   10 minutes   15 minutes

Nutritional information (per serving):
400 calories, 32 g protein, 10 g carbohydrates, 26 g fat, 0 g fiber, 120 mg cholesterol, 250 mg sodium, 350 mg potassium.

DUCK LEGS with ROSEMARY and GARLIC

Flavorful duck legs seasoned with garlic and rosemary, air-fried to crispy perfection

Ingredients:

- 2 duck legs (about 10 oz / 280 g each)
- 1 tbsp olive oil
- 2 cloves garlic, minced
- 1 tsp fresh rosemary, chopped (or 1/2 tsp dried)
- Salt and black pepper to taste
- Cooking spray

Directions:

1. Preheat the air fryer to 375°F (190°C). Pat the duck legs dry with a paper towel.
2. Rub the duck legs with olive oil, minced garlic, rosemary, salt, and black pepper until well coated.
3. Lightly spray the air fryer basket with cooking spray. Place the duck legs skin-side down in the basket.
4. Air fry for 25-30 minutes, flipping halfway through, until the skin is crispy and the internal temperature reaches 165°F (75°C).
5. Let the duck legs rest for 5 minutes before serving for the best flavor and texture.

 2 servings   10 minutes   30 minutes

Nutritional information (per serving):
420 calories, 30 g protein, 0 g carbohydrates, 34 g fat, 0 g fiber, 150 mg cholesterol, 400 mg sodium, 450 mg potassium.

MEAT

When managing diabetes, protein becomes an essential component of a balanced diet, offering stability in blood sugar levels while providing vital nutrients for overall health. Meat, in its many forms—beef, lamb, pork, poultry, and more—can play a significant role in a diabetic-friendly meal plan. The key is choosing lean cuts, cooking with minimal oil, and avoiding added sugars and carbs in marinades or sauces. The air fryer offers a game-changing solution for healthier cooking meat, using less fat while preserving flavor and texture.

Blood Sugar Control: Protein-rich foods like lean beef, lamb, and pork help to stabilize blood sugar levels by slowing the absorption of carbohydrates and preventing rapid spikes in glucose.

Nutrient-Dense: Meats provide a rich source of vital nutrients such as iron, zinc, and B vitamins, essential for energy production, immune function, and overall health.

Satiety and Weight Management: High-protein foods can help individuals feel full for longer, aiding in weight management—a crucial factor in controlling blood sugar levels.

Muscle Maintenance: Protein from meat supports muscle growth and repair. It is significant for individuals managing diabetes, as they often aim to maintain lean muscle mass to boost metabolism and improve insulin sensitivity.

Air fryers are an excellent tool for preparing meats in a way that aligns with diabetic dietary needs. Air fryers create crisp, flavorful results without excess fat by using minimal oil and cooking with high heat. This method helps reduce calories while maintaining meats' delicious, satisfying texture. Additionally, air frying helps preserve the natural nutrients in meat, making it an ideal cooking method for a health-conscious diet.

BEEF SCHNITZEL
Thinly pounded beef cutlets breaded and air-fried for a crispy texture

Ingredients:

- 8 oz (225 g) beef cutlets, pounded thin
- 1/2 cup (60 g) whole wheat breadcrumbs
- 1/4 cup (30 g) all-purpose flour
- 1 egg, beaten
- 1 tsp garlic powder
- 1/2 tsp smoked paprika
- 1/4 tsp black pepper
- 1/4 tsp salt
- Olive oil spray

Directions:

1. Preheat the air fryer to 375°F (190°C).
2. Season the beef cutlets with salt and pepper. Set up a breading station with three bowls: one for flour, one for the beaten egg, and one for the breadcrumbs mixed with garlic powder and smoked paprika.
3. Dredge each beef cutlet in flour, dip it in the egg, then coat with the seasoned breadcrumbs. Press the breadcrumbs onto the cutlets to ensure they stick.
4. Lightly spray both sides of the schnitzels with olive oil and place them in the air fryer basket. Cook for 10-12 minutes, flipping halfway through, until golden and crispy.
5. Serve with lemon wedges or your favorite side.

 2 servings 15 minutes 12 minutes

Nutritional information (per serving):
340 calories, 32 g protein, 25 g carbohydrates, 12 g fat, 2 g fiber, 120 mg cholesterol, 460 mg sodium, 500 mg potassium.

BEEF MEATBALLS

Tender meatballs seasoned with herbs, perfect for a low-carb dish

Ingredients:

- 8 oz (225 g) lean ground beef
- 1/4 cup (30 g) grated Parmesan cheese
- 1 tbsp fresh parsley, chopped (or 1 tsp dried parsley)
- 1 clove garlic, minced
- 1/4 tsp onion powder
- 1/4 tsp black pepper
- 1/4 tsp salt
- 1 egg, beaten

Directions:

1. Preheat the air fryer to 375°F (190°C).
2. In a large bowl, combine ground beef, Parmesan, parsley, garlic, onion powder, black pepper, salt, and beaten egg. Mix until well combined.
3. Roll the mixture into 1-inch (2.5 cm) meatballs and place them in the air fryer basket, ensuring they don't touch.
4. Air fry for 10-12 minutes, shaking the basket halfway through, until the meatballs are browned and cooked through (internal temperature of 160°F / 71°C).
5. Serve hot with your favorite low-carb sauce or salad.

 2 servings 10 minutes 12 minutes

Nutritional information (per serving):
250 calories, 25 g protein, 2 g carbohydrates, 16 g fat, 0 g fiber, 110 mg cholesterol, 450 mg sodium, 300 mg potassium.

BEEF STEAK BITES

Juicy steak bites seasoned and cooked to perfection in the air fryer

Ingredients:

- 10 oz (280 g) sirloin steak, cut into 1-inch cubes
- 1 tbsp olive oil
- 1 tsp garlic powder
- 1/2 tsp smoked paprika
- Salt and black pepper to taste
- 1 tsp fresh parsley, chopped (optional, for garnish)

Directions:

1. Preheat the air fryer to 400°F (200°C).
2. In a bowl, toss the steak bites with olive oil, garlic powder, smoked paprika, salt, and black pepper until evenly coated.
3. Place the steak bites in a single layer in the air fryer basket.
4. Air fry for 8-10 minutes, shaking the basket halfway through, until the steak reaches your desired level of doneness (for medium, aim for an internal temperature of 135°F / 57°C).
5. Garnish with fresh parsley and serve immediately.

 2 servings 5 minutes 10 minutes

Nutritional information (per serving):
320 calories, 32 g protein, 2 g carbohydrates, 20 g fat, 0 g fiber, 85 mg cholesterol, 400 mg sodium, 380 mg potassium.

BEEF PATTIES

Lean beef patties made healthier in the air fryer, perfect for burgers

Ingredients:

- 8 oz (225 g) lean ground beef
- 1/2 tsp garlic powder
- 1/2 tsp onion powder
- 1/4 tsp smoked paprika
- Salt and black pepper to taste
- Cooking spray

Directions:

1. Preheat the air fryer to 375°F (190°C).
2. In a bowl, mix the ground beef with garlic powder, onion powder, smoked paprika, salt, and black pepper. Form into two patties.
3. Lightly spray the air fryer basket with cooking spray and place the patties inside.
4. Air fry for 8-10 minutes, flipping halfway through, until the patties reach an internal temperature of 160°F (71°C).
5. Serve the patties on whole wheat buns or lettuce wraps with your favorite toppings.

 2 servings 5 minutes 10 minutes

Nutritional information (per serving):
250 calories, 25 g protein, 0 g carbohydrates, 17 g fat, 0 g fiber, 75 mg cholesterol, 450 mg sodium, 320 mg potassium.

BEEF JERKY

A low-carb, high-protein snack made with lean cuts of beef

Ingredients:

- 8 oz (225 g) lean beef (such as top round or flank steak), thinly sliced
- 2 tbsp soy sauce (low sodium)
- 1 tbsp Worcestershire sauce
- 1 tsp garlic powder
- 1 tsp onion powder
- 1/2 tsp black pepper
- 1/2 tsp smoked paprika
- 1/4 tsp red pepper flakes (optional, for heat)

Directions:

1. In a bowl, combine soy sauce, Worcestershire sauce, garlic powder, onion powder, black pepper, smoked paprika, and red pepper flakes. Add the beef slices and coat well. Marinate in the fridge for at least 4 hours or overnight.
2. Preheat the air fryer to 180°F (82°C). Remove the beef slices from the marinade and pat them dry with a paper towel.
3. Arrange the beef slices in a single layer in the air fryer basket.
4. Air fry for 2 hours, flipping halfway through, until the beef is dry and slightly chewy. Check for your preferred texture.
5. Let the jerky cool completely before storing in an airtight container.

 2 servings   4 hours   2 hours

Nutritional information (per serving):
160 calories, 24 g protein, 4 g carbohydrates, 4 g fat, 0 g fiber, 50 mg cholesterol, 500 mg sodium, 400 mg potassium.

BEEF KEBABS

Marinated beef skewers air-fried for a tender, flavorful meal

Ingredients:

- 8 oz (225 g) beef sirloin, cut into 1-inch cubes
- 1 tbsp olive oil
- 1 tbsp lemon juice
- 1 tsp garlic powder
- 1 tsp onion powder
- 1 tsp smoked paprika
- 1/2 tsp cumin
- Salt and black pepper to taste
- Skewers (wooden or metal)

Directions:

1. In a bowl, mix olive oil, lemon juice, garlic powder, onion powder, smoked paprika, cumin, salt, and black pepper. Add the beef cubes and coat well. Marinate for at least 1 hour in the fridge.
2. Preheat the air fryer to 400°F (200°C).
3. Thread the marinated beef cubes onto skewers, leaving a little space between each piece.
4. Place the skewers in the air fryer basket and cook for 8-10 minutes, turning halfway through, until the beef is cooked to your desired doneness.
5. Serve hot with a side of vegetables or salad.

 2 servings   1 hour 10 minutes

Nutritional information (per serving):
280 calories, 30 g protein, 2 g carbohydrates, 18 g fat, 0 g fiber, 80 mg cholesterol, 450 mg sodium, 350 mg potassium.

ROAST BEEF

A perfectly cooked roast beef with a crispy exterior and juicy interior

Ingredients:

- 12 oz (340 g) beef roast (such as top sirloin or eye of round)
- 1 tbsp olive oil
- 1 tsp garlic powder
- 1 tsp onion powder
- 1 tsp dried rosemary
- 1/2 tsp black pepper
- 1/2 tsp salt

Directions:

1. Preheat the air fryer to 380°F (190°C).
2. Rub the beef roast with olive oil, then season it with garlic powder, onion powder, rosemary, black pepper, and salt.
3. Place the roast in the air fryer basket and cook for 25-30 minutes, flipping halfway through. For medium-rare, the internal temperature should reach 130°F (54°C); for medium, 140°F (60°C).
4. Remove the roast from the air fryer, cover with foil, and let it rest for 10 minutes before slicing.
5. Serve with your favorite sides.

 2 servings   10 minutes   30 minutes

Nutritional information (per serving):
320 calories, 38 g protein, 0 g carbohydrates, 20 g fat, 0 g fiber, 110 mg cholesterol, 480 mg sodium, 400 mg potassium.

BEEF TACOS

Seasoned ground beef cooked in the air fryer, served with low-carb tortillas

Ingredients:

- 8 oz (225 g) lean ground beef
- 1 tsp chili powder
- 1/2 tsp cumin
- 1/2 tsp garlic powder
- 1/2 tsp onion powder
- 1/4 tsp smoked paprika
- Salt and pepper to taste
- 4 low-carb tortillas
- Toppings: shredded lettuce, diced tomatoes, shredded cheese, and salsa

Directions:

1. Preheat the air fryer to 375°F (190°C).
2. In a bowl, mix the ground beef with chili powder, cumin, garlic powder, onion powder, smoked paprika, salt, and pepper.
3. Place the seasoned ground beef in the air fryer basket, breaking it into small pieces. Cook for 8-10 minutes, stirring halfway through, until fully cooked.
4. Warm the low-carb tortillas in the air fryer for 1-2 minutes.
5. Assemble the tacos by filling the tortillas with the cooked beef and your favorite toppings.

 2 servings   10 minutes   12 minutes

Nutritional information (per serving):
360 calories, 28 g protein, 10 g carbohydrates, 23 g fat, 2 g fiber, 80 mg cholesterol, 500 mg sodium, 420 mg potassium.

BEEF TENDERLION

A tender and succulent beef tenderloin cooked to your preferred doneness

Ingredients:

- 10 oz (280 g) beef tenderloin
- 1 tbsp olive oil
- 1 tsp garlic powder
- 1 tsp fresh rosemary, chopped
- 1/2 tsp black pepper
- 1/2 tsp salt

Directions:

1. Preheat the air fryer to 400°F (200°C).
2. Rub the beef tenderloin with olive oil, garlic powder, rosemary, black pepper, and salt.
3. Place the beef tenderloin in the air fryer basket and cook for 12-15 minutes, depending on your preferred doneness (125°F / 52°C for medium-rare, 135°F / 57°C for medium), flipping halfway through.
4. Remove from the air fryer, cover with foil, and let rest for 5-10 minutes before slicing.
5. Serve with your favorite sides.

 2 servings   10 minutes   15 minutes

Nutritional information (per serving):
320 calories, 34 g protein, 0 g carbohydrates, 20 g fat, 0 g fiber, 100 mg cholesterol, 420 mg sodium, 350 mg potassium.

BEEF FAJITAS

Sliced beef strips with peppers and onions, a low-carb meal

Ingredients:

- 8 oz (225 g) beef sirloin, sliced into thin strips
- 1 bell pepper, sliced
- 1 small onion, sliced
- 1 tbsp olive oil
- 1 tsp chili powder
- 1/2 tsp cumin
- 1/2 tsp garlic powder
- 1/2 tsp paprika
- Salt and pepper to taste
- Low-carb tortillas or lettuce wraps (optional)

Directions:

1. Preheat the air fryer to 375°F (190°C).
2. In a bowl, mix the beef strips, bell pepper, onion, olive oil, chili powder, cumin, garlic powder, paprika, salt, and pepper until well coated.
3. Place the beef and vegetable mixture in the air fryer basket in a single layer.
4. Cook for 10-12 minutes, shaking the basket halfway through, until the beef is cooked through and the vegetables are tender.
5. Serve with low-carb tortillas or lettuce wraps for a complete meal.

 2 servings   10 minutes   12 minutes

Nutritional information (per serving):
320 calories, 28 g protein, 10 g carbohydrates, 18 g fat, 2 g fiber, 70 mg cholesterol, 460 mg sodium, 500 mg potassium.

BEEF BRISKET

A flavorful, slow-cooked brisket with a smoky, crisp finish

Ingredients:

- 12 oz (340 g) beef brisket
- 1 tbsp olive oil
- 1 tsp smoked paprika
- 1 tsp garlic powder
- 1 tsp onion powder
- 1/2 tsp cumin
- 1/2 tsp black pepper
- 1/2 tsp salt
- 1/4 tsp cayenne pepper (optional for heat)

Directions:

1. Rub the brisket with olive oil and season with smoked paprika, garlic powder, onion powder, cumin, black pepper, salt, and cayenne pepper. Let it marinate for 1 hour in the fridge.
2. Preheat the air fryer to 300°F (150°C).
3. Place the brisket in the air fryer basket, fat side up, and cook for 50-60 minutes, flipping halfway through, until the internal temperature reaches 190°F (88°C) for tender, slow-cooked results.
4. Let the brisket rest for 10 minutes before slicing.
5. Serve with your favorite sides or in sandwiches.

 2 servings   1 hour   1 hour

Nutritional information (per serving):
420 calories, 36 g protein, 1 g carbohydrates, 29 g fat, 0 g fiber, 110 mg cholesterol, 550 mg sodium, 470 mg potassium.

BEEF SHORT RIBS

Crispy short ribs cooked with minimal oil and full flavor

Ingredients:

- 1 lb (450 g) beef short ribs
- 1 tbsp olive oil
- 1 tsp garlic powder
- 1 tsp smoked paprika
- 1/2 tsp black pepper
- 1/2 tsp salt
- 1/4 tsp cayenne pepper (optional for heat)
- 1/2 tsp dried thyme

Directions:

1. Preheat the air fryer to 375°F (190°C).
2. Rub the beef short ribs with olive oil and season with garlic powder, smoked paprika, black pepper, salt, cayenne pepper (if using), and thyme.
3. Place the short ribs in the air fryer basket in a single layer.
4. Cook for 25-30 minutes, flipping halfway through, until the short ribs are crispy and the internal temperature reaches at least 145°F (63°C).
5. Let the ribs rest for a few minutes before serving.

 2 servings   10 minutes   30 minutes

Nutritional information (per serving):
520 calories, 36 g protein, 1 g carbohydrates, 42 g fat, 0 g fiber, 120 mg cholesterol, 540 mg sodium, 500 mg potassium.

BEEF STIR-FRY

A simple, healthy beef stir-fry with vegetables, cooked quickly in the air fryer

Ingredients:

- 8 oz (225 g) beef sirloin, thinly sliced
- 1 cup (150 g) broccoli florets
- 1 small bell pepper, sliced
- 1 small carrot, julienned
- 1 tbsp olive oil
- 2 tbsp soy sauce (low sodium)
- 1 tsp garlic powder
- 1 tsp ginger powder
- 1/2 tsp black pepper
- 1/4 tsp sesame oil (optional for flavor)

Directions:

1. Preheat the air fryer to 375°F (190°C).
2. Toss the sliced beef, broccoli, bell pepper, and carrot with olive oil, soy sauce, garlic powder, ginger powder, and black pepper in a bowl until well coated.
3. Spread the beef and vegetables in an even layer in the air fryer basket. Cook for 12-15 minutes, shaking the basket halfway through, until the beef is cooked through and the vegetables are tender.
4. Drizzle with sesame oil (if using) and serve hot.

 2 servings   10 minutes   15 minutes

Nutritional information (per serving):
320 calories, 28 g protein, 10 g carbohydrates, 18 g fat, 3 g fiber, 60 mg cholesterol, 730 mg sodium, 680 mg potassium.

BEEF PHILLY CHEESESTEAK

A low-carb version of the classic sandwich using air-fried beef strips

Ingredients:

- 8 oz (225 g) beef sirloin, thinly sliced
- 1 small onion, sliced
- 1 small bell pepper, sliced
- 1/2 cup (60 g) mushrooms, sliced
- 1/2 cup (60 g) shredded provolone or mozzarella cheese
- 1 tbsp olive oil
- 1 tbsp Worcestershire sauce
- 1/2 tsp garlic powder
- 1/2 tsp black pepper
- 1/4 tsp salt
- Low-carb hoagie rolls or lettuce wraps (optional)

Directions:

1. Preheat the air fryer to 375°F (190°C).
2. In a bowl, toss the beef strips, onion, bell pepper, and mushrooms with olive oil, Worcestershire sauce, garlic powder, salt, and pepper.
3. Spread the mixture evenly in the air fryer basket. Cook for 10-12 minutes, shaking halfway through, until the beef is cooked and the vegetables are tender.
4. Sprinkle the shredded cheese over the cooked beef and vegetables and cook for an additional 1-2 minutes until the cheese is melted.
5. Serve in low-carb hoagie rolls or lettuce wraps.

 2 servings   **10** minutes   **12** minutes

Nutritional information (per serving):
340 calories, 28 g protein, 8 g carbohydrates, 20 g fat, 2 g fiber, 65 mg cholesterol, 550 mg sodium, 570 mg potassium.

LAMB KEBABS

Flavorful lamb skewers with Middle Eastern spices, perfect for a quick meal

Ingredients:

- 10 oz (280 g) lamb shoulder or leg, cubed
- 1 tbsp olive oil
- 1 tsp ground cumin
- 1 tsp ground coriander
- 1/2 tsp smoked paprika
- 1/4 tsp cinnamon
- 1 clove garlic, minced
- 1/2 tsp salt
- 1/4 tsp black pepper
- 1 tbsp lemon juice
- 1 tbsp fresh parsley, chopped (for garnish)

Directions:

1. Preheat the air fryer to 400°F (200°C).
2. In a bowl, combine olive oil, cumin, coriander, paprika, cinnamon, garlic, salt, pepper, and lemon juice. Mix well.
3. Toss the lamb cubes in the marinade, coating them evenly. Thread the lamb onto skewers.
4. Place the skewers in the air fryer basket and cook for 8-10 minutes, turning halfway through, until lamb reaches your desired doneness.
5. Garnish with fresh parsley and serve.

 2 servings   **15** minutes   **10** minutes

Nutritional information (per serving):
400 calories, 30 g protein, 2 g carbohydrates, 32 g fat, 1 g fiber, 90 mg cholesterol, 580 mg sodium, 400 mg potassium.

LAMB RIBS

Crispy and juicy lamb ribs with a hint of rosemary and garlic

Ingredients:

- 1 lb (450 g) lamb ribs
- 1 tbsp (15 ml) olive oil
- 2 tsp (4 g) fresh rosemary, chopped
- 2 cloves garlic, minced
- 1/2 tsp (3 g) salt
- 1/4 tsp (1 g) black pepper

Directions:

1. Preheat your air fryer to 400°F (200°C) for 3-5 minutes.
2. In a bowl, mix olive oil, rosemary, garlic, salt, and pepper. Rub the mixture over the lamb ribs.
3. Place the seasoned lamb ribs in the air fryer basket in a single layer.
4. Air fry at 400°F (200°C) for 18-20 minutes, flipping halfway through, until crispy and golden brown.
5. Let the ribs rest for 5 minutes before serving.

 2 servings   **10** minutes   **20** minutes

Nutritional information (per serving):
640 calories, 40g protein, 0g carbohydrates, 52g fat, 0g fiber, 135mg cholesterol, 660mg sodium, 420mg potassium.

GROUND BEEF STUFFED PEPPERS

Bell peppers stuffed with ground beef and vegetables for a hearty meal

Ingredients:

- 2 medium bell peppers, tops cut off and seeds removed
- 8 oz (225 g) lean ground beef
- 1/4 cup (40 g) onion, finely chopped
- 1/4 cup (30 g) diced tomatoes
- 1/4 cup (30 g) shredded cheese (cheddar or mozzarella)
- 1/2 tsp garlic powder
- 1/2 tsp paprika
- 1/4 tsp black pepper
- 1/4 tsp salt
- 1 tbsp olive oil

Directions:

1. Preheat the air fryer to 375°F (190°C).
2. In a skillet over medium heat, cook the ground beef, onion, garlic powder, paprika, salt, and pepper until the beef is browned, about 5-7 minutes. Drain excess fat.
3. Stir in the diced tomatoes and cook for an additional 2 minutes. Remove from heat and mix in the shredded cheese.
4. Stuff the mixture into the bell peppers and drizzle the tops with olive oil.
5. Place the stuffed peppers in the air fryer basket and cook for 10-15 minutes, until the peppers are tender.

 2 servings   10 minutes   15 minutes

Nutritional information (per serving):
300 calories, 25 g protein, 10 g carbohydrates, 18 g fat, 3 g fiber, 70 mg cholesterol, 450 mg sodium, 500 mg potassium.

LAMB CHOPS

Tender lamb chops seasoned with garlic and herbs, air-fried to perfection

Ingredients:

- 4 lamb chops (approximately 6 oz/170 g each)
- 2 cloves garlic, minced
- 1 tbsp fresh rosemary, chopped
- 1 tbsp olive oil
- 1/2 tsp salt
- 1/4 tsp black pepper
- 1/2 tsp lemon zest

Directions:

1. Preheat the air fryer to 400°F (200°C).
2. In a small bowl, mix the garlic, rosemary, olive oil, salt, pepper, and lemon zest to form a marinade.
3. Rub the marinade over both sides of the lamb chops and let them marinate for 10 minutes.
4. Place the lamb chops in the air fryer basket and cook for 10-12 minutes, flipping halfway through, until the internal temperature reaches your desired doneness (medium-rare: 145°F/63°C, medium: 160°F/71°C).
5. Let the lamb chops rest for 5 minutes before serving.

 2 servings   10 minutes   12 minutes

Nutritional information (per serving):
360 calories, 30 g protein, 1 g carbohydrates, 26 g fat, 0 g fiber, 85 mg cholesterol, 350 mg sodium, 400 mg potassium.

LAMB SHOULDER

A tender and flavorful lamb shoulder roast, perfect for a special dinner

Ingredients:

- 1 lb (450 g) lamb shoulder, bone-in
- 2 tbsp (30 ml) olive oil
- 3 cloves garlic, minced
- 2 tsp (4 g) fresh rosemary, chopped
- 1 tsp (2 g) thyme
- 1/2 tsp (3 g) salt
- 1/4 tsp (1 g) black pepper

Directions:

1. Preheat the air fryer to 350°F (175°C).
2. Rub the lamb shoulder with olive oil, garlic, rosemary, thyme, salt, and pepper.
3. Place the lamb shoulder in the air fryer basket.
4. Air fry at 350°F (175°C) for 55-60 minutes, turning halfway through, until the lamb is tender and reaches an internal temperature of 145°F (63°C) for medium-rare.
5. Let the lamb rest for 10 minutes before carving and serving.

 2 servings   15 minutes   60 minutes

Nutritional information (per serving):
690 calories, 55g protein, 0g carbohydrates, 52g fat, 0g fiber, 180mg cholesterol, 750mg sodium, 490mg potassium.

LAMB MEATBALLS

Juicy lamb meatballs packed with herbs and spices, cooked with minimal oil

Ingredients:

- 8 oz (225 g) ground lamb
- 1 tbsp fresh parsley, chopped
- 1 tbsp fresh mint, chopped
- 1 clove garlic, minced
- 1/2 tsp ground cumin
- 1/2 tsp ground coriander
- 1/4 tsp ground cinnamon
- 1/4 tsp black pepper
- 1/2 tsp salt
- 1 tbsp olive oil (for brushing)

Directions:

1. In a bowl, combine the ground lamb, parsley, mint, garlic, cumin, coriander, cinnamon, salt, and pepper. Mix well.
2. Form the mixture into 10 small meatballs.
3. Preheat the air fryer to 375°F (190°C). Lightly brush the meatballs with olive oil.
4. Place the meatballs in the air fryer basket and cook for 10-12 minutes, shaking halfway through, until fully cooked and browned.
5. Serve with your favorite dipping sauce or alongside a salad.

 2 servings   10 minutes   12 minutes

Nutritional information (per serving):
300 calories, 20 g protein, 1 g carbohydrates, 24 g fat, 1 g fiber, 75 mg cholesterol, 550 mg sodium, 350 mg potassium.

LAMB SHANKS

Slow-cooked lamb shanks with a crispy finish, perfect for a hearty meal

Ingredients:

- 2 lamb shanks (approx. 1 lb each / 450 g)
- 1 tbsp (15 ml) olive oil
- 1 tsp (5 g) garlic powder
- 1 tsp (5 g) paprika
- 1 tsp (5 g) dried rosemary
- 1/2 tsp (3 g) salt
- 1/4 tsp (1 g) black pepper

Directions:

1. Preheat your air fryer to 350°F (175°C) for 5 minutes.
2. Rub the lamb shanks with olive oil, garlic powder, paprika, rosemary, salt, and pepper.
3. Place the lamb shanks in the air fryer basket and cook at 350°F (175°C) for 45-50 minutes, turning halfway through, until the lamb is tender and the exterior is crispy.
4. Let rest for 5 minutes before serving.

 2 servings   10 minutes   50 minutes

Nutritional information (per serving):
480 calories, 45g protein, 1g carbohydrates, 32g fat, 0g fiber, 160mg cholesterol, 520mg sodium, 560mg potassium.

LAMB BURGERS

Ground lamb patties made healthier in the air fryer, full of flavor

Ingredients:

- 1/2 lb (225 g) ground lamb
- 1 tsp (5 g) garlic powder
- 1/2 tsp (3 g) ground cumin
- 1/2 tsp (3 g) dried oregano
- 1/2 tsp (3 g) salt
- 1/4 tsp (1 g) black pepper
- 1 tbsp (15 ml) olive oil (for brushing the air fryer basket)
- Whole wheat buns (optional)

Directions:

1. Preheat your air fryer to 375°F (190°C) for 3-5 minutes.
2. In a bowl, mix the ground lamb, garlic powder, cumin, oregano, salt, and pepper. Form into two equal-sized patties.
3. Lightly brush the air fryer basket with olive oil to prevent sticking. Place the patties in the basket.
4. Air fry at 375°F (190°C) for 8-10 minutes, flipping halfway through, until the internal temperature reaches 160°F (71°C).
5. Serve the lamb burgers with or without buns and your favorite toppings.

 2 servings   10 minutes   10 minutes

Nutritional information (per serving):
380 calories, 22g protein, 2g carbohydrates, 32g fat, 0g fiber, 90mg cholesterol, 520mg sodium, 310mg potassium.

LAMB FAJITAS

A low-carb meal with sliced lamb, peppers, and onions

Ingredients:

- 8 oz (225 g) lamb shoulder, thinly sliced
- 1 tbsp (15 ml) olive oil
- 1/2 red bell pepper, sliced
- 1/2 green bell pepper, sliced
- 1/2 onion, sliced
- 1 tsp (2 g) chili powder
- 1/2 tsp (1 g) cumin
- 1/2 tsp (1 g) garlic powder
- 1/2 tsp (3 g) salt
- 1/4 tsp (1 g) black pepper
- 2 low-carb tortillas (optional, for serving)

Directions:

1. Preheat the air fryer to 400°F (200°C).
2. In a bowl, mix lamb slices, olive oil, chili powder, cumin, garlic powder, salt, and pepper.
3. Add bell peppers and onions to the lamb mixture and toss until evenly coated.
4. Place the mixture in the air fryer basket and cook at 400°F (200°C) for 12-15 minutes, shaking the basket halfway through.
5. Serve with low-carb tortillas or lettuce wraps.

 2 servings 10 minutes 15 minutes

Nutritional information (per serving):
360 calories, 28g protein, 12g carbohydrates, 23g fat, 4g fiber, 80mg cholesterol, 620mg sodium, 450mg potassium.

LAMB KOFTA

Spiced ground lamb skewers air-fried for a delicious and healthy snack

Ingredients:

- 8 oz (225 g) ground lamb
- 1/2 small onion, finely chopped
- 1 garlic clove, minced
- 1 tbsp (2 g) fresh parsley, chopped
- 1 tsp (2 g) ground cumin
- 1 tsp (2 g) ground coriander
- 1/2 tsp (1 g) paprika
- 1/2 tsp (3 g) salt
- 1/4 tsp (1 g) black pepper
- Wooden skewers (optional)

Directions:

1. Preheat the air fryer to 375°F (190°C).
2. In a bowl, combine ground lamb, onion, garlic, parsley, cumin, coriander, paprika, salt, and pepper. Mix until well blended.
3. Shape the lamb mixture into long, thin kofta shapes around wooden skewers if using.
4. Place the kofta in the air fryer basket and cook at 375°F (190°C) for 10-12 minutes, turning halfway through.
5. Serve hot with your favorite dip or side salad.

 2 servings 10 minutes 12 minutes

Nutritional information (per serving):
310 calories, 22g protein, 4g carbohydrates, 23g fat, 1g fiber, 75mg cholesterol, 620mg sodium, 300mg potassium.

LAMB CUTLETS

Crispy and tender lamb cutlets with a garlic-herb crust

Ingredients:

- 4 lamb cutlets (8 oz / 225 g total)
- 2 tbsp (30 ml) olive oil
- 2 garlic cloves, minced
- 1 tbsp (2 g) fresh rosemary, chopped
- 1 tbsp (2 g) fresh parsley, chopped
- 1/2 cup (50 g) whole wheat breadcrumbs
- 1/2 tsp (3 g) salt
- 1/4 tsp (1 g) black pepper

Directions:

1. Preheat the air fryer to 375°F (190°C).
2. In a small bowl, combine minced garlic, rosemary, parsley, salt, and pepper with olive oil.
3. Rub the lamb cutlets with the garlic-herb mixture and press them into the breadcrumbs to coat evenly.
4. Place the cutlets in the air fryer basket and cook at 375°F (190°C) for 8-10 minutes, turning halfway through, until crispy and golden brown.
5. Serve hot with a side of vegetables or salad.

 2 servings 10 minutes 10 minutes

Nutritional information (per serving):
380 calories, 30g protein, 12g carbohydrates, 23g fat, 2g fiber, 80mg cholesterol, 450mg sodium, 350mg potassium.

LAMB STEW

A hearty lamb stew with vegetables, slow-cooked in the air fryer

Ingredients:

- 1/2 lb (225 g) lamb shoulder, cubed
- 1 tbsp (15 ml) olive oil
- 1 carrot, sliced
- 1 potato, diced
- 1 onion, chopped
- 1 garlic clove, minced
- 1/2 cup (120 ml) low-sodium beef broth
- 1/2 tsp (1 g) dried thyme
- 1/2 tsp (1 g) dried rosemary
- Salt and pepper to taste

Directions:

1. Preheat the air fryer to 350°F (175°C).
2. In a large bowl, toss the lamb cubes with olive oil, thyme, rosemary, salt, and pepper.
3. Place lamb in the air fryer basket and cook at 350°F (175°C) for 15 minutes, stirring halfway through.
4. Add the carrot, potato, onion, garlic, and beef broth to the basket, stir well, and cook for another 20 minutes, until the vegetables are tender and the lamb is fully cooked.
5. Serve the stew warm for a hearty meal.

 2 servings   15 minutes   35 minutes

Nutritional information (per serving):
420 calories, 25g protein, 30g carbohydrates, 23g fat, 5g fiber, 80mg cholesterol, 520mg sodium, 700mg potassium.

GREEK-STYLE LAMB

Marinated lamb with lemon and oregano, air-fried for a Mediterranean-inspired dish

Ingredients:

- 1/2 lb (225 g) lamb loin or shoulder, cubed
- 2 tbsp (30 ml) olive oil
- 2 tbsp (30 ml) lemon juice
- 1 tsp (1 g) dried oregano
- 1 garlic clove, minced
- Salt and pepper to taste
- Lemon wedges for serving

Directions:

1. In a bowl, combine olive oil, lemon juice, oregano, garlic, salt, and pepper. Add lamb cubes and toss to coat. Marinate for at least 30 minutes in the fridge.
2. Preheat the air fryer to 375°F (190°C).
3. Place marinated lamb in the air fryer basket and cook at 375°F (190°C) for 12-15 minutes, shaking the basket halfway through until the lamb is cooked to your preferred doneness.
4. Serve hot with lemon wedges on the side for extra flavor.

 2 servings   40 minutes   15 minutes

Nutritional information (per serving):
360 calories, 25g protein, 2g carbohydrates, 28g fat, 1g fiber, 70mg cholesterol, 450mg sodium, 330mg potassium.

LAMB STIR-FRY

A quick and healthy lamb stir-fry with vegetables

Ingredients:

- 1/2 lb (225 g) lamb loin or shoulder, thinly sliced
- 1 tbsp (15 ml) olive oil
- 1 red bell pepper, sliced
- 1 zucchini, sliced
- 1 small onion, sliced
- 1 tbsp (15 ml) soy sauce (low-sodium)
- 1 tsp (5 ml) sesame oil
- 1/2 tsp (1 g) ground black pepper
- 1/2 tsp (1 g) garlic powder

Directions:

1. Preheat the air fryer to 375°F (190°C).
2. In a bowl, toss the lamb slices with olive oil, soy sauce, sesame oil, black pepper, and garlic powder.
3. Place the seasoned lamb and vegetables (bell pepper, zucchini, onion) in the air fryer basket.
4. Cook at 375°F (190°C) for 10-12 minutes, shaking the basket halfway through, until the lamb is cooked and vegetables are tender.
5. Serve immediately as a healthy and flavorful stir-fry.

 2 servings   10 minutes   15 minutes

Nutritional information (per serving):
320 calories, 26g protein, 12g carbohydrates, 19g fat, 3g fiber, 70mg cholesterol, 520mg sodium, 420mg potassium.

LAMB GYRO

A low-carb version of the classic Greek dish with seasoned lamb strips

Ingredients:

- 1/2 lb (225 g) lamb loin or shoulder, thinly sliced
- 1 tbsp (15 ml) olive oil
- 1 tsp (2 g) dried oregano
- 1/2 tsp (1 g) ground cumin
- 1/2 tsp (1 g) garlic powder
- 1/2 tsp (1 g) paprika
- Salt and pepper to taste
- 1/4 cup (60 g) plain Greek yogurt
- 1 small cucumber, grated
- 1 clove garlic, minced
- 2 low-carb pita bread or lettuce wraps
- Sliced tomatoes and red onions for garnish

Directions:

1. Preheat the air fryer to 375°F (190°C).
2. In a bowl, toss the lamb slices with olive oil, oregano, cumin, garlic powder, paprika, salt, and pepper.
3. Place the seasoned lamb strips in the air fryer basket and cook for 10-12 minutes, shaking halfway through, until cooked and crispy.
4. While the lamb is cooking, mix Greek yogurt, grated cucumber, and minced garlic to make a simple tzatziki sauce.
5. Serve the lamb in low-carb pita bread or lettuce wraps, topped with the tzatziki sauce, tomatoes, and red onions.

 2 servings 10 minutes 12 minutes

Nutritional information (per serving):
350 calories, 28g protein, 12g carbohydrates, 22g fat, 2g fiber, 75mg cholesterol, 620mg sodium, 480mg potassium.

LAMB TACOS

Ground lamb seasoned with cumin and paprika, served in low-carb tortillas

Ingredients:

- 1/2 lb (225 g) ground lamb
- 1 tbsp (15 ml) olive oil
- 1 tsp (2 g) ground cumin
- 1/2 tsp (1 g) paprika
- 1/2 tsp (1 g) garlic powder
- Salt and pepper to taste
- 4 low-carb tortillas
- 1/4 cup (30 g) shredded lettuce
- 1/4 cup (30 g) diced tomatoes
- 1/4 cup (30 g) shredded cheese (optional)
- Salsa and sour cream for serving

Directions:

1. Preheat the air fryer to 375°F (190°C).
2. In a bowl, mix ground lamb with olive oil, cumin, paprika, garlic powder, salt, and pepper.
3. Shape the seasoned lamb into small patties or crumbles and place them in the air fryer basket. Cook for 7-8 minutes, shaking the basket halfway through until browned and cooked through.
4. Warm the low-carb tortillas in the air fryer for 1-2 minutes, then fill them with the cooked lamb, shredded lettuce, diced tomatoes, and cheese (if using).
5. Serve with salsa and sour cream on the side.

 2 servings 10 minutes 8 minutes

Nutritional information (per serving):
400 calories, 25g protein, 15g carbohydrates, 27g fat, 3g fiber, 80mg cholesterol, 650mg sodium, 450mg potassium.

PORK CHOPS

Juicy pork chops with a golden, crispy crust, perfect for a low-carb meal

Ingredients:

- 2 bone-in pork chops (about 6 oz each, 170 g)
- 1 tbsp (15 ml) olive oil
- 1 tsp (2 g) garlic powder
- 1 tsp (2 g) paprika
- 1/2 tsp (1 g) onion powder
- Salt and pepper to taste

Directions:

1. Preheat the air fryer to 400°F (200°C).
2. Brush the pork chops with olive oil, then season both sides with garlic powder, paprika, onion powder, salt, and pepper.
3. Place the pork chops in the air fryer basket in a single layer. Cook for 10-12 minutes, flipping halfway through, until the internal temperature reaches 145°F (63°C).
4. Let the pork chops rest for 3 minutes before serving to lock in the juices.

Nutritional information (per serving):
320 calories, 32g protein, 1g carbohydrates, 21g fat, 0g fiber, 80mg cholesterol, 450mg sodium, 450mg potassium.

 2 servings 5 minutes 12 minutes

PORK TENDERLOIN

A lean and tender pork tenderloin, marinated and cooked to perfection

Ingredients:

- 1 pork tenderloin (about 12 oz / 340 g)
- 2 tbsp (30 ml) olive oil
- 1 tbsp (15 ml) soy sauce (low-sodium)
- 2 tsp (4 g) garlic powder
- 1 tsp (2 g) smoked paprika
- 1 tsp (2 g) dried oregano
- Salt and pepper to taste

Directions:

1. In a small bowl, mix olive oil, soy sauce, garlic powder, smoked paprika, oregano, salt, and pepper.
2. Rub the marinade all over the pork tenderloin and refrigerate for at least 30 minutes.
3. Preheat the air fryer to 400°F (200°C). Place the marinated pork tenderloin in the air fryer basket.
4. Cook for 12-15 minutes, turning halfway through, until the internal temperature reaches 145°F (63°C). Let it rest for 5 minutes before slicing and serving.

 2 servings 40 minutes 15 minutes

Nutritional information (per serving):
280 calories, 32g protein, 1g carbohydrates, 16g fat, 0g fiber, 85mg cholesterol, 500mg sodium, 500mg potassium.

PORK RIBS

Crispy pork ribs seasoned with spices, ideal for a flavorful meal

Ingredients:

- 1 lb (450 g) pork ribs, cut into individual ribs
- 1 tbsp (15 ml) olive oil
- 1 tsp (2 g) garlic powder
- 1 tsp (2 g) smoked paprika
- 1/2 tsp (1 g) onion powder
- 1/2 tsp (1 g) ground black pepper
- Salt to taste

Directions:

1. Preheat the air fryer to 380°F (190°C).
2. In a large bowl, rub the ribs with olive oil, garlic powder, smoked paprika, onion powder, salt, and pepper until evenly coated.
3. Arrange the ribs in the air fryer basket in a single layer, ensuring space between them for even cooking.
4. Cook for 20-25 minutes, flipping halfway through, until the ribs are crispy and cooked through, with an internal temperature of 145°F (63°C).

 2 servings 10 minutes 25 minutes

Nutritional information (per serving):
490 calories, 34g protein, 2g carbohydrates, 38g fat, 0g fiber, 120mg cholesterol, 550mg sodium, 450mg potassium.

PORK BELLY

Crispy pork belly with minimal oil, cooked to crunchy perfection

Ingredients:

- 10 oz (280 g) pork belly, skin on, cut into 1-inch cubes
- 1 tsp (5 ml) olive oil
- 1/2 tsp (1 g) garlic powder
- 1/2 tsp (1 g) smoked paprika
- Salt and pepper to taste

Directions:

1. Preheat the air fryer to 400°F (200°C).
2. In a bowl, toss the pork belly cubes with olive oil, garlic powder, smoked paprika, salt, and pepper.
3. Arrange the pork belly pieces in a single layer in the air fryer basket.
4. Cook for 20-25 minutes, flipping halfway through, until the pork belly is crispy and golden brown.

 2 servings 10 minutes 25 minutes

Nutritional information (per serving):
610 calories, 12g protein, 1g carbohydrates, 58g fat, 0g fiber, 60mg cholesterol, 470mg sodium, 300mg potassium.

PULLED PORK

A slow-cooked, tender pulled pork recipe with a crispy finish

Ingredients:

- 1 lb (450 g) pork shoulder, trimmed and cut into chunks
- 1 tbsp (15 ml) olive oil
- 1 tsp (5 g) smoked paprika
- 1/2 tsp (2 g) garlic powder
- 1/2 tsp (2 g) onion powder
- 1/2 tsp (1 g) ground cumin
- Salt and pepper to taste
- 1/4 cup (60 ml) low-sodium chicken broth (for moisture while cooking)

Directions:

1. Preheat the air fryer to 350°F (175°C).
2. In a bowl, mix the pork chunks with olive oil, smoked paprika, garlic powder, onion powder, ground cumin, salt, and pepper.
3. Place the seasoned pork in the air fryer basket. Add the chicken broth to keep it moist.
4. Cook for 45-50 minutes, turning halfway, until the pork is tender. Shred the pork using two forks.
5. Optional: Increase the air fryer temperature to 400°F (200°C) and cook for 5 minutes for a crispy finish.

 2 servings   10 minutes   50 minutes

Nutritional information (per serving):
450 calories, 42g protein, 2g carbohydrates, 30g fat, 0g fiber, 120mg cholesterol, 600mg sodium, 450mg potassium.

PORK SAUSAGE PATTIES

Homemade pork sausage patties seasoned with herbs and air-fried to a crispy texture

Ingredients:

- 8 oz (225 g) ground pork
- 1/2 tsp (2 g) garlic powder
- 1/2 tsp (2 g) onion powder
- 1/2 tsp (1 g) dried thyme
- 1/4 tsp (1 g) dried sage
- 1/4 tsp (1 g) smoked paprika
- Salt and pepper to taste

Directions:

1. Preheat the air fryer to 375°F (190°C).
2. In a mixing bowl, combine the ground pork, garlic powder, onion powder, thyme, sage, smoked paprika, salt, and pepper. Mix well.
3. Form the mixture into 4 equal-sized patties.
4. Place the patties in the air fryer basket in a single layer. Air-fry for 10-12 minutes, flipping halfway through, until golden and crispy on the outside and fully cooked inside.
5. Serve immediately or store for later use.

 2 servings   10 minutes   12 minutes

Nutritional information (per serving):
300 calories, 20g protein, 1g carbohydrates, 24g fat, 0g fiber, 80mg cholesterol, 450mg sodium, 290mg potassium.

PORK SCHNITZEL

Breaded pork cutlets air-fried for a crunchy and healthier version of schnitzel

Ingredients:

- 2 boneless pork cutlets (about 6 oz each / 170 g each)
- 1/2 cup (60 g) whole wheat breadcrumbs
- 1/4 cup (30 g) grated Parmesan cheese
- 1/2 tsp (1 g) paprika
- 1/4 tsp (1 g) garlic powder
- 1/4 tsp (1 g) black pepper
- 1/4 cup (30 g) all-purpose flour
- 1 large egg, beaten
- Olive oil spray

Directions:

1. Preheat the air fryer to 400°F (200°C).
2. In a shallow dish, mix the breadcrumbs, Parmesan, paprika, garlic powder, and black pepper. Place the flour in a second dish and the beaten egg in a third.
3. Dredge each pork cutlet in flour, dip in the beaten egg, then coat with the breadcrumb mixture, pressing the crumbs onto the cutlet to adhere well.
4. Lightly spray both sides of the cutlets with olive oil and place them in the air fryer basket in a single layer. Air-fry for 10-12 minutes, flipping halfway through, until golden and crispy.
5. Serve with lemon wedges or your favorite side dish.

 2 servings   10 minutes   12 minutes

Nutritional information (per serving):
370 calories, 35g protein, 18g carbohydrates, 17g fat, 2g fiber, 120mg cholesterol, 530mg sodium, 450mg potassium.

PORK LOIN

A juicy and tender pork loin roast, cooked with minimal oil in the air fryer

Ingredients:

- 1 lb (450 g) pork loin roast
- 1 tbsp (15 ml) olive oil
- 1 tsp (2 g) garlic powder
- 1 tsp (2 g) smoked paprika
- 1/2 tsp (1 g) black pepper
- 1/2 tsp (3 g) sea salt
- 1/2 tsp (1 g) dried thyme

Directions:

1. Preheat the air fryer to 375°F (190°C).
2. Rub the pork loin with olive oil, then season all over with garlic powder, smoked paprika, black pepper, sea salt, and dried thyme.
3. Place the pork loin in the air fryer basket. Air-fry for 25-30 minutes, flipping halfway through, until the internal temperature reaches 145°F (63°C).
4. Let the pork rest for 5 minutes before slicing and serving.

 2 servings   5 minutes   25 minutes

Nutritional information (per serving):
290 calories, 40g protein, 1g carbohydrates, 13g fat, 0g fiber, 95mg cholesterol, 510mg sodium, 610mg potassium.

PORK CARNITAS

A low-carb version of the classic Mexican dish, with crispy, shredded pork perfect for tacos or bowls

Ingredients:

- 1 lb (450 g) pork shoulder, cut into chunks
- 1 tbsp (15 ml) olive oil
- 1 tsp (2 g) cumin powder
- 1 tsp (2 g) garlic powder
- 1 tsp (2 g) smoked paprika
- 1/2 tsp (3 g) sea salt
- 1/2 tsp (1 g) black pepper
- Juice of 1 lime
- 1/4 cup (60 ml) chicken broth

Directions:

1. Preheat the air fryer to 375°F (190°C).
2. Toss the pork shoulder chunks in olive oil, cumin, garlic powder, smoked paprika, sea salt, and black pepper. Drizzle with lime juice and chicken broth.
3. Place the seasoned pork chunks in the air fryer basket and cook for 25-30 minutes, flipping halfway through, until the pork is tender and crispy.
4. Shred the pork with two forks and serve in tacos, bowls, or salads.

 2 servings   10 minutes   30 minutes

Nutritional information (per serving):
340 calories, 35g protein, 3g carbohydrates, 21g fat, 0g fiber, 110mg cholesterol, 520mg sodium, 620mg potassium.

PORK CUTLETS

Tender and crispy breaded pork cutlets, perfect for a quick and healthy meal

Ingredients:

- 2 (6 oz/170 g each) boneless pork cutlets
- 1/2 cup (60 g) whole wheat breadcrumbs
- 1/4 cup (30 g) grated Parmesan cheese
- 1/2 tsp (1 g) garlic powder
- 1/2 tsp (1 g) smoked paprika
- 1 large egg
- Salt and pepper to taste
- Olive oil spray

Directions:

1. Preheat the air fryer to 375°F (190°C).
2. In a shallow bowl, mix the breadcrumbs, Parmesan, garlic powder, smoked paprika, salt, and pepper.
3. Beat the egg in a separate bowl. Dip each pork cutlet in the egg, then coat in the breadcrumb mixture.
4. Lightly spray the air fryer basket with olive oil. Place the breaded cutlets in the basket and air fry for 12-15 minutes, flipping halfway through, until golden and cooked through.

 2 servings   10 minutes   15 minutes

Nutritional information (per serving):
320 calories, 35g protein, 12g carbohydrates, 15g fat, 2g fiber, 100mg cholesterol, 450mg sodium, 550mg potassium.

FISH AND SEAFOOD

Fish and seafood are precious additions to a diabetic-friendly diet. Rich in lean protein, healthy fats, vitamins, and minerals, these foods offer excellent nutritional value without raising blood sugar levels. For those managing Type 1 or Type 2 diabetes and those newly diagnosed or prediabetic, fish and seafood provide a satisfying way to meet nutritional needs while maintaining a low-carbohydrate, low-sugar eating plan.

The star nutrient in fish is **omega-3 fatty acids**, especially in fatty fish like salmon, sardines, and mackerel. Omega-3s are known to reduce inflammation, lower blood pressure, and improve cholesterol levels, making them essential for supporting heart health. This is particularly important for people with diabetes, who are at a higher risk of heart disease. Additionally, fish is an excellent source of **vitamin D**, **calcium**, and **B vitamins**, which help maintain bone strength, support the immune system, and aid in energy production.

Cooking fish and seafood in an air fryer offers a healthy, low-fat way to prepare meals while preserving flavor and texture. Air frying requires little to no oil, which helps keep the calorie and fat content low. Moreover, air frying ensures that fish and seafood retain moisture and nutrients, providing a delicious, nutritious, and diabetic-friendly meal.

For people managing diabetes, including fish and seafood in their diet improves overall health outcomes, helps with blood sugar management, and enhances meal satisfaction. Pairing these dishes with non-starchy vegetables, whole grains, or legumes can further boost the meal's nutritional value while keeping it low-carb and diabetes-friendly.

CRISPY FISH STICKS

Homemade fish sticks using white fish, lightly breaded, and air-fried for a healthy twist on a classic

Ingredients:

- 8 oz (227 g) white fish fillets (such as cod, haddock, or tilapia)
- ½ cup (60 g) whole wheat breadcrumbs
- ¼ cup (30 g) all-purpose flour
- 1 large egg
- ½ tsp garlic powder (2.5 g)
- ½ tsp paprika (2.5 g)
- ½ tsp salt (2.5 g)
- ¼ tsp black pepper (1.2 g)
- Cooking spray or 1 tbsp olive oil (15 ml)

Directions:

1. Preheat the air fryer to 400°F (200°C).
2. Cut the fish fillets into 1-inch-wide strips.
3. Set up a breading station with three bowls: one with flour, one with a beaten egg, and one with breadcrumbs mixed with garlic powder, paprika, salt, and pepper.
4. Coat each fish strip in flour, dip in egg, then coat with the breadcrumb mixture. Lightly spray with cooking spray or brush with olive oil.
5. Place the fish sticks in the air fryer basket in a single layer. Cook for 8-10 minutes, flipping halfway through, until golden brown and crispy.

 2 servings   15 minutes   10 minutes

Nutritional information (per serving):
290 calories, 27 g protein, 22 g carbohydrates, 11 g fat, 2 g fiber, 85 mg cholesterol, 590 mg sodium, 400 mg potassium.

SEA BASS

A tender and flaky sea bass fillet cooked with a simple garlic and lemon seasoning

Ingredients:

- 2 sea bass fillets (6 oz each / 170 g each)
- 1 tbsp olive oil (15 ml)
- 1 clove garlic, minced
- 1 tbsp lemon juice (15 ml)
- ½ tsp salt (2.5 g)
- ¼ tsp black pepper (1.2 g)
- Fresh parsley, chopped (for garnish)
- Lemon wedges (optional)

Directions:

1. Preheat your air fryer to 400°F (200°C).
2. In a small bowl, mix olive oil, garlic, lemon juice, salt, and pepper.
3. Brush the sea bass fillets with the mixture on both sides.
4. Place the fillets in the air fryer basket and cook for 8-10 minutes, or until the fish is flaky and reaches an internal temperature of 145°F (63°C).
5. Garnish with fresh parsley and serve with lemon wedges.

 2 servings 5 minutes 10 minutes

Nutritional information (per serving):
220 calories, 30 g protein, 0 g carbohydrates, 10 g fat, 0 g fiber, 70 mg cholesterol, 380 mg sodium, 450 mg potassium.

TUNA STEAKS

Juicy tuna steaks seasoned with herbs and garlic, seared to perfection in the air fryer

Ingredients:

- 2 tuna steaks (about 6 oz / 170 g each)
- 1 tbsp olive oil (15 ml)
- 2 cloves garlic, minced
- 1 tsp dried oregano (1 g)
- ½ tsp salt (2.5 g)
- ¼ tsp black pepper (1.2 g)
- 1 tbsp lemon juice (15 ml)

Directions:

1. Preheat the air fryer to 375°F (190°C).
2. In a small bowl, mix the olive oil, garlic, oregano, salt, pepper, and lemon juice.
3. Brush the tuna steaks with the seasoning mixture, coating both sides.
4. Place the tuna steaks in the air fryer basket and cook for 6-8 minutes, flipping halfway through, until seared on the outside but still pink in the center.

 2 servings 5 minutes 8 minutes

Nutritional information (per serving):
220 calories, 35 g protein, 1 g carbohydrates, 9 g fat, 0 g fiber, 75 mg cholesterol, 320 mg sodium, 650 mg potassium.

LEMON GARLIC SALMON

Delicate salmon fillets marinated in lemon juice and garlic, air-fried for a perfectly flaky texture

Ingredients:

- 2 salmon fillets (6 oz each / 170 g each)
- 2 tbsp lemon juice (30 ml)
- 2 cloves garlic, minced
- 1 tbsp olive oil (15 ml)
- ½ tsp salt (2.5 g)
- ¼ tsp black pepper (1.2 g)
- Lemon slices (optional, for garnish)
- Fresh parsley (optional, for garnish)

Directions:

1. In a small bowl, mix lemon juice, garlic, olive oil, salt, and pepper to make the marinade.
2. Marinate the salmon fillets in the lemon-garlic mixture for at least 10 minutes.
3. Preheat the air fryer to 400°F (200°C). Place the marinated salmon fillets in the air fryer basket.
4. Cook the salmon for 7-8 minutes, or until it flakes easily with a fork and reaches an internal temperature of 145°F (63°C).
5. Garnish with lemon slices and parsley before serving.

2 servings 10 minutes 8 minutes

Nutritional information (per serving):
280 calories, 34 g protein, 1 g carbohydrates, 16 g fat, 0 g fiber, 85 mg cholesterol, 450 mg sodium, 750 mg potassium.

COD with DILL

Light and tender cod fillets seasoned with fresh dill and lemon for a refreshing, flavorful dish

Ingredients:

- 2 cod fillets (6 oz each / 170 g each)
- 1 tbsp olive oil (15 ml)
- 1 tbsp fresh dill, chopped (or 1 tsp dried dill)
- 1 tbsp lemon juice (15 ml)
- ½ tsp salt (2.5 g)
- ¼ tsp black pepper (1.2 g)
- Lemon wedges (optional, for garnish)

Directions:

1. Preheat the air fryer to 375°F (190°C).
2. In a small bowl, mix olive oil, dill, lemon juice, salt, and pepper to create a seasoning mixture.
3. Brush the cod fillets with the dill and lemon mixture on both sides.
4. Place the seasoned cod fillets in the air fryer basket. Cook for 8-10 minutes, or until the fillets are cooked through and flake easily with a fork.
5. Serve with lemon wedges for an extra burst of flavor.

 2 servings 10 minutes 10 minutes

Nutritional information (per serving):
220 calories, 35 g protein, 1 g carbohydrates, 8 g fat, 0 g fiber, 85 mg cholesterol, 460 mg sodium, 700 mg potassium.

FISH TACOS

Seasoned white fish fillets served in low-carb tortillas with fresh salsa and avocado

Ingredients:

- 2 white fish fillets (6 oz / 170 g each, such as cod or tilapia)
- 1 tbsp olive oil (15 ml)
- 1 tsp chili powder (2 g)
- ½ tsp cumin (1 g)
- ½ tsp garlic powder (1 g)
- ½ tsp salt (2.5 g)
- ¼ tsp black pepper (1.2 g)
- 4 low-carb tortillas
- 1 avocado, sliced
- ½ cup fresh salsa (120 ml)

Directions:

1. Preheat the air fryer to 375°F (190°C).
2. In a small bowl, mix the olive oil, chili powder, cumin, garlic powder, salt, and pepper. Brush the mixture onto both sides of the fish fillets.
3. Place the fish fillets in the air fryer basket and cook for 8-10 minutes, flipping halfway, until the fish is flaky.
4. Assemble the tacos by placing the fish in tortillas and topping with fresh salsa and avocado slices.

 2 servings 10 minutes 10 minutes

Nutritional information (per serving):
400 calories, 35 g protein, 25 g carbohydrates, 18 g fat, 8 g fiber, 55 mg cholesterol, 680 mg sodium, 750 mg potassium.

TILAPIA with HERB CRUST

Mild and flaky tilapia fillets, air-fried with a crisp herb and Parmesan coating

Ingredients:

- 2 tilapia fillets (6 oz / 170 g each)
- ½ cup grated Parmesan cheese (45 g)
- ½ cup breadcrumbs (60 g, preferably whole wheat)
- 2 tbsp fresh parsley, chopped (8 g)
- 1 tsp garlic powder (2 g)
- 1 tsp dried oregano (1 g)
- ½ tsp salt (2.5 g)
- ¼ tsp black pepper (1.2 g)
- 1 tbsp olive oil (15 ml)
- 1 egg, beaten

Directions:

1. Preheat the air fryer to 400°F (200°C).
2. In a shallow bowl, combine Parmesan, breadcrumbs, parsley, garlic powder, oregano, salt, and pepper.
3. Dip each tilapia fillet into the beaten egg, then coat with the herb and Parmesan mixture.
4. Lightly spray or brush the air fryer basket with olive oil, place the fillets inside, and cook for 8-10 minutes until the coating is golden and the fish is flaky.

 2 servings 10 minutes 10 minutes

Nutritional information (per serving):
350 calories, 36 g protein, 12 g carbohydrates, 18 g fat, 2 g fiber, 105 mg cholesterol, 690 mg sodium, 450 mg potassium.

BLACKENED CATFISH

Spicy, Southern-style catfish fillets with a crispy, flavorful crust

Ingredients:

- 2 catfish fillets (6 oz / 170 g each)
- 1 tbsp olive oil (15 ml)
- 1 tbsp paprika (7 g)
- 1 tsp garlic powder (2 g)
- 1 tsp onion powder (2 g)
- 1 tsp dried thyme (1 g)
- 1 tsp cayenne pepper (optional for heat, 1 g)
- ½ tsp salt (2.5 g)
- ½ tsp black pepper (1.2 g)
- Lemon wedges (for serving)

Directions:

1. Preheat the air fryer to 400°F (200°C).
2. In a small bowl, mix together the paprika, garlic powder, onion powder, thyme, cayenne pepper, salt, and black pepper.
3. Brush the catfish fillets with olive oil, then coat both sides evenly with the spice mixture.
4. Place the seasoned fillets in the air fryer basket and cook for 8-10 minutes until the fish is flaky and the seasoning forms a crispy crust.
5. Serve with lemon wedges.

 2 servings 5 minutes 10 minutes

Nutritional information (per serving):
280 calories, 30 g protein, 2 g carbohydrates, 17 g fat, 1 g fiber, 90 mg cholesterol, 500 mg sodium, 400 mg potassium.

MAHI-MAHI with CITRUS GLAZE

Succulent mahi-mahi fillets drizzled with a tangy citrus glaze for a light, refreshing meal

Ingredients:

- 2 mahi-mahi fillets (6 oz / 170 g each)
- 1 tbsp olive oil (15 ml)
- Salt and pepper, to taste
- 1 tbsp orange juice (15 ml)
- 1 tbsp lemon juice (15 ml)
- 1 tsp honey (7 g)
- ½ tsp Dijon mustard (2.5 g)
- ½ tsp garlic powder (1.2 g)
- Zest of ½ lemon and ½ orange

Directions:

1. Preheat the air fryer to 400°F (200°C).
2. Brush the mahi-mahi fillets with olive oil and season with salt and pepper on both sides.
3. In a small bowl, mix together the orange juice, lemon juice, honey, Dijon mustard, garlic powder, and citrus zest to create the glaze.
4. Place the mahi-mahi fillets in the air fryer basket and cook for 6-8 minutes, until the fish flakes easily with a fork.
5. Drizzle the citrus glaze over the cooked fillets and serve.

 2 servings 10 minutes 8 minutes

Nutritional information (per serving):
290 calories, 35 g protein, 7 g carbohydrates, 12 g fat, 1 g fiber, 95 mg cholesterol, 250 mg sodium, 500 mg potassium.

HADDOCK with LEMON PEPPER

Tender haddock fillets seasoned with lemon pepper and air-fried until golden

Ingredients:

- 2 haddock fillets (6 oz / 170 g each)
- 1 tbsp olive oil (15 ml)
- 1 tsp lemon pepper seasoning (5 g)
- ½ tsp garlic powder (2.5 g)
- Salt, to taste
- 1 lemon, sliced for garnish

Directions:

1. Preheat the air fryer to 400°F (200°C).
2. Brush the haddock fillets with olive oil and sprinkle with lemon pepper seasoning, garlic powder, and a pinch of salt.
3. Place the fillets in the air fryer basket and cook for 8-10 minutes, until golden and the fish flakes easily with a fork.
4. Serve with fresh lemon slices for garnish.

 2 servings 5 minutes 10 minutes

Nutritional information (per serving):
220 calories, 35 g protein, 2 g carbohydrates, 9 g fat, 0 g fiber, 75 mg cholesterol, 350 mg sodium, 450 mg potassium.

HALIBUT with HERB BUTTER

A delicate halibut fillet, air-fried and served with a dollop of fresh herb butter

Ingredients:

- 2 halibut fillets (6 oz / 170 g each)
- 1 tbsp olive oil (15 ml)
- Salt and pepper, to taste
- 2 tbsp unsalted butter (30 g), softened
- 1 tsp fresh parsley, chopped
- 1 tsp fresh dill, chopped
- 1 clove garlic, minced
- 1 lemon (zested and juiced)

Directions:

1. Preheat the air fryer to 375°F (190°C).
2. Pat the halibut fillets dry, drizzle with olive oil, and season with salt and pepper.
3. Place the fillets in the air fryer basket and cook for 8-10 minutes, until the fish flakes easily with a fork.
4. In a small bowl, combine butter, parsley, dill, garlic, lemon zest, and juice. Top each fillet with a dollop of the herb butter before serving.

 2 servings 10 minutes 10 minutes

Nutritional information (per serving):
320 calories, 35 g protein, 1 g carbohydrates, 20 g fat, 0 g fiber, 90 mg cholesterol, 180 mg sodium, 750 mg potassium.

TROUT with FRESH HERBS

Whole trout air-fried with a lemon-herb marinade, offering a perfectly cooked, flaky meal.

Ingredients:

- 2 whole trout (8 oz / 225 g each), cleaned and gutted
- 2 tbsp olive oil (30 ml)
- 1 lemon, thinly sliced
- 2 cloves garlic, minced
- 2 tbsp fresh parsley, chopped
- 1 tbsp fresh thyme leaves
- Salt and pepper, to taste

Directions:

1. Preheat the air fryer to 375°F (190°C).
2. In a small bowl, mix olive oil, garlic, parsley, thyme, salt, and pepper. Rub the mixture inside and outside of the trout. Stuff lemon slices inside the fish.
3. Place the trout in the air fryer basket and cook for 10-12 minutes, flipping halfway through, until the fish is golden and flaky.
4. Serve with extra lemon wedges if desired.

 2 servings 10 minutes 12 minutes

Nutritional information (per serving):
340 calories, 40 g protein, 2 g carbohydrates, 20 g fat, 0 g fiber, 120 mg cholesterol, 190 mg sodium, 900 mg potassium.

FISH CAKES

Savory fish cakes made with canned fish or fresh fillets, lightly breaded and air-fried to crisp perfection

Ingredients:

- 8 oz (225 g) canned fish (tuna, salmon, or fresh white fish fillets, cooked)
- 1/2 cup (60 g) breadcrumbs
- 1 large egg
- 1 tbsp mayonnaise (15 ml)
- 1 tbsp Dijon mustard (15 ml)
- 1 tbsp fresh parsley, chopped
- 1 tsp lemon juice (5 ml)
- 1/4 tsp garlic powder
- Salt and pepper, to taste
- 1 tbsp olive oil spray

Directions:

1. In a bowl, combine the fish, egg, mayonnaise, Dijon mustard, parsley, lemon juice, garlic powder, salt, and pepper. Mix well.
2. Form the mixture into 4 small patties. Coat each patty with breadcrumbs, pressing lightly to adhere.
3. Preheat the air fryer to 375°F (190°C). Lightly spray both sides of the fish cakes with olive oil spray.
4. Place the fish cakes in the air fryer basket in a single layer. Cook for 8-10 minutes, flipping halfway through, until golden and crispy.

 2 servings 15 minutes 10 minutes

Nutritional information (per serving):
320 calories, 25 g protein, 18 g carbohydrates, 15 g fat, 1 g fiber, 95 mg cholesterol, 420 mg sodium, 420 mg potassium.

SARDINES with LEMON

Crispy sardines seasoned with olive oil and lemon for a nutritious, Omega-3-packed snack

Ingredients:

- 6 fresh sardines (about 1 lb / 450 g total)
- 1 tbsp olive oil (15 ml)
- 1 lemon (zested and juiced)
- Salt and pepper, to taste
- Fresh parsley, for garnish (optional)

Directions:

1. Preheat the air fryer to 375°F (190°C).
2. Rinse and pat dry the sardines. Rub them with olive oil, lemon zest, lemon juice, salt, and pepper.
3. Place the sardines in the air fryer basket in a single layer and cook for 7-8 minutes, or until crispy and golden brown.
4. Garnish with fresh parsley and serve with lemon wedges.

 2 servings 5 minutes 8 minutes

Nutritional information (per serving):
250 calories, 30 g protein, 1 g carbohydrates, 14 g fat, 0 g fiber, 95 mg cholesterol, 300 mg sodium, 400 mg potassium.

BARRAMUNDI

A mild, flaky fish perfect for air-frying, served with a garlic-butter drizzle

Ingredients:

- 2 barramundi fillets (6 oz / 170 g each)
- 1 tbsp olive oil (15 ml)
- 1/2 tsp garlic powder
- Salt and pepper, to taste
- 2 tbsp butter (28 g)
- 1 garlic clove, minced
- 1 tsp lemon juice (5 ml)
- Fresh parsley, chopped, for garnish

Directions:

1. Preheat the air fryer to 375°F (190°C). Pat the barramundi fillets dry with a paper towel.
2. Drizzle olive oil over the fillets and season with garlic powder, salt, and pepper.
3. Place the fillets in the air fryer basket and cook for 8-10 minutes, or until the fish is flaky and cooked through.
4. While the fish cooks, melt butter in a small saucepan over low heat, stir in minced garlic, and cook for 1-2 minutes. Add lemon juice and remove from heat.
5. Drizzle the garlic-butter mixture over the cooked barramundi fillets and garnish with fresh parsley before serving.

 2 servings 10 minutes 10 minutes

Nutritional information (per serving):
300 calories, 34 g protein, 0 g carbohydrates, 18 g fat, 0 g fiber, 95 mg cholesterol, 290 mg sodium, 450 mg potassium.

SHRIMP with GARLIC and PAPRIKA

Juicy, seasoned shrimp cooked to perfection, perfect for a snack or a light meal

Ingredients:

- 12 oz (340 g) large shrimp, peeled and deveined
- 1 tbsp olive oil (15 ml)
- 2 garlic cloves, minced
- 1/2 tsp smoked paprika
- 1/4 tsp salt
- 1/4 tsp black pepper
- Lemon wedges, for serving
- Fresh parsley, chopped (optional garnish)

Directions:

1. Preheat the air fryer to 400°F (200°C).
2. In a bowl, toss the shrimp with olive oil, minced garlic, paprika, salt, and pepper until evenly coated.
3. Place the shrimp in a single layer in the air fryer basket and cook for 6-8 minutes, shaking the basket halfway through, until shrimp are pink and cooked through.
4. Serve with lemon wedges and garnish with fresh parsley, if desired.

 2 servings 5 minutes 8 minutes

Nutritional information (per serving):
210 calories, 32 g protein, 2 g carbohydrates, 9 g fat, 0 g fiber, 230 mg cholesterol, 550 mg sodium, 260 mg potassium.

CRAB CAKES

Healthy, crispy crab cakes made with lump crab meat, lightly breaded, and air-fried

Ingredients:

- 8 oz (225 g) lump crab meat
- 1/4 cup (30 g) whole wheat breadcrumbs
- 1 tbsp (15 g) mayonnaise
- 1 tsp Dijon mustard
- 1 egg, beaten
- 1/2 tsp Old Bay seasoning
- 1 tbsp fresh parsley, chopped
- 1/2 tsp lemon juice
- Cooking spray

Directions:

1. Preheat the air fryer to 375°F (190°C).
2. In a large bowl, combine crab meat, breadcrumbs, mayonnaise, Dijon mustard, beaten egg, Old Bay seasoning, parsley, and lemon juice. Mix gently until just combined.
3. Form the mixture into 4 small patties. Lightly spray each side with cooking spray.
4. Place the crab cakes in a single layer in the air fryer basket and cook for 10-12 minutes, flipping halfway, until golden brown and crispy.

 2 servings 10 minutes 12 minutes

Nutritional information (per serving):
230 calories, 22 g protein, 14 g carbohydrates, 10 g fat, 1 g fiber, 115 mg cholesterol, 600 mg sodium, 350 mg potassium.

LOBSTER TAILS

Tender lobster tails seasoned with butter and herbs, air-fried until just right

Ingredients:

- 2 lobster tails (about 6 oz each)
- 2 tbsp (28 g) unsalted butter, melted
- 1 tsp garlic, minced
- 1/2 tsp paprika
- 1 tbsp fresh parsley, chopped
- 1 tbsp lemon juice
- Salt and pepper, to taste
- Cooking spray

Directions:

1. Preheat the air fryer to 380°F (190°C).
2. Using kitchen shears, cut the top of the lobster shells and pull the meat slightly out while keeping it attached at the base.
3. In a small bowl, mix melted butter, garlic, paprika, parsley, lemon juice, salt, and pepper.
4. Brush the butter mixture over the lobster meat. Place the lobster tails in the air fryer basket and cook for 6-8 minutes, until the meat is opaque and slightly golden.

 2 servings 10 minutes 8 minutes

Nutritional information (per serving):
200 calories, 25 g protein, 2 g carbohydrates, 10 g fat, 0 g fiber, 130 mg cholesterol, 400 mg sodium, 200 mg potassium.

COCOUNT SHRIMP

Crispy, coconut-coated shrimp with a delicious crunch and tropical flavor

Ingredients:

- 12 large shrimp (about 6 oz), peeled and deveined
- 1/2 cup (50 g) unsweetened shredded coconut
- 1/4 cup (30 g) panko breadcrumbs
- 1/4 cup (30 g) all-purpose flour
- 1 large egg, beaten
- 1/4 tsp paprika
- 1/4 tsp garlic powder
- Salt and pepper, to taste
- Cooking spray

Directions:

1. Preheat the air fryer to 375°F (190°C).
2. In a bowl, mix shredded coconut, panko breadcrumbs, paprika, garlic powder, salt, and pepper. Place flour in a separate bowl and the beaten egg in another.
3. Coat each shrimp in flour, dip in the beaten egg, then press into the coconut mixture to coat evenly.
4. Lightly spray the shrimp with cooking spray and place in the air fryer basket in a single layer. Cook for 8-10 minutes, flipping halfway through, until golden brown and crispy.

 2 servings 15 minutes 10 minutes

Nutritional information (per serving):
280 calories, 20 g protein, 22 g carbohydrates, 12 g fat, 2 g fiber, 185 mg cholesterol, 380 mg sodium, 180 mg potassium.

CALAMARI RINGS

Lightly breaded calamari rings air-fried until crispy, served with a tangy dipping sauce

Ingredients:

- 8 oz (225 g) calamari rings
- 1/2 cup (60 g) all-purpose flour
- 1/4 cup (30 g) panko breadcrumbs
- 1 large egg, beaten
- 1/4 tsp paprika
- 1/4 tsp garlic powder
- Salt and pepper, to taste
- Cooking spray
- Lemon wedges, for serving
- Tangy dipping sauce (optional)

Directions:

1. Preheat the air fryer to 400°F (200°C).
2. In one bowl, combine flour, paprika, garlic powder, salt, and pepper. In another bowl, place the beaten egg. In a third bowl, combine panko breadcrumbs.
3. Dip each calamari ring into the flour mixture, then the egg, and finally coat with the panko breadcrumbs.
4. Place the calamari rings in a single layer in the air fryer basket, spray lightly with cooking spray, and cook for 6-8 minutes, flipping halfway through, until golden and crispy.

 2 servings 10 minutes 8 minutes

Nutritional information (per serving):
230 calories, 18 g protein, 24 g carbohydrates, 8 g fat, 1 g fiber, 195 mg cholesterol, 420 mg sodium, 270 mg potassium.

CLAMS with GARLIC BUTTER

Garlicky clams air-fried and served with a light butter sauce for a delicious seafood appetizer

Ingredients:

- 1 lb (450 g) fresh clams, cleaned
- 2 tbsp (30 g) unsalted butter, melted
- 2 garlic cloves, minced
- 1 tbsp fresh parsley, chopped
- 1 tbsp lemon juice
- Salt and pepper, to taste
- Lemon wedges, for serving

Directions:

1. Preheat the air fryer to 375°F (190°C).
2. In a small bowl, combine melted butter, minced garlic, parsley, lemon juice, salt, and pepper.
3. Place cleaned clams in the air fryer basket in a single layer. Drizzle the garlic butter mixture evenly over the clams.
4. Air-fry for 6-8 minutes, or until clams open. Discard any unopened clams. Serve with lemon wedges.

 2 servings 10 minutes 8 minutes

Nutritional information (per serving):
230 calories, 18 g protein, 5 g carbohydrates, 14 g fat, 0 g fiber, 75 mg cholesterol, 510 mg sodium, 420 mg potassium.

SCALLOPS with LEMON BUTTER

Seared scallops with a golden crust, drizzled with lemon butter for a decadent dish

Ingredients:

- 8 large sea scallops (about 8 oz / 225 g)
- 2 tbsp (30 g) unsalted butter, melted
- 1 tbsp lemon juice
- 1 garlic clove, minced
- 1 tbsp fresh parsley, chopped
- Salt and pepper, to taste
- Lemon wedges, for serving

Directions:

1. Preheat the air fryer to 400°F (200°C).
2. Pat the scallops dry and season with salt and pepper. Place them in the air fryer basket in a single layer.
3. Air-fry for 6-8 minutes, flipping halfway through, until scallops are golden and opaque.
4. In a small bowl, combine melted butter, lemon juice, and minced garlic. Drizzle the lemon butter over the scallops and garnish with fresh parsley. Serve with lemon wedges.

 2 servings 5 minutes 8 minutes

Nutritional information (per serving):
250 calories, 22 g protein, 3 g carbohydrates, 17 g fat, 0 g fiber, 75 mg cholesterol, 350 mg sodium, 420 mg potassium.

MUSSELS

Mussels air-fried with garlic, parsley, and a splash of white wine for a flavorful seafood treat

Ingredients:

- 1 lb (450 g) fresh mussels, cleaned and debearded
- 2 tbsp (30 ml) white wine
- 1 tbsp (15 g) unsalted butter, melted
- 2 garlic cloves, minced
- 1 tbsp fresh parsley, chopped
- Salt and pepper, to taste
- Lemon wedges, for serving

Directions:

1. Preheat the air fryer to 375°F (190°C).
2. Toss the mussels with white wine, melted butter, minced garlic, salt, and pepper.
3. Place the mussels in the air fryer basket in a single layer and air-fry for 6-8 minutes, until the shells open and the mussels are cooked through.
4. Garnish with fresh parsley and serve with lemon wedges.

 2 servings 5 minutes 8 minutes

Nutritional information (per serving):
220 calories, 20 g protein, 5 g carbohydrates, 10 g fat, 0 g fiber, 45 mg cholesterol, 600 mg sodium, 450 mg potassium.

SHRIMP SKEWERS

Skewered shrimp marinated in herbs and grilled to perfection in the air fryer

Ingredients:

- 12 large shrimp (about 1/2 lb or 225 g), peeled and deveined
- 2 tbsp (30 ml) olive oil
- 2 garlic cloves, minced
- 1 tbsp fresh lemon juice
- 1 tsp dried oregano
- Salt and pepper, to taste
- Fresh parsley, for garnish
- Wooden skewers, soaked in water for 10 minutes

Directions:

1. Preheat the air fryer to 375°F (190°C).
2. In a bowl, mix olive oil, garlic, lemon juice, oregano, salt, and pepper. Add shrimp and toss to coat. Let marinate for 10 minutes.
3. Thread the shrimp onto the soaked skewers and place them in the air fryer basket in a single layer.
4. Air-fry for 6-8 minutes, flipping halfway through, until shrimp are pink and cooked through.
5. Garnish with fresh parsley and serve immediately.

 2 servings 10 minutes 8 minutes

Nutritional information (per serving):
240 calories, 24 g protein, 1 g carbohydrates, 16 g fat, 0 g fiber, 180 mg cholesterol, 480 mg sodium, 220 mg potassium.

GARLIC BUTTER SHRIMP

Shrimp tossed in garlic butter and quickly cooked in the air fryer for a simple and satisfying dish

Ingredients:

- 12 large shrimp (about 1/2 lb or 225 g), peeled and deveined
- 2 tbsp (28 g) unsalted butter, melted
- 2 garlic cloves, minced
- 1 tbsp (15 ml) lemon juice
- 1 tbsp (4 g) fresh parsley, chopped
- Salt and pepper, to taste
- Lemon wedges, for serving (optional)

Directions:

1. Preheat the air fryer to 375°F (190°C).
2. In a small bowl, mix melted butter, garlic, lemon juice, parsley, salt, and pepper. Toss the shrimp in the garlic butter mixture to coat evenly.
3. Arrange the shrimp in a single layer in the air fryer basket.
4. Air fry for 6-8 minutes, flipping halfway through, until the shrimp are pink and fully cooked.
5. Serve with extra garlic butter sauce and lemon wedges, if desired.

 2 servings 10 minutes 8 minutes

Nutritional information (per serving):
260 calories, 24 g protein, 2 g carbohydrates, 18 g fat, 0 g fiber, 195 mg cholesterol, 480 mg sodium, 240 mg potassium.

CLAM STRIPS

Crispy air-fried clam strips perfect for snacking or serving with a dipping sauce

Ingredients:

- 8 oz (225 g) clam strips, thawed if frozen
- 1/2 cup (60 g) all-purpose flour
- 1/2 cup (60 g) cornmeal
- 1 tsp (2.6 g) garlic powder
- 1 tsp (2.6 g) paprika
- 1 large egg, beaten
- Salt and pepper, to taste
- Cooking spray

Directions:

1. Preheat the air fryer to 375°F (190°C).
2. In a shallow dish, combine flour, cornmeal, garlic powder, paprika, salt, and pepper.
3. Dip clam strips into the beaten egg, then dredge in the flour mixture, pressing to adhere.
4. Arrange the coated clam strips in a single layer in the air fryer basket and lightly spray with cooking spray.
5. Air fry for 6-8 minutes, shaking halfway through, until golden and crispy. Serve with your favorite dipping sauce.

 2 servings   10 minutes   8 minutes

Nutritional information (per serving):
280 calories, 20 g protein, 28 g carbohydrates, 8 g fat, 1 g fiber, 90 mg cholesterol, 520 mg sodium, 300 mg potassium.

LOBSTER TAILS with LEMON GARLIC

Buttery lobster tails air-fried with a lemon-garlic butter sauce for a simple yet luxurious meal

Ingredients:

- 2 lobster tails (about 5 oz / 140 g each)
- 2 tbsp (28 g) unsalted butter, melted
- 2 cloves garlic, minced
- 1 tbsp (15 ml) fresh lemon juice
- 1/2 tsp (1 g) paprika
- Salt and pepper, to taste
- Fresh parsley, for garnish (optional)
- Lemon wedges for serving

Directions:

1. Preheat the air fryer to 380°F (193°C).
2. In a small bowl, mix melted butter, garlic, lemon juice, paprika, salt, and pepper.
3. Using kitchen shears, carefully cut down the top of the lobster shells to expose the meat. Brush the lobster tails generously with the lemon-garlic butter sauce.
4. Place lobster tails in the air fryer basket, shell-side down and cook for 6-8 minutes until the meat is opaque and cooked through.
5. Serve with extra lemon-garlic butter, garnish with parsley, and add lemon wedges on the side.

 2 servings   10 minutes   8 minutes

Nutritional information (per serving):
240 calories, 26 g protein, 1 g carbohydrates, 14 g fat, 0 g fiber, 140 mg cholesterol, 310 mg sodium, 250 mg potassium.

STUFFED CLAMS

Stuffed clams with a breadcrumb and herb mixture, air-fried until golden and crisp

Ingredients:

- 6 large clams, cleaned and shells reserved
- 1/2 cup (60 g) breadcrumbs
- 2 tbsp (28 g) unsalted butter, melted
- 1 tbsp (15 ml) olive oil
- 2 cloves garlic, minced
- 1 tbsp (15 ml) fresh lemon juice
- 1 tbsp (3 g) fresh parsley, chopped
- Salt and pepper, to taste
- 1/4 tsp (0.5 g) paprika (optional)

Directions:

1. Preheat the air fryer to 375°F (190°C).
2. In a bowl, mix breadcrumbs, melted butter, olive oil, garlic, lemon juice, parsley, salt, pepper, and paprika until well mixed.
3. Stuff each clam with the breadcrumb mixture and place the stuffed clams in the air fryer basket.
4. Air fry for 8-10 minutes, or until the tops are golden brown and crispy.
5. Serve hot with lemon wedges for squeezing over the clams.

2 servings   15 minutes   10 minutes

Nutritional information (per serving):
280 calories, 12 g protein, 25 g carbohydrates, 14 g fat, 2 g fiber, 45 mg cholesterol, 410 mg sodium, 150 mg potassium.

BACON-WRAPPED SCALLOPS

Scallops wrapped in turkey bacon and air-fried for a crispy, savory bite

Ingredients:

- 6 large sea scallops
- 3 slices turkey bacon, cut in half
- 1 tbsp (15 ml) olive oil
- 1/2 tsp (1 g) garlic powder
- 1/2 tsp (1 g) paprika
- Salt and pepper, to taste
- Toothpicks, for securing

Directions:

1. Preheat the air fryer to 400°F (200°C).
2. Wrap each scallop with a half-slice of turkey bacon and secure with a toothpick.
3. In a small bowl, mix olive oil, garlic powder, paprika, salt, and pepper, then brush over the bacon-wrapped scallops.
4. Place scallops in the air fryer basket in a single layer and cook for 8-10 minutes, turning halfway through, until the bacon is crispy and scallops are opaque.
5. Serve hot as an appetizer or with a dipping sauce.

 2 servings   10 minutes   10 minutes

Nutritional information (per serving):
210 calories, 24 g protein, 3 g carbohydrates, 10 g fat, 0 g fiber, 45 mg cholesterol, 620 mg sodium, 230 mg potassium.

SHRIMP and VEGETABLE STIR-FRY

A quick and easy shrimp stir-fry with veggies, made even healthier in the air fryer

Ingredients:

- 12 oz (340 g) large shrimp, peeled and deveined
- 1 cup (150 g) bell peppers, sliced
- 1 cup (150 g) broccoli florets
- 1/2 cup (75 g) zucchini, sliced
- 2 tbsp (30 ml) olive oil
- 1 tbsp (15 ml) low-sodium soy sauce
- 1 tsp (2 g) garlic powder
- 1/2 tsp (1 g) ginger powder
- Salt and pepper, to taste

Directions:

1. Preheat the air fryer to 375°F (190°C).
2. Toss shrimp and vegetables with olive oil, soy sauce, garlic powder, ginger powder, salt, and pepper in a bowl.
3. Spread shrimp and vegetables in a single layer in the air fryer basket.
4. Air fry for 10-12 minutes, shaking the basket halfway through until shrimp are cooked and vegetables are tender.
5. Serve hot, optionally with a side of rice or quinoa.

 2 servings   10 minutes   12 minutes

Nutritional information (per serving):
320 calories, 32 g protein, 14 g carbohydrates, 16 g fat, 4 g fiber, 230 mg cholesterol, 720 mg sodium, 690 mg potassium.

SCALLOPS with GARLIC BUTTER

Buttery, garlicky scallops cooked to perfection in the air fryer with a crispy exterior

Ingredients:

- 8 oz (225 g) large sea scallops
- 2 tbsp (30 g) unsalted butter, melted
- 1 clove garlic, minced
- 1 tbsp (15 ml) lemon juice
- 1/2 tsp (1 g) paprika
- Salt and pepper, to taste
- Fresh parsley, for garnish (optional)

Directions:

1. Preheat the air fryer to 400°F (200°C).
2. Pat scallops dry with paper towels. In a bowl, mix melted butter, garlic, lemon juice, paprika, salt, and pepper.
3. Toss the scallops in the butter mixture, ensuring they are evenly coated.
4. Place scallops in the air fryer basket in a single layer. Air fry for 6-8 minutes, flipping halfway through, until golden and cooked through.
5. Garnish with parsley and serve hot.

 2 servings   5 minutes   8 minutes

Nutritional information (per serving):
240 calories, 22 g protein, 2 g carbohydrates, 16 g fat, 0 g fiber, 60 mg cholesterol, 450 mg sodium, 420 mg potassium.

VEGETABLES

Incorporating a wide variety of vegetables into your daily meals is crucial when managing diabetes. **Vegetables are naturally low in carbohydrates and sugars,** making them an excellent choice for people with diabetes or those looking to maintain healthy blood sugar levels. Rich in fiber, vitamins, and minerals, vegetables help regulate digestion, improve heart health, and provide a steady energy source without spiking blood glucose levels. Including more vegetables in your diet can promote weight management, control cholesterol, and reduce the risk of complications associated with diabetes.

Air fryers offer an innovative way to prepare quick, easy, and healthy vegetables. With the air fryer, you can enjoy crispy, flavorful vegetables with little to no added oil, making it an ideal method for creating diabetic-friendly dishes. Air-fried vegetables retain their nutrients while achieving the desired crispiness without excess fats, making it easier to meet your dietary goals without sacrificing flavor.

For individuals managing diabetes, keeping meals low in carbohydrates and sugars is essential. Air-frying vegetables create delicious, satisfying side dishes or snacks that fit seamlessly into a low-carb, low-sugar meal plan. You can also experiment with herbs, spices, and marinades to enhance flavor without relying on high-sodium or high-sugar additives.

By incorporating these simple and affordable air-fryer vegetable recipes into your daily meals, you'll add nutrient-dense, flavorful options that support a low-carb, low-sugar diet—perfect for managing diabetes. These healthy vegetable options can be served as sides, snacks, or even light meals, making it easier to maintain a low-carb, low-sugar diet while enjoying delicious food.

CRISPY BRUSSELS SPROUTS

Crispy Brussels sprouts seasoned with garlic and a drizzle of balsamic vinegar

Ingredients:

- 8 oz (225 g) Brussels sprouts, trimmed and halved
- 1 tbsp (15 ml) olive oil
- 1 clove garlic, minced
- 1 tbsp (15 ml) balsamic vinegar
- Salt and pepper to taste

Directions:

1. Preheat the air fryer to 375°F (190°C).
2. In a bowl, toss the Brussels sprouts with olive oil, garlic, salt, and pepper until evenly coated.
3. Place the Brussels sprouts in the air fryer basket and cook for 12 minutes, shaking the basket halfway through to ensure even cooking.
4. Once crispy and golden, remove from the air fryer and drizzle with balsamic vinegar before serving.

 2 servings

 5 minutes

 12 minutes

Nutritional information (per serving):
120 calories, 3g protein, 12g carbohydrates, 7g fat, 4g fiber, 0mg cholesterol, 130mg sodium, 380mg potassium.

ROASTED CAULIFLOWER

Tender cauliflower florets with a hint of paprika and olive oil.

Ingredients:

- 1 small head of cauliflower (about 12 oz / 340 g), cut into florets
- 1 tbsp (15 ml) olive oil
- 1/2 tsp (2.5 g) paprika
- Salt and pepper to taste

Directions:

1. Preheat the air fryer to 400°F (200°C).
2. In a bowl, toss the cauliflower florets with olive oil, paprika, salt, and pepper until well-coated.
3. Place the cauliflower florets in the air fryer basket in a single layer and cook for 12-15 minutes, shaking the basket halfway through, until tender and lightly browned.
4. Serve immediately.

 2 servings 5 minutes 15 minutes

Nutritional information (per serving):
100 calories, 3g protein, 10g carbohydrates, 6g fat, 4g fiber, 0mg cholesterol, 180mg sodium, 450mg potassium.

GARLIC GREEN BEANS

Crisp-tender green beans seasoned with garlic and a touch of salt

Ingredients:

- 8 oz (225 g) fresh green beans, trimmed
- 1 tbsp (15 ml) olive oil
- 2 garlic cloves, minced
- Salt and pepper to taste

Directions:

1. Preheat the air fryer to 375°F (190°C).
2. Toss the green beans with olive oil, minced garlic, salt, and pepper in a bowl until evenly coated.
3. Place the green beans in the air fryer basket in a single layer. Air fry for 7-8 minutes, shaking the basket halfway through, until crisp-tender.
4. Serve immediately.

 2 servings 5 minutes 8 minutes

Nutritional information (per serving):
110 calories, 2g protein, 8g carbohydrates, 7g fat, 3g fiber, 0mg cholesterol, 180mg sodium, 200mg potassium.

ZUCCHINI FRIES

Low-carb zucchini sticks coated in Parmesan, air-fried to perfection

Ingredients:

- 1 medium zucchini (about 7 oz/200 g), cut into sticks
- 1/4 cup (25 g) grated Parmesan cheese
- 1/4 cup (30 g) almond flour (or breadcrumbs for non-low-carb)
- 1 large egg, beaten
- 1/2 tsp (2.5 ml) garlic powder
- Salt and pepper to taste
- Cooking spray

Directions:

1. Preheat the air fryer to 400°F (200°C).
2. In one bowl, mix Parmesan, almond flour, garlic powder, salt, and pepper. In a second bowl, place the beaten egg.
3. Dip each zucchini stick into the egg, then coat it with the Parmesan mixture.
4. Arrange the zucchini fries in a single layer in the air fryer basket and spray lightly with cooking spray. Air fry for 8-10 minutes, shaking the basket halfway through, until golden and crispy.
5. Serve immediately with your favorite dipping sauce.

 2 servings 10 minutes 10 minutes

Nutritional information (per serving):
220 calories, 11g protein, 7g carbohydrates, 16g fat, 3g fiber, 95mg cholesterol, 310mg sodium, 350mg potassium.

SWEET POTATO WEDGES

Seasoned sweet potato wedges, crispy on the outside and soft on the inside

Ingredients:

- 1 large sweet potato (about 10 oz/280 g), cut into wedges
- 1 tbsp (15 ml) olive oil
- 1/2 tsp (2.5 ml) smoked paprika
- 1/2 tsp (2.5 ml) garlic powder
- Salt and pepper to taste
- Cooking spray

Directions:

1. Preheat the air fryer to 400°F (200°C).
2. In a bowl, toss the sweet potato wedges with olive oil, smoked paprika, garlic powder, salt, and pepper until evenly coated.
3. Place the wedges in a single layer in the air fryer basket and lightly spray with cooking spray.
4. Air fry for 12-15 minutes, shaking the basket halfway through until the wedges are crispy on the outside and tender on the inside.
5. Serve immediately with your favorite dipping sauce or as a side dish.

 2 servings   5 minutes   15 minutes

Nutritional information (per serving):
180 calories, 2g protein, 28g carbohydrates, 7g fat, 4g fiber, 0mg cholesterol, 230mg sodium, 450mg potassium.

BROCCOLI with LEMON

Roasted broccoli with a zesty lemon dressing for a tangy twist

Ingredients:

- 2 cups (150 g) broccoli florets
- 1 tbsp (15 ml) olive oil
- 1/2 tsp (2.5 ml) garlic powder
- Salt and pepper to taste
- Zest and juice of 1/2 lemon
- Cooking spray

Directions:

1. Preheat the air fryer to 375°F (190°C).
2. Toss the broccoli florets with olive oil, garlic powder, salt, and pepper in a bowl until evenly coated.
3. Spread the broccoli in a single layer in the air fryer basket and lightly spray with cooking spray.
4. Air fry for 8-10 minutes, shaking the basket halfway through until the broccoli is tender and slightly crispy.
5. Drizzle with lemon juice and zest before serving.

 2 servings   5 minutes   10 minutes

Nutritional information (per serving):
110 calories, 3g protein, 10g carbohydrates, 7g fat, 4g fiber, 0mg cholesterol, 160mg sodium, 400mg potassium.

ASPARAGUS with PARMESAN

Parmesan-crusted asparagus spears roasted until tender and crisp

Ingredients:

- 1/2 lb (225 g) asparagus spears, trimmed
- 1 tbsp (15 ml) olive oil
- 1/4 cup (25 g) grated Parmesan cheese
- 1/2 tsp (2.5 ml) garlic powder
- Salt and pepper to taste
- Cooking spray

Directions:

1. Preheat the air fryer to 375°F (190°C).
2. Toss the asparagus spears in a bowl with olive oil, garlic powder, salt, and pepper.
3. Sprinkle the Parmesan cheese evenly over the asparagus and toss to coat.
4. Arrange the asparagus in a single layer in the air fryer basket and lightly spray with cooking spray.
5. Air fry for 7-8 minutes until the asparagus is tender and the Parmesan is golden and crispy.

 2 servings   5 minutes   8 minutes

Nutritional information (per serving):
170 calories, 6g protein, 5g carbohydrates, 13g fat, 3g fiber, 15mg cholesterol, 240mg sodium, 350mg potassium.

BUTTERNUT SQUASH CUBES

Sweet butternut squash cubes roasted with a sprinkle of cinnamon

Ingredients:

- 2 cups (300 g) butternut squash, peeled and cubed
- 1 tbsp (15 ml) olive oil
- 1/2 tsp (2.5 g) ground cinnamon
- Salt to taste
- Cooking spray

Directions:

1. Preheat the air fryer to 400°F (200°C).
2. In a bowl, toss the butternut squash cubes with olive oil, cinnamon, and a pinch of salt.
3. Arrange the squash cubes in a single layer in the air fryer basket and lightly spray with cooking spray.
4. Air fry for 15 minutes, shaking the basket halfway through until the squash is tender and lightly caramelized.

 2 servings   5 minutes   15 minutes

Nutritional information (per serving):
130 calories, 1g protein, 23g carbohydrates, 5g fat, 4g fiber, 0mg cholesterol, 80mg sodium, 580mg potassium.

ROASTED BELL PEPPERS

Vibrant bell peppers air-fried to smoky, caramelized perfection

Ingredients:

- 2 large bell peppers (about 12 oz / 340 g), sliced into strips
- 1 tbsp (15 ml) olive oil
- Salt and pepper to taste
- Cooking spray

Directions:

1. Preheat the air fryer to 375°F (190°C).
2. Toss the bell pepper strips with olive oil, salt, and pepper in a bowl.
3. Arrange the peppers in a single layer in the air fryer basket, making sure they aren't overcrowded.
4. Air fry for 12 minutes, shaking the basket halfway through until the peppers are tender and slightly charred.

 2 servings   5 minutes   12 minutes

Nutritional information (per serving):
100 calories, 1g protein, 9g carbohydrates, 7g fat, 3g fiber, 0mg cholesterol, 150mg sodium, 260mg potassium.

CRISPY KALE CHIPS

Light and crunchy kale chips seasoned with sea salt

Ingredients:

- 4 cups (about 3.5 oz / 100 g) kale leaves, stems removed and torn into bite-sized pieces
- 1 tbsp (15 ml) olive oil
- 1/2 tsp (2.5 ml) sea salt
- Cooking spray

Directions:

1. Preheat the air fryer to 350°F (175°C).
2. Toss the kale leaves with olive oil and sprinkle with sea salt.
3. Arrange the kale in a single layer in the air fryer basket, ensuring pieces do not overlap.
4. Air fry for 5-8 minutes, shaking the basket halfway through until the kale is crispy and lightly browned.

 2 servings   5 minutes   8 minutes

Nutritional information (per serving):
70 calories, 3g protein, 7g carbohydrates, 4.5g fat, 2g fiber, 0mg cholesterol, 150mg sodium, 300mg potassium.

MUSHROOMS with BALSAMIC GLAZE

Juicy mushrooms roasted with a rich balsamic glaze

Ingredients:

- 8 oz (225 g) mushrooms, halved or quartered
- 1 tbsp (15 ml) olive oil
- 1 tbsp (15 ml) balsamic vinegar
- 1 tsp (5 ml) soy sauce (optional)
- 1 clove garlic, minced
- Salt and pepper to taste
- Cooking spray

Directions:

1. Preheat the air fryer to 400°F (200°C).
2. In a bowl, toss the mushrooms with olive oil, balsamic vinegar, soy sauce (if using), garlic, salt, and pepper.
3. Lightly spray the air fryer basket with cooking spray, then add the seasoned mushrooms.
4. Air fry for 12-15 minutes, shaking the basket halfway through until the mushrooms are tender and caramelized.

 2 servings 5 minutes 15 minutes

Nutritional information (per serving):
100 calories, 2g protein, 7g carbohydrates, 7g fat, 2g fiber, 0mg cholesterol, 150mg sodium, 250mg potassium.

STUFFED MINI PEPPERS

Mini bell peppers stuffed with a savory quinoa and vegetable filling, air-fried until tender and slightly crisp

Ingredients:

- 8 mini bell peppers
- 1/2 cup (90 g) cooked quinoa
- 1/4 cup (40 g) diced zucchini
- 1/4 cup (30 g) diced red onion
- 2 tbsp (15 g) grated Parmesan cheese
- 1 tbsp (15 ml) olive oil
- 1/2 tsp (2.5 ml) garlic powder
- Salt and pepper to taste
- Cooking spray

Directions:

1. Preheat the air fryer to 375°F (190°C).
2. Cut the tops off the mini bell peppers and remove the seeds. In a bowl, mix cooked quinoa, zucchini, red onion, Parmesan, olive oil, garlic powder, salt, and pepper.
3. Stuff the peppers with the quinoa mixture and arrange them in the air fryer basket, which has been lightly sprayed with cooking spray.
4. Air fry for 8-10 minutes until the peppers are tender and slightly crisp on the edges.

 2 servings 15 minutes 10 minutes

Nutritional information (per serving):
180 calories, 5g protein, 25g carbohydrates, 7g fat, 4g fiber, 5mg cholesterol, 200mg sodium, 400mg potassium.

PARMESAN-CRUSTED CAULIFLOWER

Crispy cauliflower florets coated in Parmesan and herbs, perfect as a crunchy side or healthy snack

Ingredients:

- 2 cups (200 g) cauliflower florets
- 1/4 cup (25 g) grated Parmesan cheese
- 1 tbsp (15 ml) olive oil
- 1/2 tsp (2.5 g) garlic powder
- 1/2 tsp (2.5 g) dried oregano
- Salt and pepper to taste
- Cooking spray

Directions:

1. Preheat the air fryer to 375°F (190°C).
2. In a bowl, toss cauliflower florets with olive oil, garlic powder, oregano, salt, and pepper. Add the Parmesan cheese and mix until the cauliflower is well-coated.
3. Place the cauliflower in the air fryer basket in a single layer, sprayed lightly with cooking spray.
4. Air fry for 10-12 minutes, shaking the basket halfway through, until golden and crispy.

 2 servings 10 minutes 12 minutes

Nutritional information (per serving):
180 calories, 8g protein, 10g carbohydrates, 12g fat, 3g fiber, 15mg cholesterol, 320mg sodium, 350mg potassium.

ROASTED BEETS

Sweet earthy beets roasted to tender perfection in the air fryer, great for salads or as a standalone side

Ingredients:

- 2 medium beets (about 200 g), peeled and cut into 1-inch cubes
- 1 tbsp (15 ml) olive oil
- Salt and pepper to taste
- 1/2 tsp (2.5 g) garlic powder (optional)

Directions:

1. Preheat the air fryer to 380°F (190°C).
2. In a bowl, toss the beet cubes with olive oil, salt, pepper, and garlic powder (if using) until evenly coated.
3. Place the beets in the air fryer basket in a single layer. Roast for 18-20 minutes, shaking the basket halfway through cooking, until the beets are tender and slightly crispy on the edges.
4. Serve warm as a side dish or add to your favorite salad.

 2 servings 5 minutes 20 minutes

Nutritional information (per serving):
110 calories, 2g protein, 14g carbohydrates, 6g fat, 4g fiber, 0mg cholesterol, 200mg sodium, 400mg potassium.

ARTICHOKE

Hearts Tender artichoke hearts lightly seasoned with herbs and olive oil, roasted until crispy and golden

Ingredients:

- 1 cup (150 g) canned or jarred artichoke hearts, drained and halved
- 1 tbsp (15 ml) olive oil
- 1/2 tsp (1 g) dried Italian herbs (such as oregano and basil)
- Salt and pepper to taste
- Optional: 1 tbsp (4 g) grated Parmesan for extra flavor

Directions:

1. Preheat the air fryer to 375°F (190°C).
2. In a bowl, toss the artichoke hearts with olive oil, Italian herbs, salt, and pepper until evenly coated.
3. Place the artichoke hearts in the air fryer basket in a single layer and cook for 8-10 minutes, shaking halfway through, until crispy and golden brown.
4. Optionally, sprinkle with Parmesan after cooking for extra flavor and serve warm.

 2 servings 5 minutes 10 minutes

Nutritional information (per serving):
110 calories, 2g protein, 6g carbohydrates, 9g fat, 3g fiber, 0mg cholesterol, 150mg sodium, 200mg potassium.

GARLIC ROASTED RADISHES

A low-carb potato alternative, seasoned with garlic and herbs

Ingredients:

- 1 lb (450 g) radishes, trimmed and halved
- 1 tbsp olive oil
- 1 tsp garlic powder
- 1/2 tsp dried thyme
- Salt and pepper, to taste

Directions:

1. Preheat the air fryer to 380°F (193°C).
2. In a mixing bowl, toss radishes with olive oil, garlic powder, thyme, salt, and pepper until well-coated.
3. Place the radishes in a single layer in the air fryer basket and cook for 10-12 minutes, shaking halfway through, until the radishes are tender and the edges are crispy.
4. Serve warm as a low-carb alternative to roasted potatoes.

 2 servings 5 minutes 12 minutes

Nutritional information (per serving):
70 calories, 1g protein, 4g carbohydrates, 5g fat, 2g fiber, 0mg cholesterol, 5mg sodium, 230mg potassium.

BEET CHIPS

Thinly sliced beets with a light seasoning for a crunchy, low-carb snack

Ingredients:

- 2 medium beets (about 8 oz / 225 g), peeled and thinly sliced
- 1/2 tbsp olive oil
- 1/4 tsp sea salt
- Optional: 1/8 tsp black pepper or paprika for extra flavor

Directions:

1. Preheat the air fryer to 350°F (177°C).
2. Toss beet slices in a bowl with olive oil, salt, and optional seasonings until evenly coated.
3. Arrange beets in a single layer in the air fryer basket, working in batches if needed.
4. Air fry for 12-15 minutes, shaking the basket halfway through, until chips are crispy.
5. Let cool slightly before serving.

 2 servings 5 minutes 15 minutes

Nutritional information (per serving):
70 calories, 1g protein, 14g carbohydrates, 2g fat, 3g fiber, 0mg cholesterol, 150mg sodium, 270mg potassium.

CARAMELIZED ONIONS

Sweet, golden-brown onions perfect as a side or topping

Ingredients:

- 1 large onion (about 10 oz / 280 g), thinly sliced
- 1/2 tbsp olive oil
- 1/4 tsp salt
- 1/8 tsp black pepper (optional)

Directions:

1. Preheat the air fryer to 300°F (149°C).
2. In a bowl, toss the onion slices with olive oil, salt, and optional pepper until evenly coated.
3. Place the onions in the air fryer basket in a single layer or as close to a single layer as possible.
4. Air fry for 12-15 minutes, shaking the basket every 5 minutes, until onions are golden brown and caramelized.
5. Serve warm as a side or topping for sandwiches, salads, or main dishes.

 2 servings 5 minutes 15 minutes

Nutritional information (per serving):
55 calories, 0.5g protein, 10g carbohydrates, 2g fat, 1.5g fiber, 0mg cholesterol, 150mg sodium, 120mg potassium.

STUFFED ZUCCHINI BOATS

Zucchini halves are filled with a seasoned vegetable or low-carb filling

Ingredients:

- 1 medium zucchini (about 8 oz / 225 g), halved lengthwise
- 1/4 cup bell pepper, diced (1 oz / 28 g)
- 1/4 cup cherry tomatoes, diced (1.5 oz / 42 g)
- 1/4 cup shredded mozzarella cheese (1 oz / 28 g)
- 1/4 tsp garlic powder
- 1/4 tsp Italian seasoning
- Salt and pepper to taste
- Fresh basil, chopped (optional garnish)

Directions:

1. Preheat the air fryer to 350°F (177°C).
2. Using a spoon, scoop out the center of each zucchini half to create a "boat."
3. In a bowl, mix diced bell pepper, tomatoes, cheese, garlic powder, Italian seasoning, salt, and pepper.
4. Spoon the vegetable mixture into each zucchini boat and place them in the air fryer basket.
5. Air fry for 10-15 minutes until zucchini is tender and cheese is melted. Garnish with basil if desired, and serve warm.

 2 servings 10 minutes 15 minutes

Nutritional information (per serving):
80 calories, 4g protein, 6g carbohydrates, 5g fat, 1.5g fiber, 10mg cholesterol, 120mg sodium, 250mg potassium.

RAINBOW CARROTS

Colorful carrots roasted until tender with a hint of garlic and herbs

Ingredients:

- 8 oz (225 g) rainbow carrots, peeled and cut into 2-inch pieces
- 1/2 tbsp olive oil (7.5 ml)
- 1/4 tsp garlic powder
- 1/4 tsp dried thyme
- Salt and pepper to taste

Directions:

1. Preheat the air fryer to 380°F (193°C).
2. In a bowl, toss the carrots with olive oil, garlic powder, thyme, salt, and pepper until well coated.
3. Place the seasoned carrots in the air fryer basket in a single layer.
4. Air fry for 12-15 minutes, shaking halfway until the carrots are tender and slightly caramelized.
5. Serve warm and enjoy the colorful, flavorful side dish!

 2 servings **5** minutes  **15** minutes

Nutritional information (per serving):
80 calories, 1g protein, 10g carbohydrates, 4g fat, 3g fiber, 0mg cholesterol, 100mg sodium, 250mg potassium.

STUFFED BELL PEPPERS

Mini bell peppers stuffed with a flavorful mixture of vegetables and spices

Ingredients:

- 6 mini bell peppers, halved and deseeded
- 1/2 cup (75 g) diced zucchini
- 1/4 cup (30 g) diced tomatoes
- 1/4 cup (25 g) diced onion
- 1/4 tsp garlic powder
- 1/4 tsp smoked paprika
- Salt and pepper to taste
- 1/4 cup (30 g) shredded cheese (optional)

Directions:

1. Preheat the air fryer to 360°F (182°C).
2. In a mixing bowl, combine zucchini, tomatoes, onion, garlic powder, smoked paprika, salt, and pepper. Mix well.
3. Spoon the vegetable mixture into each bell pepper half, filling them evenly. Sprinkle with shredded cheese if desired.
4. Place the stuffed peppers in the air fryer basket in a single layer. Air fry for 12-15 minutes, or until the peppers are tender and the cheese is melted.
5. Serve warm and enjoy these flavorful, veggie-packed bites!

 2 servings **10** minutes **15** minutes

Nutritional information (per serving):
120 calories, 3g protein, 16g carbohydrates, 6g fat, 3g fiber, 5mg cholesterol, 180mg sodium, 250mg potassium.

CAULIFLOWER STEAKS

Thick cauliflower slices roasted to golden perfection with a hint of paprika

Ingredients:

- 1 medium cauliflower head, sliced into 1-inch (2.5 cm) thick steaks
- 1 tbsp (15 ml) olive oil
- 1/2 tsp paprika
- 1/4 tsp garlic powder
- Salt and pepper, to taste

Directions:

1. Preheat the air fryer to 400°F (200°C).
2. In a small bowl, mix olive oil, paprika, garlic powder, salt, and pepper. Brush this mixture onto both sides of each cauliflower steak.
3. Place the cauliflower steaks in the air fryer basket in a single layer. Air fry for 12-15 minutes, flipping halfway, until golden and tender.
4. Serve hot as a delicious, low-carb side or main dish.

 2 servings **5** minutes **15** minutes

Nutritional information (per serving):
110 calories, 3g protein, 10g carbohydrates, 8g fat, 3g fiber, 0mg cholesterol, 170mg sodium, 300mg potassium.

TOMATO BASIL BITES

Fresh tomatoes with basil and a touch of olive oil, air-fried to bring out the sweetness

Ingredients:

- 1 cup (150 g) cherry tomatoes, halved
- 1 tbsp (15 ml) olive oil
- 1/4 tsp salt
- 1/4 tsp black pepper
- 1/4 cup (5 g) fresh basil leaves, roughly chopped

Directions:

1. Preheat the air fryer to 375°F (190°C).
2. In a mixing bowl, toss cherry tomato halves with olive oil, salt, and pepper.
3. Place the seasoned tomatoes in the air fryer basket in a single layer. Air fry for 8 minutes, shaking the basket halfway through, until tomatoes are softened and slightly caramelized.
4. Sprinkle fresh basil over the tomatoes and serve warm as a flavorful appetizer or side.

 2 servings 5 minutes 8 minutes

Nutritional information (per serving):
80 calories, 1g protein, 6g carbohydrates, 6g fat, 2g fiber, 0mg cholesterol, 150mg sodium, 300mg potassium.

ACORN SQUASH SLICES

Thin acorn squash slices lightly spiced with cinnamon and nutmeg

Ingredients:

- 1 small acorn squash (about 1 lb / 450 g), seeded and sliced into thin rings
- 1 tbsp (15 ml) olive oil
- 1/4 tsp ground cinnamon
- 1/8 tsp ground nutmeg
- Salt, to taste

Directions:

1. Preheat the air fryer to 380°F (193°C).
2. In a bowl, toss the acorn squash slices with olive oil, cinnamon, nutmeg, and a pinch of salt until evenly coated.
3. Arrange the slices in a single layer in the air fryer basket. Air fry for 12-15 minutes, flipping halfway through, until tender and golden brown.
4. Serve warm as a sweet and savory side dish.

 2 servings 5 minutes 15 minutes

Nutritional information (per serving):
100 calories, 1g protein, 17g carbohydrates, 4g fat, 3g fiber, 0mg cholesterol, 5mg sodium, 400mg potassium.

GARLIC-PARMESAN MUSHROOMS

Mushrooms tossed with garlic and Parmesan, air-fried until tender and savory

Ingredients:

- 8 oz (225 g) button or cremini mushrooms, cleaned and halved
- 1 tbsp (15 ml) olive oil
- 1 tbsp (15 g) grated Parmesan cheese
- 1 clove garlic, minced
- Salt and pepper, to taste
- 1 tsp fresh parsley, chopped (optional, for garnish)

Directions:

1. Preheat the air fryer to 380°F (193°C).
2. In a bowl, toss the mushrooms with olive oil, Parmesan, garlic, salt, and pepper until well-coated.
3. Place the mushrooms in a single layer in the air fryer basket. Air fry for 8-10 minutes, shaking the basket halfway, until mushrooms are tender and golden.
4. Garnish with fresh parsley, if desired, and serve warm.

 2 servings 5 minutes 10 minutes

Nutritional information (per serving):
120 calories, 4g protein, 6g carbohydrates, 9g fat, 1g fiber, 3mg cholesterol, 160mg sodium, 300mg potassium.

DAIRY PRODUCTS

Dairy products are often highlighted in nutritional discussions for their essential nutrients, and they play an important role in diabetes management, particularly for people with Type 1 and Type 2 diabetes or those newly diagnosed. Dairy offers an excellent source of calcium, protein, and vitamins D and B12, crucial for bone health, immune function, and muscle maintenance. Regarding a diabetic-friendly diet, dairy in moderation can contribute positively, particularly low-fat and high-protein varieties that support blood sugar control and provide long-lasting satiety. Additionally, studies indicate that some dairy products with probiotics, like yogurt, support gut health, which is beneficial for metabolic health and may improve insulin sensitivity.

For people with diabetes, choosing the right dairy products is vital. Opting for low-sugar, low-fat, and high-protein options, such as Greek yogurt, cottage cheese, or part-skim cheeses, can help manage calorie intake and support blood glucose stability. Including dairy recipes in your cooking repertoire adds flavor and nutritional balance to meals without requiring complex preparation. Using an air fryer to prepare dairy-inclusive recipes allows for healthier versions of traditionally fried foods, as it uses minimal oil, making dishes lighter and lower in calories and fat.

COTTAGE CHEESE PANCAKES

Light, fluffy pancakes made with cottage cheese for extra protein

Ingredients:

- 1/2 cup (120 g) cottage cheese
- 1/2 cup (60 g) almond flour
- 2 large eggs
- 1/4 tsp baking powder
- 1/4 tsp vanilla extract
- 1/8 tsp salt
- Cooking spray or a small amount of oil for greasing

Directions:

1. Preheat the air fryer to 350°F (175°C).
2. In a medium bowl, blend together the cottage cheese, almond flour, eggs, baking powder, vanilla extract, and salt until smooth.
3. Grease a small oven-safe dish or silicone muffin molds with cooking spray or a small amount of oil. Pour the batter into the prepared dish or divide between the muffin molds to make pancake-sized portions.
4. Place the dish or molds in the air fryer basket and cook for 8–10 minutes, or until the pancakes are firm and golden on top. Check for doneness and add 1-2 minutes if necessary.
5. Remove and let cool slightly. Serve with your favorite low-sugar toppings or enjoy as is.

 2 servings   5 minutes   10 minutes

Nutritional information (per serving):
210 calories, 15 g protein, 6 g carbohydrates, 14 g fat, 2 g fiber, 140 mg cholesterol, 320 mg sodium, 150 mg potassium.

FETA-STUFFED PEPPERS

Mini peppers filled with feta cheese, roasted until tender

Ingredients:

- 6 mini sweet peppers
- 1/3 cup (50 g) feta cheese, crumbled
- 1/4 tsp dried oregano
- 1/8 tsp black pepper
- Olive oil spray

Directions:

1. Preheat the air fryer to 375°F (190°C).
2. Slice the tops off the mini peppers and remove any seeds inside.
3. In a small bowl, mix the feta cheese, oregano, and black pepper. Stuff each mini pepper with the feta mixture.
4. Lightly spray the stuffed peppers with olive oil and place them in the air fryer basket.
5. Cook for 8–10 minutes, or until the peppers are tender and the feta is slightly golden. Serve warm.

 2 servings 5 minutes 10 minutes

Nutritional information (per serving):
140 calories, 5 g protein, 7 g carbohydrates, 10 g fat, 2 g fiber, 20 mg cholesterol, 280 mg sodium, 120 mg potassium.

YOGURT-MARINATED CHICKEN

Chicken marinated in yogurt and spices for a flavorful main dish

Ingredients:

- 2 boneless, skinless chicken breasts (about 8 oz/225 g each)
- 1/2 cup (120 ml) plain Greek yogurt
- 1 tbsp lemon juice (15 ml)
- 1/2 tsp ground cumin
- 1/2 tsp smoked paprika
- 1/4 tsp garlic powder
- 1/4 tsp ground coriander
- Salt and pepper, to taste
- Olive oil spray

Directions:

1. In a bowl, mix the yogurt, lemon juice, cumin, smoked paprika, garlic powder, ground coriander, salt, and pepper.
2. Coat the chicken breasts with the yogurt marinade, cover, and refrigerate for at least 30 minutes.
3. Preheat the air fryer to 380°F (193°C). Lightly spray the air fryer basket with olive oil.
4. Place the marinated chicken breasts in the basket and cook for 12–15 minutes, flipping halfway, until the internal temperature reaches 165°F (74°C).
5. Let the chicken rest for a few minutes before slicing and serving.

 2 servings 40 minutes 15 minutes

Nutritional information (per serving):
210 calories, 32 g protein, 4 g carbohydrates, 7 g fat, 0 g fiber, 85 mg cholesterol, 320 mg sodium, 350 mg potassium.

RICOTTA-STUFFED MUSHROOMS

Mushroom caps filled with creamy ricotta and herbs

Ingredients:

- 8 large mushroom caps (about 6 oz/170 g)
- 1/3 cup (80 g) ricotta cheese
- 1 tbsp (4 g) grated Parmesan cheese
- 1/2 tsp dried Italian herbs
- 1 clove garlic, minced
- Salt and pepper, to taste
- Olive oil spray
- Fresh parsley, chopped, for garnish (optional)

Directions:

1. In a small bowl, mix the ricotta, Parmesan, Italian herbs, garlic, salt, and pepper.
2. Spoon the ricotta mixture into each mushroom cap until filled.
3. Preheat the air fryer to 375°F (190°C). Lightly spray the air fryer basket with olive oil.
4. Place the stuffed mushrooms in the basket and cook for 8–10 minutes, until mushrooms are tender and the filling is slightly golden.
5. Garnish with fresh parsley, if desired, and serve warm.

 2 servings 10 minutes 10 minutes

Nutritional information (per serving):
140 calories, 7 g protein, 6 g carbohydrates, 10 g fat, 1 g fiber, 20 mg cholesterol, 150 mg sodium, 220 mg potassium.

BRIE and APPLE BITES

Warm brie and apple slices wrapped in phyllo dough

Ingredients:

- 4 sheets of phyllo dough, thawed (about 8"x8" sheets)
- 4 slices (1 oz/28 g) brie cheese
- 1/2 medium apple, thinly sliced (about 2 oz/56 g)
- 1 tsp honey or maple syrup (optional)
- Olive oil spray

Directions:

1. Preheat the air fryer to 350°F (175°C). Lay out one phyllo sheet on a flat surface and lightly spray with olive oil. Place a second phyllo sheet on top, spray again, and repeat with the remaining sheets.
2. Cut the layered phyllo sheets into 4 equal squares. Place a slice of brie and a few apple slices in the center of each square. Drizzle with honey or maple syrup, if desired.
3. Fold the corners of the phyllo over the filling to form a small bundle. Lightly spray the tops with olive oil.
4. Place the bundles in the air fryer basket and cook for 6–8 minutes or until the phyllo is golden brown and crispy.
5. Serve warm and enjoy!

 2 servings 5 minutes 8 minutes

Nutritional information (per serving):
160 calories, 5 g protein, 13 g carbohydrates, 10 g fat, 1 g fiber, 20 mg cholesterol, 210 mg sodium, 70 mg potassium.

TOFU and COTTAGE CHEESE BITES

Protein-packed bites with tofu and cottage cheese

Ingredients:

- 1/2 cup (120 g) firm tofu, drained and diced
- 1/4 cup (60 g) cottage cheese
- 1/4 cup (30 g) breadcrumbs
- 1 tbsp (8 g) grated Parmesan cheese
- 1/4 tsp garlic powder
- 1/4 tsp onion powder
- Salt and pepper to taste
- Olive oil spray

Directions:

1. Preheat the air fryer to 375°F (190°C).
2. In a mixing bowl, gently combine the diced tofu and cottage cheese. Add breadcrumbs, Parmesan, garlic powder, onion powder, salt, and pepper. Mix until well combined.
3. Form the mixture into small, bite-sized balls, pressing them firmly so they hold their shape.
4. Lightly spray the air fryer basket with olive oil and place the bites in a single layer. Lightly spray the tops with olive oil.
5. Air fry for 10–12 minutes or until golden and crispy, turning halfway through.

 2 servings 10 minutes 12 minutes

Nutritional information (per serving):
180 calories, 14 g protein, 12 g carbohydrates, 8 g fat, 2 g fiber, 10 mg cholesterol, 290 mg sodium, 150 mg potassium.

MASCARPONE-STUFFED DATES

Sweet dates stuffed with mascarpone cheese

Ingredients:

- 6 large Medjool dates
- 1/4 cup (60 g) mascarpone cheese
- Optional: 1/4 tsp cinnamon or honey drizzle for added sweetness

Directions:

1. Preheat the air fryer to 350°F (175°C).
2. Slice each date lengthwise, remove the pit, and create a small pocket for filling.
3. Using a small spoon or piping bag, fill each date with about 1 teaspoon of mascarpone cheese. Optionally, sprinkle with a pinch of cinnamon or drizzle with honey.
4. Place the stuffed dates in the air fryer basket in a single layer and cook for 3–4 minutes until the dates are warm and slightly caramelized.

 2 servings 5 minutes 4 minutes

Nutritional information (per serving):
150 calories, 2 g protein, 27 g carbohydrates, 6 g fat, 3 g fiber, 5 mg cholesterol, 15 mg sodium, 180 mg potassium.

BLUE CHEESE BRUSSELS SPROUTS

Roasted Brussels sprouts with a sprinkle of blue cheese for a sharp, tangy finish

Ingredients:

- 8 oz (225 g) Brussels sprouts, halved
- 1 tbsp (15 ml) olive oil
- Salt and pepper, to taste
- 1 oz (28 g) blue cheese, crumbled

Directions:

1. Preheat the air fryer to 375°F (190°C).
2. In a bowl, toss Brussels sprouts with olive oil, salt, and pepper until evenly coated.
3. Place Brussels sprouts in the air fryer basket in a single layer and cook for 10-12 minutes, shaking halfway through, until tender and slightly crispy.
4. Transfer Brussels sprouts to a serving dish and sprinkle with blue cheese while still warm. Serve immediately.

 2 servings   5 minutes   12 minutes

Nutritional information (per serving):
170 calories, 6 g protein, 12 g carbohydrates, 12 g fat, 5 g fiber, 10 mg cholesterol, 250 mg sodium, 400 mg potassium.

COTTAGE CHEESE BALLS

Crispy on the outside and creamy on the inside, these cottage cheese bites make an excellent snack

Ingredients:

- 1 cup (240 g) cottage cheese, drained
- 1/4 cup (30 g) breadcrumbs
- 1/4 cup (30 g) grated Parmesan cheese
- 1 large egg
- 1/4 tsp garlic powder
- Salt and pepper, to taste
- Cooking spray

Directions:

1. Preheat the air fryer to 375°F (190°C).
2. In a bowl, combine cottage cheese, breadcrumbs, Parmesan, egg, garlic powder, salt, and pepper. Mix until well combined.
3. Form the mixture into small balls about 1 inch in diameter.
4. Lightly spray the air fryer basket with cooking spray. Place the cottage cheese balls in the basket in a single layer, ensuring they don't touch.
5. Cook for 10-12 minutes, shaking halfway through, until golden and crispy on the outside. Serve warm.

 2 servings   10 minutes   12 minutes

Nutritional information (per serving):
190 calories, 13 g protein, 15 g carbohydrates, 8 g fat, 1 g fiber, 55 mg cholesterol, 360 mg sodium, 150 mg potassium.

CRUSTLESS QUICHE with SWISS CHEESE

A low-carb quiche with Swiss cheese, eggs, and a mix of veggies

Ingredients:

- 4 large eggs
- 1/4 cup (60 ml) milk or cream
- 1/2 cup (55 g) shredded Swiss cheese
- 1/4 cup (30 g) chopped bell peppers
- 1/4 cup (30 g) chopped spinach
- Salt and pepper, to taste
- Cooking spray

Directions:

1. Preheat the air fryer to 320°F (160°C).
2. In a bowl, whisk together the eggs, milk, salt, and pepper until smooth. Stir in the Swiss cheese, bell peppers, and spinach.
3. Lightly spray two small oven-safe ramekins or baking dishes with cooking spray. Divide the mixture evenly between the two dishes.
4. Place the ramekins in the air fryer basket and cook for 12-15 minutes or until the quiche is set and golden on top. Let cool slightly before serving.

 2 servings   5 minutes   8 minutes

Nutritional information (per serving):
220 calories, 15 g protein, 5 g carbohydrates, 16 g fat, 1 g fiber, 210 mg cholesterol, 270 mg sodium, 210 mg potassium.

GOAT CHEESE–STUFFED MUSHROOMS
Portobello mushrooms filled with creamy goat cheese and roasted to perfection

Ingredients:

- 4 large portobello mushrooms
- 1/4 cup (60 g) goat cheese, softened
- 1 tsp (5 ml) olive oil
- 1/2 tsp dried thyme
- Salt and pepper, to taste
- Fresh parsley, chopped (optional garnish)

Directions:

1. Preheat the air fryer to 370°F (190°C).
2. Clean the mushrooms and remove the stems. Lightly brush the caps with olive oil and season with salt and pepper.
3. In a small bowl, mix the goat cheese with thyme. Spoon the goat cheese mixture into each mushroom cap.
4. Place the mushrooms in the air fryer basket and cook for 10-12 minutes until they are tender and the cheese is golden.
5. Garnish with fresh parsley, if desired, and serve warm.

 2 servings 10 minutes 12 minutes

Nutritional information (per serving):
150 calories, 7 g protein, 5 g carbohydrates, 11 g fat, 1 g fiber, 20 mg cholesterol, 180 mg sodium, 340 mg potassium.

CAULIFLOWER and CHEDDAR CHEESE BAKE
Cauliflower florets coated with cheddar for a quick, cheesy side dish

Ingredients:

- 2 cups (240 g) cauliflower florets
- 1/2 cup (60 g) shredded cheddar cheese
- 1 tbsp (15 ml) olive oil
- Salt and pepper, to taste
- 1/4 tsp garlic powder (optional)

Directions:

1. Preheat the air fryer to 375°F (190°C).
2. In a mixing bowl, toss the cauliflower florets with olive oil, salt, pepper, and garlic powder (if using).
3. Place the cauliflower in the air fryer basket and cook for 8 minutes.
4. Sprinkle the shredded cheddar over the cauliflower and cook for 3-4 minutes, until cheese is melted and bubbly.
5. Serve warm and enjoy your cheesy cauliflower bake!

 2 servings 5 minutes 12 minutes

Nutritional information (per serving):
200 calories, 9 g protein, 7 g carbohydrates, 16 g fat, 2 g fiber, 25 mg cholesterol, 240 mg sodium, 340 mg potassium.

RICOTTA and HERB FRITTERS
Light and fluffy ricotta fritters flavored with fresh herbs and garlic

Ingredients:

- 1/2 cup (120 g) ricotta cheese
- 1/4 cup (30 g) grated Parmesan cheese
- 1/4 cup (30 g) all-purpose flour
- 1 large egg
- 1 clove garlic, minced
- 1 tbsp (15 g) fresh parsley, chopped
- Salt and pepper, to taste
- Olive oil spray

Directions:

1. Preheat the air fryer to 375°F (190°C).
2. In a mixing bowl, combine ricotta, Parmesan, flour, egg, garlic, parsley, salt, and pepper, stirring until well mixed.
3. Scoop small spoonfuls of the mixture to form fritters, shaping them gently with your hands.
4. Spray the air fryer basket with olive oil spray and place the fritters in a single layer. Lightly spray the tops of the fritters.
5. Air fry for 8 minutes, flipping halfway through, until golden and slightly crisp. Serve warm.

 2 servings 10 minutes 8 minutes

Nutritional information (per serving):
210 calories, 11 g protein, 12 g carbohydrates, 13 g fat, 1 g fiber, 65 mg cholesterol, 300 mg sodium, 150 mg potassium.

CREAM CHEESE JALAPENO POPPERS

Spicy jalapeños filled with cream cheese and coated lightly

Ingredients:

- 4 large jalapeño peppers
- 1/4 cup (60 g) cream cheese, softened
- 2 tbsp (15 g) shredded cheddar cheese
- 1/4 tsp garlic powder
- Salt and pepper, to taste
- Olive oil spray

Directions:

1. Preheat the air fryer to 375°F (190°C).
2. Slice each jalapeño in half lengthwise, removing the seeds and membranes for a milder flavor.
3. In a small bowl, mix cream cheese, shredded cheddar, garlic powder, salt, and pepper.
4. Fill each jalapeño half with the cream cheese mixture, then place them in a single layer in the air fryer basket. Lightly spray the tops with olive oil.
5. Air fry for 8 minutes, or until the tops are golden and jalapeños are tender. Serve warm.

 2 servings   10 minutes   8 minutes

Nutritional information (per serving):
180 calories, 4 g protein, 5 g carbohydrates, 15 g fat, 1 g fiber, 35 mg cholesterol, 220 mg sodium, 150 mg potassium.

HALLUMI FRIES

Thick slices of halloumi cheese air-fried to golden perfection

Ingredients:

- 7 oz (200 g) halloumi cheese, cut into thick fries
- 1 tbsp olive oil or cooking spray
- Optional: 1/4 tsp paprika or garlic powder for extra flavor

Directions:

1. Preheat the air fryer to 375°F (190°C).
2. Pat the halloumi dry with paper towels, then brush or spray lightly with olive oil.
3. Place halloumi fries in the air fryer basket in a single layer. Sprinkle with paprika or garlic powder if desired.
4. Air fry for 8–10 minutes, turning halfway through, until golden and crispy on the edges. Serve warm.

 2 servings   5 minutes   10 minutes

Nutritional information (per serving):
300 calories, 18 g protein, 2 g carbohydrates, 24 g fat, 0 g fiber, 65 mg cholesterol, 1000 mg sodium, 100 mg potassium.

LEMON RICOTTA COOKIES

Light, lemony cookies made with ricotta for a soft, melt-in-your-mouth treat

Ingredients:

- 1/2 cup (120 g) ricotta cheese
- 2 tbsp (28 g) unsalted butter, softened
- 1/4 cup (50 g) granulated sugar
- 1/2 cup (60 g) all-purpose flour
- 1/2 tsp baking powder
- Zest of 1/2 lemon
- 1/2 tbsp lemon juice
- Pinch of salt

Directions:

1. Preheat the air fryer to 325°F (160°C) and line the basket with parchment paper.
2. In a mixing bowl, cream together the ricotta cheese, softened butter, and sugar until smooth.
3. Stir in the flour, baking powder, lemon zest, lemon juice, and salt until combined.
4. Scoop small spoonfuls of the dough onto the parchment paper in the air fryer basket, leaving space between each.
5. Air fry for 8 minutes or until the edges are lightly golden. Let cool before serving.

 2 servings   10 minutes   8 minutes

Nutritional information (per serving):
280 calories, 6 g protein, 32 g carbohydrates, 15 g fat, 1 g fiber, 45 mg cholesterol, 180 mg sodium, 60 mg potassium.

SNACKS

For individuals managing diabetes, snacking can help maintain stable blood sugar levels throughout the day. However, choosing the right snacks is essential, as traditional high-carb, sugar-laden options can lead to spikes in glucose levels. This is where the air fryer comes in, offering a way to prepare delicious, low-carb, low-sugar snacks that are both satisfying and nourishing.

Air-fried snacks can help you enjoy your favorite flavors and textures with a fraction of the oil and calories found in traditional fried foods. From crispy, savory bites to sweet, low-sugar treats, these recipes are designed to make snacking enjoyable and health-conscious.

Lower Carbs and Sugar: Most recipes focus on minimal sugar and slow-digesting carbs, which are vital for stabilizing blood sugar.

High Fiber: Ingredients like vegetables and whole grains add fiber, helping with satiety and slower glucose absorption.

Healthy Fats and Protein: Many snacks incorporate nuts, seeds, cheese, and lean meats, providing sustained energy and preventing blood sugar dips.

Quick and Convenient: The air fryer reduces cooking time, making healthy snacking more convenient.

ZUCCHINI CHIPS
Thinly sliced zucchini with a crisp coating for a low-carb crunch

Ingredients:
- 1 medium zucchini (about 7 oz or 200 g), thinly sliced
- 1/4 cup grated Parmesan cheese (1 oz or 28 g)
- 1/4 cup almond flour (1 oz or 28 g)
- 1/4 tsp garlic powder
- 1/4 tsp paprika
- Salt and pepper to taste
- Olive oil spray

Directions:
1. In a bowl, mix Parmesan, almond flour, garlic powder, paprika, salt, and pepper.
2. Lightly spray zucchini slices with olive oil and coat each slice with the cheese mixture.
3. Arrange the coated zucchini slices in a single layer in the air fryer basket.
4. Air fry at 375°F (190°C) for 10-12 minutes, flipping halfway, until golden and crispy.

 2 servings   10 minutes   12 minutes

Nutritional information (per serving):
140 calories, 6g protein, 4g carbohydrates, 10g fat, 2g fiber, 10mg cholesterol, 180mg sodium, 200mg potassium.

CAULIFLOWER BITES

Lightly breaded cauliflower with a hint of garlic, a great low-carb snack

Ingredients:

- 1/2 medium cauliflower head (about 7 oz or 200 g), cut into bite-sized florets
- 1/4 cup almond flour (1 oz or 28 g)
- 1/4 cup grated Parmesan cheese (1 oz or 28 g)
- 1/4 tsp garlic powder
- Salt and pepper to taste
- Olive oil spray

Directions:

1. Mix almond flour, Parmesan cheese, garlic powder, salt, and pepper in a mixing bowl.
2. Lightly spray the cauliflower florets with olive oil, then toss them in the bowl to coat with the flour mixture.
3. Arrange the cauliflower bites in a single layer in the air fryer basket.
4. Air fry at 375°F (190°C) for 10-12 minutes, shaking halfway through, until golden and crispy.

 2 servings 10 minutes 12 minutes

Nutritional information (per serving):
160 calories, 7g protein, 7g carbohydrates, 11g fat, 3g fiber, 10mg cholesterol, 180mg sodium, 270mg potassium.

APPLE CHIPS

Lightly spiced apple slices with no added sugar, perfect for a sweet snack

Ingredients:

- 1 large apple (about 6 oz or 170 g), thinly sliced
- 1/4 tsp ground cinnamon

Directions:

1. Preheat the air fryer to 300°F (150°C).
2. Arrange the apple slices in a single layer in the air fryer basket, ensuring they don't overlap.
3. Sprinkle cinnamon evenly over the slices.
4. Air fry for 15 minutes, flipping halfway through until the apple slices are crispy.

 2 servings 5 minutes 15 minutes

Nutritional information (per serving):
80 calories, 0g protein, 22g carbohydrates, 0g fat, 4g fiber, 0mg cholesterol, 0mg sodium, 160mg potassium.

CAPRESE SKEWERS with TOMATOES and MOZZARELLA

A quick, delicious appetizer with blistered cherry tomatoes, creamy mozzarella, and fresh basil

Ingredients:

- 8 cherry tomatoes
- 8 small fresh mozzarella balls (about 4 oz or 115 g)
- 8 fresh basil leaves
- 1 tbsp (15 ml) olive oil
- Salt and pepper to taste
- Balsamic glaze for drizzling (optional)

Directions:

1. Preheat the air fryer to 375°F (190°C).
2. Thread each skewer with one cherry tomato, one mozzarella ball, and a fresh basil leaf, repeating if desired.
3. Brush skewers lightly with olive oil and season with salt and pepper.
4. Place skewers in the air fryer basket in a single layer and air fry for 3 minutes until tomatoes start to blister slightly.
5. Drizzle with balsamic glaze before serving, if desired.

 2 servings 5 minutes 3 minutes

Nutritional information (per serving):
180 calories, 8g protein, 6g carbohydrates, 15g fat, 1g fiber, 30mg cholesterol, 220mg sodium, 100mg potassium.

MINI QUICHES

Bite-sized mini quiches filled with eggs, cheese, and your choice of veggies or meat

Ingredients:

- 4 large eggs
- 1/4 cup (60 ml) milk
- 1/4 cup (30 g) shredded cheddar cheese
- 1/4 cup (30 g) diced ham or bacon (optional)
- 2 tbsp (10 g) chopped spinach or bell peppers
- Salt and pepper to taste

Directions:

1. In a bowl, whisk together eggs, milk, salt, and pepper.
2. Add cheese, ham, bacon, and vegetables, and stir to combine.
3. Grease a mini muffin tin or small quiche mold and pour the mixture evenly.
4. Air fry at 350°F (175°C) for 10-12 minutes or until quiches are set and golden.

 2 servings   5 minutes   15 minutes

Nutritional information (per serving):
150 calories, 12 g protein, 2 g carbohydrates, 10 g fat, 0 g fiber, 180 mg cholesterol, 300 mg sodium, 100 mg potassium.

PROSCIUTTO-WRAPPED MELON

Sweet melon cubes wrapped in savory prosciutto, air-fried to a crispy, flavorful perfection

Ingredients:

- 4 slices prosciutto (approx. 2 oz / 60 g)
- 8 melon cubes (cantaloupe or honeydew, approx. 1 cup / 150 g)
- 1 tsp olive oil spray
- Freshly ground black pepper, to taste

Directions:

1. Wrap each melon cube with a slice of prosciutto, securing it with a toothpick if needed.
2. Lightly spray the wrapped melon with olive oil for extra crispiness.
3. Place in the air fryer basket in a single layer. Air fry at 375°F (190°C) for 5-8 minutes or until the prosciutto is crispy.
4. Season with a touch of black pepper and serve warm.

 2 servings   5 minutes   8 minutes

Nutritional information (per serving):
120 calories, 8g protein, 5g carbohydrates, 7g fat, 1g fiber, 25mg cholesterol, 520mg sodium, 200mg potassium.

SPICY ROASTED ALMONDS

Crunchy almonds with a bold kick of smoked paprika and cayenne, perfect for snacking

Ingredients:

- 1 cup (150 g) raw almonds
- 1/2 tsp olive oil
- 1/2 tsp smoked paprika
- 1/4 tsp cayenne pepper
- 1/4 tsp garlic powder
- 1/4 tsp sea salt

Directions:

1. In a bowl, toss the almonds with olive oil, smoked paprika, cayenne pepper, garlic powder, and salt until well coated.
2. Preheat the air fryer to 350°F (175°C).
3. Place the almonds in a single layer in the air fryer basket and cook for 8-10 minutes, shaking the basket halfway through until golden and aromatic.
4. Allow almonds to cool slightly for optimal crunch before serving.

 2 servings   5 minutes   10 minutes

Nutritional information (per serving):
170 calories, 6g protein, 5g carbohydrates, 15g fat, 4g fiber, 0mg cholesterol, 100mg sodium, 200mg potassium.

DEVILED EGGS

A creative take on deviled eggs with a crisp exterior

Ingredients:

- 4 large eggs
- 2 tbsp mayonnaise
- 1 tsp Dijon mustard
- 1/4 tsp smoked paprika, plus more for garnish
- Salt and pepper to taste
- Fresh chives, for garnish

Directions:

1. Preheat the air fryer to 270°F (132°C). Place eggs in the air fryer basket and cook for 15 minutes.
2. Once cooked, transfer eggs to an ice bath to cool for 5 minutes, then peel.
3. Slice eggs in half lengthwise, remove yolks, and place yolks in a small bowl. Mash yolks with mayonnaise, mustard, smoked paprika, salt, and pepper until smooth.
4. Spoon or pipe the yolk mixture back into egg whites. Sprinkle with additional smoked paprika and garnish with chives before serving.

 2 servings   10 minutes   15 minutes

Nutritional information (per serving):
140 calories, 6g protein, 1g carbohydrates, 12g fat, 0g fiber, 210mg cholesterol, 230mg sodium, 60mg potassium.

VEGGIE SPRING ROLLS

Freshly rolled veggies wrapped and air-fried for a crispy bite

Ingredients:

- 4 spring roll wrappers
- 1/2 cup (75g) shredded carrots
- 1/2 cup (75g) shredded cabbage
- 1/4 cup (35g) sliced bell peppers
- 1/4 cup (35g) bean sprouts
- 1 tbsp soy sauce
- 1 tsp sesame oil
- Olive oil spray

Directions:

1. In a bowl, combine carrots, cabbage, bell peppers, bean sprouts, soy sauce, and sesame oil. Mix well.
2. Place a spring roll wrapper on a clean surface and add 2 tbsp of the veggie filling. Roll tightly, folding in the sides and sealing the edge with a bit of water.
3. Preheat the air fryer to 375°F (190°C). Spray the spring rolls lightly with olive oil spray.
4. Place spring rolls in the air fryer basket, avoiding overlap, and cook for 10 minutes or until golden and crispy, flipping halfway through.

 2 servings   15 minutes   10 minutes

Nutritional information (per serving):
160 calories, 4g protein, 24g carbohydrates, 5g fat, 3g fiber, 0mg cholesterol, 350mg sodium, 180mg potassium.

SHRIMP and AVOCADO LETTUCE WRAPS

Fresh and flavorful, these air fryer shrimp and avocado lettuce wraps are a quick and low-carb perfect meal

Ingredients:

- 8 oz (225 g) large shrimp, peeled and deveined
- 1 tbsp olive oil
- Salt and pepper, to taste
- 1/4 tsp garlic powder
- 1/4 tsp smoked paprika
- 1 avocado, sliced
- 4 large lettuce leaves (romaine or butter lettuce work well)
- 1 tbsp lime juice
- Fresh cilantro for garnish (optional)

Directions:

1. Toss the shrimp in olive oil, salt, pepper, garlic powder, and smoked paprika to coat evenly.
2. Preheat the air fryer to 400°F (200°C). Place shrimp in a single layer in the basket and cook for 5-6 minutes, turning halfway, until pink and opaque.
3. Arrange lettuce leaves on a plate. Divide avocado slices among the lettuce leaves, then add cooked shrimp.
4. Drizzle with lime juice and garnish with fresh cilantro if desired. Serve immediately.

 2 servings   10 minutes   6 minutes

Nutritional information (per serving):
320 calories, 20g protein, 12g carbohydrates, 22g fat, 8g fiber, 145mg cholesterol, 420mg sodium, 600mg potassium.

BRUSCHETTA with TOMATOES and BASIL

Crispy baguette slices topped with fresh tomatoes, basil, and a hint of balsamic

Ingredients:

- 4 slices of baguette (about 1/2 inch thick)
- 1/2 cup (75g) diced tomatoes
- 1 tbsp fresh basil, chopped
- 1/2 tsp balsamic vinegar
- 1/2 tsp olive oil
- Salt and pepper to taste
- Olive oil spray

Directions:

1. Preheat the air fryer to 375°F (190°C).
2. Spray both sides of baguette slices lightly with olive oil and place them in the air fryer. Cook for 3-5 minutes until golden and crispy.
3. In a bowl, combine diced tomatoes, basil, balsamic vinegar, olive oil, salt, and pepper.
4. Spoon the tomato mixture onto the toasted baguette slices and serve immediately.

 2 servings 10 minutes 5 minutes

Nutritional information (per serving):
120 calories, 3g protein, 20g carbohydrates, 3g fat, 2g fiber, 0mg cholesterol, 170mg sodium, 150mg potassium.

HERB and CHEESE-STUFFED MUSHROOMS

Savory mushroom caps filled with a creamy herb and cheese mixture, air-fried to golden perfection

Ingredients:

- 8 large white mushrooms, stems removed (about 4 oz / 115 g)
- 2 oz (57 g) cream cheese, softened
- 1/4 cup (20 g) shredded Parmesan cheese
- 1/4 tsp garlic powder
- 1/4 tsp dried Italian herbs
- 1/8 tsp salt
- Freshly ground black pepper to taste
- Cooking spray

Directions:

1. In a small bowl, combine the cream cheese, Parmesan, garlic powder, Italian herbs, salt, and pepper. Mix well until creamy.
2. Spoon the cheese mixture evenly into each mushroom cap.
3. Preheat the air fryer to 375°F (190°C) and lightly spray the basket with cooking spray.
4. Place the stuffed mushrooms in the basket and air fry for 7-8 minutes or until mushrooms are tender and the tops are golden.

 2 servings 10 minutes 8 minutes

Nutritional information (per serving):
180 calories, 6g protein, 4g carbohydrates, 15g fat, 1g fiber, 35mg cholesterol, 320mg sodium, 90mg potassium.

BAKED AVOCADO FRIES

Crispy on the outside and creamy on the inside air fryer avocado fries make a delicious and healthy snack

Ingredients:

- 1 large avocado, ripe but firm
- 1/4 cup (30g) all-purpose flour
- 1/4 tsp salt
- 1/4 tsp black pepper
- 1/4 tsp smoked paprika
- 1/4 cup (60ml) milk or plant-based milk
- 1/2 cup (30g) panko breadcrumbs

Directions:

1. Preheat the air fryer to 400°F (200°C).
2. Slice avocado into thick wedges. Mix flour, salt, pepper, and smoked paprika in a small bowl. Add milk in a separate bowl, and place the panko breadcrumbs in a third bowl.
3. Dredge each avocado slice in flour mixture, dip in milk, and coat with panko breadcrumbs.
4. Arrange coated avocado slices in a single layer in the air fryer basket. Cook for 8 minutes, flipping halfway through, until golden and crispy.
5. Serve warm with your favorite dipping sauce.

 2 servings 10 minutes 8 minutes

Nutritional information (per serving):
210 calories, 4g protein, 20g carbohydrates, 14g fat, 6g fiber, 0mg cholesterol, 250mg sodium, 550mg potassium.

DESSERTS

Desserts can be part of a healthy diet, even for individuals managing diabetes, thanks to thoughtful recipe adjustments and mindful ingredient choices. For people with Type 1 or Type 2 diabetes, prediabetic, or newly diagnosed, the air fryer offers a fantastic way to indulge in sweet treats while keeping blood sugar levels in check. This unique cooking tool reduces unhealthy fats and sugars without sacrificing flavor or satisfaction. By focusing on low-carb, low-sugar options, it's possible to enjoy a variety of desserts that align with a diabetes-friendly lifestyle.

The air fryer's versatility means you can create all sorts of diabetic-friendly dessert options, from baked fruit crisps to nut-based cookies, without the need for excessive oils or high-glycemic ingredients. It's easy to whip up everything from cookies to crisps that support balanced blood sugar levels using alternatives like almond flour, low-carb sweeteners, and fresh fruits.

CHOCOLATE CHIP COOKIES
A chewy, sugar-free cookie with almond flour and dark chocolate

Ingredients:

- 1/2 cup (60 g) almond flour
- 2 tbsp (30 g) unsalted butter, softened
- 2 tbsp (24 g) sugar-free sweetener (e.g., erythritol or monk fruit)
- 1/2 tsp vanilla extract
- 1/4 tsp baking powder
- 1/8 tsp salt
- 2 tbsp (28 g) sugar-free chocolate chips

Directions:

1. Preheat the air fryer to 320°F (160°C).
2. In a small bowl, mix almond flour, butter, sweetener, vanilla extract, baking powder, and salt until well combined.
3. Fold in the chocolate chips, then form the dough into small, round cookies and flatten slightly.
4. Place cookies in the air fryer basket lined with parchment paper. Air fry for 7-8 minutes or until golden brown.
5. Allow to cool slightly before serving.

 2 servings 5 minutes 8 minutes

Nutritional information (per serving):
240 calories, 4g protein, 6g carbohydrates, 22g fat, 3g fiber, 15mg cholesterol, 120mg sodium, 40mg potassium.

BERRY CRISP
A mixed berry crisp with an almond and coconut topping for a sweet and tangy dessert

Ingredients:

- 1 cup (150 g) mixed berries (e.g., blueberries, strawberries, raspberries)
- 2 tbsp (16 g) almond flour
- 1 tbsp (8 g) rolled oats
- 1 tbsp (12 g) chopped nuts (e.g., almonds or pecans)
- 1 tbsp (15 g) melted butter
- 1 tbsp (12 g) sugar-free sweetener
- 1/2 tsp cinnamon

Directions:

1. Preheat the air fryer to 350°F (175°C).
2. In a small bowl, mix almond flour, oats, nuts, melted butter, sweetener, and cinnamon until it is crumbly.
3. Place Sprinkle the crumble mixture on top of the berries in a small oven-safe dish.
4. Air fry for 8-10 minutes or until the topping is golden and the berries are bubbling.
5. Let cool slightly before serving.

 2 servings 5 minutes 10 minutes

Nutritional information (per serving):
210 calories, 3g protein, 15g carbohydrates, 16g fat, 5g fiber, 10mg cholesterol, 50mg sodium, 120mg potassium.

ALMOND FLOUR BROWNIES

Rich and chocolatey brownies without refined sugars

Ingredients:

- 1/2 cup (48 g) almond flour
- 2 tbsp (14 g) unsweetened cocoa powder
- 1/4 cup (50 g) sugar-free sweetener
- 1/4 tsp baking powder
- 1/8 tsp salt
- 1 large egg
- 2 tbsp (28 g) melted butter
- 1/2 tsp vanilla extract

Directions:

1. Preheat the air fryer to 325°F (160°C).
2. In a mixing bowl, combine almond flour, cocoa powder, sweetener, baking powder, and salt.
3. Add the egg, melted butter, and vanilla extract, stirring until well-mixed.
4. Pour the batter into a small, greased, air fryer-safe dish.
5. Air fry for 10-12 minutes or until a toothpick inserted into the center comes out mostly clean. Let cool before serving.

 2 servings   5 minutes   12 minutes

Nutritional information (per serving):

230 calories, 6g protein, 9g carbohydrates, 20g fat, 3g fiber, 70mg cholesterol, 120mg sodium, 100mg potassium.

BANANA BREAD BITES

Mini banana bread pieces, perfect for portion control

Ingredients:

- 1/2 cup (60 g) almond flour
- 1 small ripe banana, mashed (about 1/4 cup or 60 ml)
- 1/4 tsp baking powder
- 1/4 tsp ground cinnamon
- 1/8 tsp salt
- 1 tbsp (15 ml) maple syrup or sugar-free sweetener
- 1/4 tsp vanilla extract
- 1 tbsp (15 ml) milk of choice

Directions:

1. Preheat the air fryer to 330°F (165°C).
2. In a bowl, mix almond flour, mashed banana, baking powder, cinnamon, salt, maple syrup, vanilla, and milk until smooth.
3. Divide the batter into small, greased muffin molds or silicone cups, filling each about halfway.
4. Place molds in the air fryer basket and cook for 8 minutes, or until golden and set.
5. Let cool slightly, then remove from molds and serve warm.

 2 servings   5 minutes   8 minutes

Nutritional information (per serving):

140 calories, 3g protein, 18g carbohydrates, 6g fat, 3g fiber, 5mg cholesterol, 100mg sodium, 160mg potassium.

CINNAMON WALNUTS

A crunchy and sweet nut treat with a hint of cinnamon spice

Ingredients:

- 1 cup (120 g) walnut halves
- 1 tbsp (15 ml) maple syrup
- 1/2 tsp ground cinnamon
- 1/8 tsp salt

Directions:

1. Preheat the air fryer to 350°F (175°C).
2. In a bowl, toss the walnuts with maple syrup, cinnamon, and salt until well-coated.
3. Place the walnuts in the air fryer basket in a single layer.
4. Air fry for 5 minutes, shaking the basket halfway through, until walnuts are toasted and crisp.
5. Allow to cool slightly before serving; they will become crunchier as they cool.

 2 servings   3 minutes   5 minutes

Nutritional information (per serving):

180 calories, 4g protein, 7g carbohydrates, 16g fat, 2g fiber, 0mg cholesterol, 70mg sodium, 125mg potassium.

LEMON RICOTTA CAKE

Light and zesty, with a creamy texture from ricotta cheese

Ingredients:

- 1/2 cup (125 g) ricotta cheese
- 1/4 cup (60 g) granulated sugar
- 1/4 cup (30 g) almond flour
- 1 large egg
- 1 tbsp (15 ml) lemon juice
- Zest of 1/2 lemon
- 1/4 tsp baking powder
- Pinch of salt

Directions:

1. Preheat the air fryer to 320°F (160°C) and grease a small 4-inch (10 cm) baking pan.
2. In a mixing bowl, combine ricotta, sugar, almond flour, egg, lemon juice, lemon zest, baking powder, and salt. Stir until smooth and well-mixed.
3. Pour the batter into the prepared pan and smooth the top.
4. Place the pan in the air fryer and bake for 15 minutes or until the cake is set and a toothpick inserted in the center comes out clean.
5. Allow the cake to cool slightly before serving.

 2 servings   5 minutes   15 minutes

Nutritional information (per serving):
210 calories, 7g protein, 20g carbohydrates, 11g fat, 1g fiber, 55mg cholesterol, 80mg sodium, 90mg potassium.

SUGAR-FREE CARAMELIZED PEACHES

Juicy peach halves with a natural caramel flavor

Ingredients:

- 2 ripe peaches, halved and pits removed
- 1 tbsp (15 ml) melted butter
- 1/2 tsp ground cinnamon
- 1/4 tsp vanilla extract

Directions:

1. Preheat the air fryer to 350°F (175°C).
2. In a small bowl, mix the melted butter, cinnamon, and vanilla extract. Brush the peach halves with the mixture.
3. Place the peaches in the air fryer basket, cut side up, and cook for 8-10 minutes or until soft and slightly caramelized.
4. Allow to cool slightly before serving.

 2 servings   5 minutes   10 minutes

Nutritional information (per serving):
70 calories, 1g protein, 10g carbohydrates, 3g fat, 2g fiber, 0mg cholesterol, 0mg sodium, 285mg potassium.

ALMOND BUTTER COOKIES

Soft, satisfying cookies made with almond butter and low-carb sweeteners

Ingredients:

- 1/4 cup (60 ml) almond butter
- 2 tbsp (30 ml) almond flour
- 1 tbsp (15 ml) sugar substitute (e.g., erythritol or stevia)
- 1/4 tsp baking powder
- 1/4 tsp vanilla extract

Directions:

1. Preheat the air fryer to 350°F (175°C).
2. In a mixing bowl, combine almond butter, almond flour, sugar substitute, baking powder, and vanilla extract until smooth.
3. Roll the dough into small balls (about 1 inch/2.5 cm) and flatten slightly.
4. Place the cookies in the air fryer basket, leaving space between each, and cook for 6-8 minutes or until lightly golden.
5. Allow the cookies to cool before serving.

 2 servings   5 minutes   8 minutes

Nutritional information (per serving):
180 calories, 6g protein, 4g carbohydrates, 15g fat, 3g fiber, 0mg cholesterol, 60mg sodium, 190mg potassium.

BLUEBERRY MUFFINS

Mini blueberry muffins, low in carbs and bursting with fresh berries

Ingredients:

- 1/4 cup (30 g) all-purpose flour
- 1/4 cup (60 ml) almond milk or regular milk
- 2 tbsp (30 ml) sugar substitute (e.g., erythritol)
- 1/4 tsp baking powder
- 1/4 cup (50 g) fresh blueberries
- 1/2 tbsp (7 ml) vegetable oil
- 1/4 tsp vanilla extract
- Pinch of salt

Directions:

1. Preheat the air fryer to 320°F (160°C).
2. In a bowl, mix flour, sugar substitute, baking powder, and salt. Add milk, oil, and vanilla extract, and stir until smooth. Gently fold in the blueberries.
3. Pour the batter into silicone muffin cups, filling each about 3/4 full.
4. Place the muffin cups in the air fryer basket and bake for 8-10 minutes or until a toothpick inserted comes out clean.
5. Let the muffins cool slightly before serving.

 2 servings   5 minutes   10 minutes

Nutritional information (per serving):
130 calories, 3g protein, 20g carbohydrates, 5g fat, 2g fiber, 0mg cholesterol, 90mg sodium, 60mg potassium.

PEAR SLICES with HONEY and ALMONDS

Delicately sweet pear slices topped with almond slivers and a drizzle of honey

Ingredients:

- 1 large pear, sliced into 1/4-inch (0.6 cm) thick slices
- 1 tbsp (15 ml) honey
- 2 tbsp (15 g) sliced almonds
- 1/4 tsp ground cinnamon

Directions:

1. Preheat the air fryer to 350°F (175°C).
2. Arrange the pear slices in a single layer in the air fryer basket.
3. Drizzle honey over the pear slices, sprinkle with cinnamon, and top with sliced almonds.
4. Air fry for 6-8 minutes until pears are tender and almonds are golden.
5. Let cool slightly before serving.

 2 servings   5 minutes   8 minutes

Nutritional information (per serving):
150 calories, 1g protein, 25g carbohydrates, 5g fat, 4g fiber, 0mg cholesterol, 0mg sodium, 150mg potassium.

CHEESECAKE BITES

Mini cheesecakes made with cream cheese and a hint of vanilla

Ingredients:

- 4 oz (115 g) cream cheese, softened
- 1 tbsp (15 g) granulated sugar or sugar substitute
- 1/4 tsp vanilla extract
- 1 large egg
- 1/4 cup (30 g) graham cracker crumbs
- Optional: fresh berries or a sprinkle of cinnamon for garnish

Directions:

1. Preheat the air fryer to 320°F (160°C).
2. In a bowl, mix the cream cheese, sugar, vanilla extract, and egg until smooth.
3. Grease a mini muffin pan or silicone mold and sprinkle graham cracker crumbs at the bottom of each cup.
4. Pour the cream cheese mixture into each cup, filling about halfway.
5. Air fry for 6-7 minutes, or until the cheesecake bites are set. Allow them to cool before removing from the mold.

 2 servings   10 minutes 7 minutes

Nutritional information (per serving):
190 calories, 4g protein, 8g carbohydrates, 16g fat, 0g fiber, 55mg cholesterol, 110mg sodium, 40mg potassium.

CHOCOLATE HAZELNUT MUG CAKE

Single-serving, low-carb chocolate cake with a hint of hazelnut

Ingredients:

- 4 tbsp (60 ml) milk
- 4 tbsp (32 g) all-purpose flour
- 2 tbsp (16 g) cocoa powder
- 1/4 tsp baking powder
- 2 tbsp (30 g) hazelnut spread (like Nutella)
- 1 tbsp (12 g) sugar or sugar substitute
- 1 tbsp (15 ml) vegetable oil

Directions:

1. In a bowl, combine milk, flour, cocoa powder, baking powder, sugar, and oil; stir until smooth.
2. Divide batter between two air fryer-safe mugs. Drop 1 tbsp of hazelnut spread into the center of each mug.
3. Preheat the air fryer to 350°F (175°C). Air fry the mugs for 7-8 minutes until the cake is set.
4. Let cool slightly before enjoying directly from the mug.

 2 servings   5 minutes   8 minutes

Nutritional information (per serving):
300 calories, 5g protein, 34g carbohydrates, 16g fat, 2g fiber, 15mg cholesterol, 120mg sodium, 90mg potassium.

LOW-CARB PUMPKIN SPICE MUFFINS

Soft and moist muffins perfect for autumn cravings

Ingredients:

- 1/2 cup (60 g) almond flour
- 1/4 cup (60 g) pumpkin puree
- 1 large egg
- 2 tbsp (30 ml) unsweetened almond milk
- 2 tbsp (24 g) granulated erythritol or preferred low-carb sweetener
- 1/2 tsp baking powder
- 1/2 tsp pumpkin spice blend
- 1/4 tsp vanilla extract
- Pinch of salt

Directions:

1. Preheat the air fryer to 330°F (165°C).
2. In a medium bowl, whisk together almond flour, erythritol, baking powder, pumpkin spice, and salt.
3. Add pumpkin puree, egg, almond milk, and vanilla extract to the dry ingredients, mixing until smooth.
4. Divide the batter between two silicone muffin cups, filling each about 3/4 full.
5. Place muffin cups in the air fryer basket and bake for 10 minutes, or until a toothpick inserted comes out clean. Allow to cool slightly before serving.

 2 servings   10 minutes   10 minutes

Nutritional information (per serving):
130 calories, 5g protein, 6g carbohydrates, 10g fat, 2g fiber, 35mg cholesterol, 160mg sodium, 100mg potassium.

PEANUT BUTTER BALLS

Bite-sized peanut butter snacks, sweetened with stevia

Ingredients:

- 1/4 cup (60 g) creamy peanut butter
- 2 tbsp (30 g) almond flour
- 1 tbsp (15 g) coconut flour
- 1 tbsp (15 g) sugar-free chocolate chips
- 1/2 tbsp (7 ml) melted coconut oil

Directions:

1. In a medium bowl, mix the peanut butter, almond flour, and coconut flour until a thick dough forms.
2. Roll the mixture into small balls, about 1 inch in diameter, and place on a small tray.
3. In a separate bowl, combine the chocolate chips and melted coconut oil. Place in the air fryer at 300°F (150°C) for 1 minute to melt, stirring until smooth.
4. Dip each peanut butter ball in the melted chocolate, ensuring an even coating.
5. Place the coated balls in the air fryer at 320°F (160°C) for 3–5 minutes, until slightly firm. Allow to cool before serving.

2 servings   10 minutes   5 minutes

Nutritional information (per serving):
190 calories, 5g protein, 8g carbohydrates, 16g fat, 2g fiber, 0mg cholesterol, 90mg sodium, 110mg potassium.

COCONUT MACAROONS

Light and fluffy coconut bites with no added sugars

Ingredients:

- 1 cup (75 g) unsweetened shredded coconut
- 1/4 cup (60 ml) sweetened condensed milk
- 1/2 tsp vanilla extract
- 1 large egg white

Directions:

1. In a bowl, mix shredded coconut, sweetened condensed milk, and vanilla extract until well combined.
2. In a separate bowl, whisk the egg white until frothy, then gently fold it into the coconut mixture.
3. Preheat the air fryer to 320°F (160°C). Shape the mixture into small balls or mounds and place on parchment paper in the air fryer basket.
4. Air fry for 6-8 minutes until the tops are golden brown. Allow to cool before serving.

 2 servings 5 minutes 8 minutes

Nutritional information (per serving):
150 calories, 2g protein, 18g carbohydrates, 8g fat, 4g fiber, 5mg cholesterol, 50mg sodium, 100mg potassium.

CHOCOLATE-COVERED STRAWBERRIES

A quick and easy way to create a chocolate treat without added sugars

Ingredients:

- 1/2 cup (90 g) dark chocolate chips
- 10 fresh strawberries
- 1/2 tsp coconut oil (optional for a smoother chocolate coating)

Directions:

1. Preheat the air fryer to 350°F (175°C).
2. In a heat-safe bowl, combine chocolate chips and coconut oil. Place the bowl in the air fryer basket and heat for about 3-5 minutes, stirring halfway until melted and smooth.
3. Dip each strawberry into the melted chocolate, allowing any excess to drip off.
4. Place on a parchment-lined plate and refrigerate for 10 minutes to set before serving.

 2 servings   5 minutes 5 minutes

Nutritional information (per serving):
150 calories, 1g protein, 15g carbohydrates, 10g fat, 2g fiber, 0mg cholesterol, 5mg sodium, 130mg potassium.

LEMON POPPY SEED MUFFINS

Light, lemony muffins with a hint of poppy seed

Ingredients:

- 1/2 cup (60 g) almond flour
- 1/4 cup (60 ml) Greek yogurt
- 1 tbsp (15 ml) lemon juice
- 1 tbsp (15 g) sugar-free sweetener (granulated)
- 1 large egg
- 1/2 tsp (2.5 ml) vanilla extract
- 1/2 tbsp (7 g) poppy seeds
- 1/2 tsp (2 g) baking powder
- Zest of 1/2 lemon

Directions:

1. Mix the almond flour, Greek yogurt, lemon juice, sweetener, egg, vanilla extract, poppy seeds, baking powder, and lemon zest in a mixing bowl. Stir until a smooth batter forms.
2. Divide the batter evenly into two silicone muffin cups or liners.
3. Place the muffin cups in the air fryer basket. Set the air fryer to 330°F (165°C) and bake for 12 minutes until a toothpick inserted in the center comes out clean.
4. Allow to cool before serving.

 2 servings 5 minutes 12 minutes

Nutritional information (per serving):
200 calories, 8g protein, 10g carbohydrates, 15g fat, 3g fiber, 55mg cholesterol, 110mg sodium, 90mg potassium.

CHOCOLATE ALMOND BARK

Dark chocolate almond bark made with sugar-free chocolate

Ingredients:

- 1/2 cup (90 g) dark chocolate chips (sugar-free if desired)
- 1/4 cup (30 g) almonds, roughly chopped
- 1/2 tsp (2.5 ml) coconut oil

Directions:

1. In a microwave-safe bowl, melt the chocolate chips and coconut oil for 15-20 seconds, stirring in between, until smooth.
2. Mix the chopped almonds into the melted chocolate.
3. Pour the mixture onto a parchment-lined air fryer-safe dish, spreading it into an even layer.
4. Place in the air fryer at 320°F (160°C) for 4-5 minutes to set.
5. Let it cool completely before breaking into pieces.

 2 servings   5 minutes   5 minutes

Nutritional information (per serving):
220 calories, 4g protein, 15g carbohydrates, 18g fat, 4g fiber, 0mg cholesterol, 15mg sodium, 160mg potassium.

KETO DONUTS

Low-carb donuts with a sprinkle of cinnamon on top

Ingredients:

- 1/2 cup (56 g) almond flour
- 2 tbsp (28 g) coconut flour
- 2 tbsp (28 g) granulated erythritol (or preferred keto sweetener)
- 1/2 tsp (2.5 ml) baking powder
- 1/4 tsp salt
- 1/4 cup (60 ml) unsweetened almond milk
- 1 large egg
- 1/2 tsp (2.5 ml) vanilla extract
- 1 tbsp (14 g) melted butter

Directions:

1. In a mixing bowl, combine almond flour, coconut flour, erythritol, baking powder, and salt.
2. In a separate bowl, whisk almond milk, egg, vanilla extract, and melted butter.
3. Combine the wet and dry ingredients, stirring until smooth.
4. Pour the batter into a donut mold, filling each cavity halfway.
5. Air fry at 350°F (175°C) for 7-8 minutes, until golden and firm to the touch. Let cool slightly before serving.

 2 servings   10 minutes   8 minutes

Nutritional information (per serving):
180 calories, 6g protein, 4g carbohydrates, 15g fat, 3g fiber, 60mg cholesterol, 120mg sodium, 180mg potassium.

CINNAMON-SPICED PECANS

Crispy pecans with a hint of cinnamon spice

Ingredients:

- 1 cup (100 g) pecan halves
- 1 tbsp (15 ml) melted coconut oil or butter
- 1/2 tsp (1 g) ground cinnamon
- 1/2 tbsp (7 g) granulated sweetener or sugar substitute
- Pinch of salt

Directions:

1. Preheat the air fryer to 320°F (160°C).
2. In a bowl, mix pecans with melted coconut oil, cinnamon, sweetener, and salt until well-coated.
3. Place pecans in the air fryer basket in an even layer. Air fry for 5 minutes, shaking halfway through, until golden and fragrant.
4. Allow pecans to cool slightly before serving.

 2 servings   5 minutes   5 minutes

Nutritional information (per serving):
200 calories, 2g protein, 6g carbohydrates, 20g fat, 4g fiber, 0mg cholesterol, 5mg sodium, 125mg potassium.

CHOCOLATE AVOCADO BROWNIES

Fudgy brownies with healthy fats from avocado

Ingredients:

- 1/2 medium avocado (about 1/4 cup or 50 g), mashed
- 1/4 cup (60 ml) almond butter or nut butter of choice
- 1/4 cup (25 g) unsweetened cocoa powder
- 1/4 cup (40 g) granulated sweetener or sugar substitute
- 1 large egg
- 1/2 tsp (2.5 ml) vanilla extract
- 1/8 tsp baking powder
- Pinch of salt
- Optional: 1 tbsp (15 g) dark chocolate chips

Directions:

1. Preheat the air fryer to 320°F (160°C).
2. Mix the mashed avocado, almond butter, cocoa powder, sweetener, egg, vanilla extract, baking powder, and salt in a medium bowl until smooth.
3. Pour the brownie batter into a small greased pan or ramekins that fit inside your air fryer. Sprinkle with chocolate chips if desired.
4. Air fry for 12–15 minutes or until a toothpick inserted into the center is clean. Allow to cool slightly before serving.

 2 servings   10 minutes   15 minutes

Nutritional information (per serving):
250 calories, 6g protein, 20g carbohydrates, 16g fat, 6g fiber, 55mg cholesterol, 60mg sodium, 400mg potassium.

ALMOND JOY BITES

A low-carb twist on the classic coconut, almond, and chocolate candy

Ingredients:

- 1/2 cup (45 g) unsweetened shredded coconut
- 2 tbsp (30 g) almond butter
- 1 tbsp (15 ml) coconut oil, melted
- 1 tbsp (15 g) sugar-free chocolate chips
- 1 tbsp (10 g) whole almonds

Directions:

1. In a bowl, mix shredded coconut, almond butter, and melted coconut oil until thoroughly combined.
2. Form small balls from the mixture (about 1 inch each) and place an almond on top of each ball.
3. Arrange the bites in the air fryer basket and cook at 350°F (175°C) for 5–8 minutes until golden and slightly crisp.
4. Once cooled, melt the chocolate chips in the microwave and drizzle over the bites.

 2 servings   10 minutes   8 minutes

Nutritional information (per serving):
220 calories, 3g protein, 10g carbohydrates, 18g fat, 4g fiber, 0mg cholesterol, 5mg sodium, 150mg potassium.

COCONUT FLOUR SHORTBREAD

Buttery, crumbly cookies made with coconut flour

Ingredients:

- 1/4 cup (30 g) coconut flour
- 2 tbsp (30 g) softened butter or coconut oil
- 1 tbsp (15 ml) maple syrup or sugar-free sweetener
- 1/2 tsp vanilla extract
- Pinch of salt

Directions:

1. In a bowl, mix the coconut flour, butter or coconut oil, maple syrup, vanilla extract, and salt until a dough forms.
2. Shape the dough into small, round cookies, about 1/4 inch thick, and place them in the air fryer basket.
3. Air fry at 320°F (160°C) for 8–10 minutes or until edges are lightly golden.
4. Let the cookies cool before serving for the best texture.

 2 servings   5 minutes   10 minutes

Nutritional information (per serving):
160 calories, 2g protein, 7g carbohydrates, 14g fat, 3g fiber, 10mg cholesterol, 55mg sodium, 80mg potassium.

BERRY COMPOTE

A naturally sweet compote to top your favorite desserts

Ingredients:

- 1 cup (150 g) mixed berries (blueberries, strawberries, raspberries)
- 1 tbsp (15 ml) water
- 1/2 tbsp (7 ml) honey or sugar-free sweetener
- 1/4 tsp lemon zest

Directions:

1. In a small, heat-safe dish, combine berries, water, honey, and lemon zest. Stir well.
2. Place the dish in the air fryer basket and air fry at 350°F (175°C) for 10 minutes, stirring halfway through.
3. Once cooked, stir the compote and let it cool slightly before serving.

 2 servings   2 minutes 10 minutes

Nutritional information (per serving):
60 calories, 0.5g protein, 15g carbohydrates, 0g fat, 3g fiber, 0mg cholesterol, 1mg sodium, 50mg potassium.

LOW-CARB CREME BRULEE

A decadent, sugar-free version of this creamy classic

Ingredients:

- 1/2 cup (120 ml) heavy cream
- 1/2 tsp vanilla extract
- 2 large egg yolks
- 1 tbsp (12 g) powdered sugar substitute (erythritol or monk fruit)
- 1/2 tsp granulated sugar substitute (for topping)

Directions:

1. In a small saucepan, warm the heavy cream over low heat until it steams. Remove from heat and stir in the vanilla extract.
2. In a mixing bowl, whisk the egg yolks and powdered sugar substitute until smooth. Slowly add the warm cream to the yolks, whisking continuously.
3. Pour the mixture into two small ramekins. Place the ramekins in the air fryer basket and cook at 300°F (150°C) for 20 minutes until the custard is set but still slightly jiggly in the center.
4. Let the ramekins cool, then refrigerate for at least 1 hour. Before serving, sprinkle each with a thin layer of granulated sugar substitute and use a kitchen torch to caramelize the topping.

 2 servings   5 minutes   20 minutes

Nutritional information (per serving):
220 calories, 2g protein, 3g carbohydrates, 22g fat, 0g fiber, 220mg cholesterol, 20mg sodium, 35mg potassium.

VANILLA BEAN PUDDING

Creamy, vanilla-flavored pudding made without added sugars

Ingredients:

- 1 cup (240 ml) whole milk
- 1/2 cup (120 ml) heavy cream
- 1 tbsp (12 g) granulated sugar or sugar substitute
- 1 vanilla bean, split, and seeds scraped (or 1 tsp vanilla extract)
- 2 large egg yolks

Directions:

1. In a small saucepan, heat the milk, heavy cream, and vanilla bean seeds over low heat until warm but not boiling. Remove from heat.
2. In a separate bowl, whisk the egg yolks with the sugar until smooth. Slowly add the warm milk mixture to the yolks, whisking continuously.
3. Pour the mixture into two small ramekins. Place the ramekins in the air fryer basket and cook at 300°F (150°C) for 15 minutes, or until the pudding is set but still slightly jiggly in the center.
4. Allow the puddings to cool, then refrigerate for at least 1 hour before serving.

 2 servings   5 minutes   15 minutes

Nutritional information (per serving):
220 calories, 2g protein, 3g carbohydrates, 22g fat, 0g fiber, 220mg cholesterol, 20mg sodium, 35mg potassium.

30-DAY MEAL PLAN

	Week 1			
	Breakfast	**Lunch**	**Snack**	**Dinner**
Day 1	Avocado Toast with a Twist	Shrimp and Quinoa Salad	Zucchini Chips	Lemon Garlic Chicken Garlic Green Beans Low-Carb Chocolate Chip Cookies
Day 2	French Toast Sticks	Crispy Tofu and Spinach Salad	Spicy Roasted Almonds	BBQ Chicken Thighs Roasted Bell Peppers Berry Crisp
Day 3	Veggie Omelette Cups	Black Bean Tacos	Deviled Eggs	Lamb Kofta Broccoli with Lemon Almond Flour Brownies
Day 4	Cottage Cheese Pancakes	Mushroom Soup	Apple Chips	Sea Bass Rainbow Carrots Sugar-Free Caramelized Peaches
Day 5	Blueberry Protein Pancake Bites	Kale and Sweet Potato Salad	Baked Avocado Fries	Turkey Meatballs Parmesan-Crusted Cauliflower Blueberry Muffins
Day 6	Zucchini and Mushroom Frittata Slices	Barley-Stuffed Bell Peppers	Air Fryer Baked Avocado Fries	Duck Breast Rainbow Carrots Coconut Macaroons
Day 7	Sweet Potato Breakfast Hash	Quinoa-Stuffed Bell Peppers	Shrimp and Avocado Lettuce Wraps	Ground Turkey Tacos Asparagus with Parmesan Chocolate-Covered Strawberries
	Week 2			
	Breakfast	**Lunch**	**Snack**	**Dinner**
Day 8	Mini Breakfast Pizza	Broccoli with Lemon	Prosciutto-Wrapped Melon	Lamb Gyro Carrot Fries Pear Slices with Honey and Almonds
Day 9	Cottage Cheese Balls	Lentil and Spinach Patties	Apple Cinnamon Oatmeal Bites	Shrimp Skewers Eggplant Chips Keto Donuts
Day 10	English Muffin	Cauliflower Soup	Air Fryer Peanut Butter Balls	Fish Tacos Butternut Squash Cubes Lemon Ricotta Cookies

	Breakfast	Lunch	Snack	Dinner
Day 11	Breakfast Sandwiches Cinnamon Chia Breakfast Bites	Roasted Vegetable Salad	Zucchini Fries	Beef Schnitzel Spaghetti Squash Cheesecake Bites
Day 12	Sweet Potato Breakfast Hash	Falafel Salad	Veggie Spring Rolls	Chicken and Broccoli Roasted Beets Almond Joy Bites
Day 13	Crustless Quiche with Swiss Cheese	Chicken Caesar Salad	Air Fryer Almond Butter Cookies	Pork Chops Crispy Kale Chips Air Fryer Berry Compote
Day 14	Banana Pancake Bites	Turkey and Veggie Patties	Caprese Skewers with Mozzarella	Lamb Chops Garlic-Parmesan Mushrooms Low-Carb Creme Brulee

Week 3

	Breakfast	Lunch	Snack	Dinner
Day 15	Cottage Cheese Pancakes	Spiced Black Beans and Rice	Mascarpone-Stuffed Dates	Beef Tacos Green Peas Cinnamon-Spiced Pecans
Day 16	Spinach and Feta Breakfast Wraps	Butternut Squash Soup	Apple Chips	Pork Carnitas Artichoke Hearts Low-Carb Pumpkin Spice Muffins
Day 17	Breakfast Quesadilla	Millet Veggie Nuggets	Zucchini Chips	Duck Legs with Rosemary and Garlic Broccoli with Lemon Vanilla Bean Pudding
Day 18	Crispy Bacon and Egg Cups	Salmon Salad with Avocado	Herb and Cheese-Stuffed Mushrooms	Lamb Fajitas Caramelized Onions Chocolate Avocado Brownies
Day 19	Zucchini Fries	Red Pepper and Lentil Soup	Cauliflower Bites	Turkey Cutlets Cauliflower Steaks Air Fryer Cheesecake Bites
Day 20	Apple Cinnamon Oatmeal Bites	Shrimp and Quinoa Salad	Spicy Roasted Almonds	Mahi Mahi with Citrus Glaze Beet Chips Chocolate Hazelnut Mug Cake

	Breakfast	Lunch	Snack	Dinner
Day 21	Low-Carb Egg and Cheese Muffins	Blackened Catfish	Air Fryer Peanut Butter Balls	Chicken Drumsticks Garlic Green Beans Lemon Poppy Seed Muffins

Week 4

	Breakfast	Lunch	Snack	Dinner
Day 22	Cheesy Cauliflower Hash Browns	Chickpea and Kale Fritters	Zucchini Chips	Crispy Chicken Wings Garlic Roasted Radishes Chocolate Almond Bark
Day 23	Sweet Potato Breakfast Hash	Shrimp Skewers	Cottage Cheese Balls	BBQ Pork Ribs Stuffed Mini Peppers Pear Slices with Honey and Almonds
Day 24	Avocado Toast with a Twist	Roasted Cauliflower	Herb and Cheese-Stuffed Mushrooms	Philly Cheesesteak Spaghetti Squash Low-Carb Chocolate Chip Cookies
Day 25	Mini Breakfast Pizza	Barley and Veggie Patties	Apple Cinnamon Oatmeal Bites	Tuna Steaks Sweet Potato Wedges Air Fryer Cheesecake Bites
Day 26	Zucchini and Mushroom Frittata Slices	Polenta Fries	Air Fryer Almond Butter Cookies	Pork Schnitzel Parmesan-Crusted Cauliflower Coconut Flour Shortbread
Day 27	English Muffin Breakfast Sandwiches	Turkey Stuffed Peppers	Mascarpone-Stuffed Dates	Lamb Shoulder Baby Potatoes Berry Compote
Day 28	Spinach and Feta Breakfast Wraps	Zucchini and Leek Soup	Deviled Eggs	Bacon-Wrapped Scallops Asparagus with Parmesan Almond Flour Brownies

Week 5

	Breakfast	Lunch	Snack	Dinner
Day 29	Cottage Cheese Pancakes	Quinoa-Crusted Chicken Tenders	Spicy Roasted Almonds	Halibut with Herb Butter Carrot Fries Coconut Macaroons
Day 30	French Toast Sticks	Crispy Farro Salad Bites	Caprese Skewers with Mozzarella	Roast Beef Crispy Brussels Sprouts Vanilla Bean Pudding

INDEX

Cod with Dill	82
Corn on the Cob	50
Cottage Cheese Balls	103
Cottage Cheese Pancakes	100
Crab Cakes	86
Cream Cheese Jalapeño Poppers	105
Crispy Air Fryer Wild Rice Cakes	35
Crispy Bacon and Egg Cups	22
Crispy Breakfast Sausage Patties	23
Crispy Brussels Sprouts	44
Crispy Brussels Sprouts	91
Crispy Chicken Wings	59
Crispy Cinnamon Walnuts	112
Crispy Farro Salad Bites	31
Crispy Fish Sticks	80
Crispy Kale Chips	48
Crispy Kale Chips	94
Crispy Lentil Fritters	31
Crispy Tofu and Spinach Salad	37
Crispy Turkey Bacon Strips	27
Crustless Quiche with Swiss Cheese	103

D

Deviled Eggs	109
Duck Breast	64
Duck Legs	64
Duck Legs with Rosemary and Garlic	65
Duck Nuggets	64
Duck Wings	65
Duck with Orange Glaze	65

E

Easy Breakfast Burritos	26
Eggplant Chips	48
English Muffin Breakfast Sandwiches	27

F

Falafel Salad	36
Feta-Stuffed Peppers	101
Fish Cakes	84
Fish Tacos	82
French Toast Sticks	22

G

Garlic Butter Shrimp	88
Garlic Green Beans	45
Garlic Green Beans	92
Garlic Roasted Radishes	96
Garlic-Parmesan Mushrooms	99
Goat Cheese-Stuffed Mushrooms	104
Greek-Style Lamb	75
Green Peas	51
Ground Beef Stuffed Peppers	72
Ground Turkey Tacos	57

H

Haddock with Lemon Pepper	83
Halibut with Herb Butter	84
Halloumi Fries	105
Herb and Cheese-Stuffed Mushrooms	110
Herb-Crusted Turkey Cutlets	54

K

Kale and Sweet Potato Salad	38
Keto Donuts	117
Kidney Bean and Corn Patties	33

L

Lamb Burgers	73
Lamb Chops	72
Lamb Cutlets	74
Lamb Fajitas	74
Lamb Gyro	76
Lamb Kebabs	71
Lamb Kofta	74
Lamb Meatballs	73
Lamb Ribs	71
Lamb Shanks	73
Lamb Shoulder	72
Lamb Stew	75
Lamb Stir-Fry	75
Lamb Tacos	76
Lemon Garlic Chicken	60
Lemon Garlic Salmon	81
Lemon Poppy Seed Muffins	116
Lemon Ricotta Cake	113
Lemon Ricotta Cookies	105
Lentil and Spinach Patties	34
Lobster Tails	86
Lobster Tails with Lemon Garlic	89
Low-Carb Chocolate Chip Cookies	111
Low-Carb Creme Brulee	119
Low-Carb Egg and Cheese Muffins	23
Low-Carb Pumpkin Spice Muffins	115

M

Mahi Mahi with Citrus Glaze	83
Mascarpone-Stuffed Dates	102
Millet Veggie Nuggets	30
Mini Breakfast Pizza	28
Mini Quiches	108
Mushroom Soup	41
Mushrooms with Balsamic Glaze	95
Mussels	88

O

Oatmeal and Raisin Bars	34
Okra Fries	52

P

Parmesan Crusted Cauliflower	49
Parmesan-Crusted Cauliflower	95
Pear Slices with Honey and Almonds	114
Philly Cheesesteak	71

**I genuinely look forward to hearing from you
and
appreciate your response!**

Thank you for selecting this cookbook.
Your input is significant and aids me in providing you
with excellent recipes and content.
If you have liked these recipes, kindly consider leaving a review
on the Amazon page.
Your feedback can assist other readers in discovering this cookbook.
I value your support!

Warm regards,

Deb Corbin